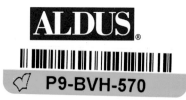

P9-BVH-570

User Manual

Your complete guide to
SuperPaint's tools and features

Version 3.0 for use with Apple® Macintosh® computers

First Edition

June 1993

Aldus Corporation
Consumer Division

5120 Shoreham Place

San Diego, CA 92122-5926

For service and Technical Support in the United States and Canada, call Aldus Consumer Division at (619) 558-6000. For service and support outside the United States and Canada, please contact your local distributor or dealer.

000-746
ISBN 1-56026-090-4
Printed in the USA

Table of Contents US 30-3500-0000183490

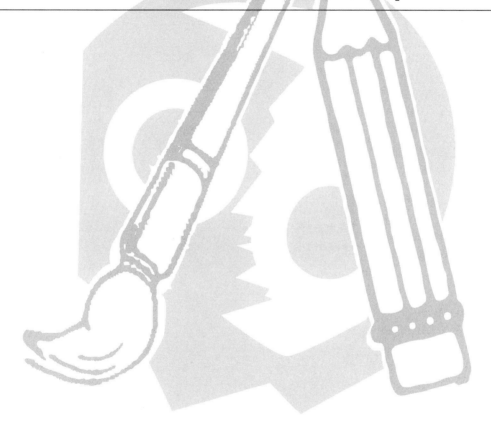

Part 1: Introduction to SuperPaint

Introduction to SuperPaint

Welcome to SuperPaint! This section of the manual introduces you to SuperPaint and tells you how to get started using the program.

What is SuperPaint?

SuperPaint combines the features of Macintosh paint, draw, and image-processing programs in one powerful, easy-to-use graphics program. This combination spares you the expense of purchasing three products, and the inconvenience of learning and working with three separate programs — which in turn can dramatically increase your productivity.

The basis of SuperPaint is the ability to work in two different "layers": a paint (or bitmapped) layer, and a draw (or object-oriented) layer. The layers are superimposed on the screen, and in your printouts, to produce a single image.

Paint-layer graphics are patterns of dots with no special relationship to each other — paint images tend to have a "textural" look. Working in the Paint layer is like sketching with a pencil or painting with a brush: you have areas of the paper or canvas that have been covered, and areas that haven't.

Paint graphic.

Items in the Draw layer are treated as discrete, mathematically defined objects (hence the term "object-oriented"). This means, among other things, that working in the Draw layer is similar to cutting out smooth shapes and laying them out in a collage.

Draw graphic.

Both layers have advantages and drawbacks. Fortunately SuperPaint allows you to move graphics back and forth easily to take advantage of the strengths of each. Generally speaking, the Paint layer lets you be spontaneous and creative, while the Draw layer provides smooth precision at the maximum resolution of your output device.

Whether you're a novice or an experienced Macintosh user, whether you're an artist or someone who can't draw a straight line unaided, whether you're creating art for business or pleasure, SuperPaint provides a complete graphics environment. SuperPaint's simple, elegant interface provides power without sacrificing ease of use.

New Features

SuperPaint has been completely restructured and powerful features have been added, without compromising the ease of use that is a SuperPaint hallmark. The features are completely integrated; for instance, you can create a complex fill composed of a pattern, with a background color and a foreground color, texture, or gradient, and then apply it with any of the tools in either layer. This intuitive integration of features allows you to concentrate on your work rather than the limitations of the program.

This version of SuperPaint includes some exciting new capabilities:

Color — SuperPaint supports full real-time color; you can work in 1-bit black-and-white documents (spot color assignments are still available), and you can work in 8-bit, 16-bit, and 32-bit color documents. All Paint and Draw tools are fully supported for color work, and you can use color Paint and Draw plug-in modules.

Basic Image Enhancement — Brightness & Contrast and Color Balance controls, along with selection masking, a Smudge tool, and diffuse, lighten, darken, and invert functions provide everything you need for image enhancement.

Gradients — You can select one of the six graduated fills that are provided, or you can define your own using up to 256 colors (selected from nearly 16.8 million), for use with all of the tools. There are four gradient paths: linear, rectangular, circular, and peaked. In addition, a gradient can be combined with a pattern as part of a custom fill.

8-bit Gradients palette.

High-resolution text filled with a gradient.

Textures — You can save as a "texture" any image you create or import; the texture can then be applied with any of the tools as a continuous fill. The texture image can be virtually any size, and the repetition of the image is seamless. For example, using a scanned image, you could "paint with a fish." In addition, the texture can be combined with a pattern as part of a custom fill.

Top: Painting over an unmasked graphic.
Bottom: Painting over a masked graphic.

Masking — In the Paint layer, the selection tools can be used to create areas that function as masks or inverted masks. A masked area cannot be painted on or erased, while an inverted mask acts like a stencil: the selection area is the only area that can be altered.

Hot Keys — Pressing a single key on the keyboard allows you to toggle to a tool other than the one currently selected, and to most of the floating palettes, without deselecting the current tool.

Virtual Documents — SuperPaint lets you work with large documents: up to six feet by six feet, depending on available disk storage space (i. e., you are no longer limited by the amount of RAM in your system).

On-line Help — Immediate assistance with features and options is available from within the program.

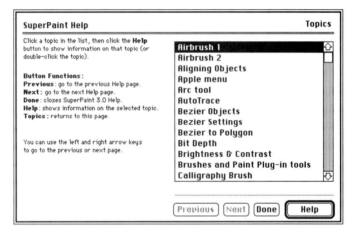

Image Formats — SuperPaint can work with documents in a variety of graphics formats, including PICT, TIFF and EPS (without loss of resolution). In addition, with the appropriate plug-in modules, images can be brought directly into the program from scanners and other image-acquisition devices.

Simplified Text Formatting — Text attributes (font, size, style, justification, and spacing) can be changed individually from the Text and Font menus, or all together in the Text Settings dialog box.

The Frequent Fills palette.

Frequent Fills Palette — The twelve most-recent fill combinations are saved on this palette, meaning you don't have to try to recreate them — just click the one you want.

Custom Lines — You can specify horizontal and vertical line thickness individually (up to 99 pixels each); define complex fills for the lines; and choose from a selection of arrow and dash schemes, or create your own.

Of course, the features that made the previous versions of SuperPaint so popular are still available. For example:

- Editable Bezier curves add flexibility and control to the precision of the Draw layer.

- AutoTrace automatically traces bitmapped shapes, creating objects in the Draw layer; you control the definition of the objects.

- SuperBits lets you convert bitmapped images to Draw objects and edit them at any resolution; that is, you're not restricted by the limitations of the Macintosh screen.

- Transfer Modes provide control over the interaction with the background of paint, paste, and fill operations; the modes are Opaque, Paint on Darker, Invert, Translucent, Transparent (as a percentage), and Transparent Background (the last two are new to SuperPaint 3.0).

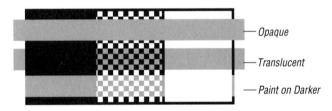

- Transformation commands allow scaling, free rotation, flipping, and slanting of text and graphics in both the Paint and Draw layers. In addition, distortion and perspective can be applied in the Paint layer.

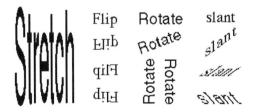

Getting Started

Before using SuperPaint, you should be familiar with basic Macintosh operations like clicking, dragging, and choosing from menus. If you're not, please consult your Macintosh user manual.

Before doing anything else, check the SuperPaint box to be sure you have all the items listed in the "Package Contents" section. Then follow the procedures in the "System Requirements and Installation Card" included in your SuperPaint package.

Package Contents

In addition to this manual, you should have the following items:

- Four disks

- A Quick Reference Card

- A Registration Card

- A System Requirements and Installation Card

- How Are We Doing Card

- Services and Support Card

- An Addendum

If your package does not include all of these items, call Customer Service at (619) 558-6000. Outside the U.S. or Canada, contact your local Aldus dealer or distributor.

Before opening the disk package, be sure to read the Aldus License Agreement carefully.

System Requirements

A hard disk is required. For black-and-white documents, SuperPaint needs at least 2 megabytes of RAM and System 6.0.5 (or later). Color requires a minimum of 2 megabytes of RAM (4 megabytes is recommended), System 6.0.5 (or later), and 32-bit QuickDraw. (Large 32-bit documents may require additional RAM for satisfactory performance.)

Note: SuperPaint also requires at least the 128K ROM version of the Macintosh. If you've upgraded an original 128K (RAM) Macintosh, or a 512K with more memory, but haven't upgraded the ROMs, Super-Paint still won't run. A quick check: if an early Macintosh has been upgraded with an 800K internal floppy drive, it has the 128K ROMs, too.

Registration & Technical Support

There are many advantages to being a registered SuperPaint user. Take a moment now to fill out the enclosed Registration Card, and check Part 6, *Services & Support*, for additional registration information.

If you're having problems with SuperPaint, or just can't figure out how to use one of its features correctly, you can call our Technical Support department. Again, check *Services & Support* for more details.

Read the Book!

It's possible that no one has ever really read an entire user's manual. Some programs, like SuperPaint, are so easy to use that a manual hardly seems necessary.

However, this doesn't mean that all its capabilities are obvious, or that you will discover them just by using the program. To learn the fine points, you really should take the time to go through the manual, especially Part 4, *Using SuperPaint*. (For instance, there's a way to bypass the Scale Selection dialog box if you want to use the same scaling factors you used before. But, you won't find this shortcut in the menu, or in the dialog box — it's only in the manual.)

So, please: read the book!

International Variations

The default values for settings such as units of measurement, paper size and so on, vary according to the version in use. Thus, if you are using the International-English version of SuperPaint, you may find occasional differences between the default settings and the screen samples printed in the SuperPaint manual and the items displayed on your computer.

The International-English and Canadian-English versions of the software include these specific differences from the U.S. version:

- Units of measurement default to millimeters.

- Default paper size is US Letter for the Canadian-English version, and A4 Letter for the International-English version.

- The default currency symbol varies by country. For example, the Canadian system uses the dollar sign ($), and the British system uses the pound sign (£).

Using This Manual

This manual is divided into seven parts (including the *Index*). You're reading the *Introduction to SuperPaint* right now, but what you read next depends on your Macintosh background.

To Get Started Right Now...

You can start right away with the program and discover things on your own. You might want to skim through Part 2, *Tutorial*, or Part 3, *Guide to Tools and Menus*.

For a Guided Tour...

Turn to Part 2, *Tutorial*, and follow the instructions step by step.

For Quick Reference...

Read Part 3, *Guide to Tools and Menus*, put the Quick Reference Card by your keyboard, and perhaps look through the list of topics in the on-line Help dialog box.

For Detailed Reference...

Turn to Part 4, *Using SuperPaint*. You can go through the chapters in order, or skip right to the one that contains the information you need.

For Extra Hints...

Read Part 5, *Tips & Techniques*. This is a selection of hints, tips, and techniques to achieve special results, drawn from the experience of our current users, testers, technical support staff, and design team.

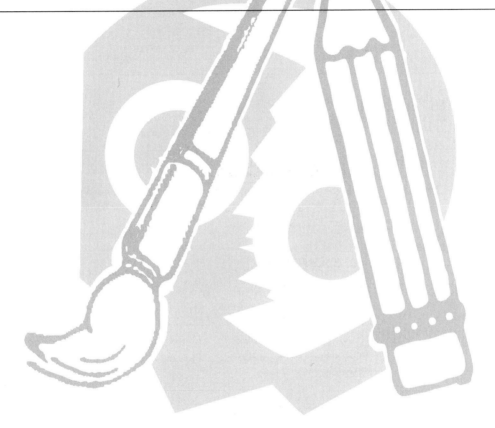

Part 2: Tutorial

Tutorial

If you're new to Macintosh graphics programs in general, and Super-Paint in particular, this section is for you. Just reading through it will give you an idea of what SuperPaint can do, but to get that all-important feel for the program, you should follow the instructions presented here.

If you are familiar with previous versions of SuperPaint, you may want to read the sections on fills, and then go on to Part 3, *Tools and Menus*, and Part 5, *Tips and Techniques*.

Introduction

This tutorial introduces some of the features of SuperPaint. Not everything is covered here; "everything" is covered in Part 4, *Using Super-Paint*. But the tutorial is enough of a sampler to get you going and give you some experience that will illuminate Part 4.

Don't feel you have to obediently follow the tutorial step by step — experiment! Try different things to see what happens. You won't do any harm and you'll become familiar with SuperPaint more quickly.

As much as possible, we use standard Macintosh terminology — to select a tool, you click its icon; dragging means moving the pointer while pressing the mouse button; Option-clicking means holding down the Option key while pressing the mouse button; and so on. If you are not familiar with this terminology, please refer to your Apple user's manual. The term "pop-up," or more correctly, "pop-up palette," refers to a palette of similar items that pops out of a drop-shadowed box on the main Tools palette or the Line & Fill palette (all of the pop-up palettes are defined and illustrated in Part 4).

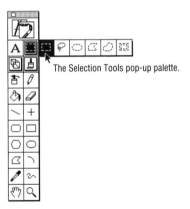

The Selection Tools pop-up palette.

SuperPaint's Layers

The basis of SuperPaint's integrated graphics capabilities is the ability to work in two different "layers." These layers are superimposed on the screen, and in your printouts, to produce a single image. The two layers are a Paint (or *bitmapped*) layer, and a Draw (or *object-oriented*) layer.

Paint layer.　　　　　　Draw layer.　　　　　　Paint and Draw layers
　　　　　　　　　　　　　　　　　　　　　　　superimposed.

Both layers have some common tools and commands; there are also a few tools and commands that are specific to each. You can easily move graphic items from one layer to the other, you can move either layer from front to back, and you can hide the back layer.

The Paint Layer

The Paint layer is the one "in front" when you begin SuperPaint. The graphics you create in this layer are simply collections of dots (the dots on your screen are also called *pixels*). For instance, if you paint a circle, you create a collection of dots with no special relationship to each other. If you paint a square that intersects the circle, you are simply adding dots to the image. The two shapes may be clear to you, but SuperPaint doesn't recognize them as distinct shapes at all. This means that paint graphics, once created, are dealt with on a pixel-by-pixel basis — you can erase part of the circle, for instance, and with it, any overlapping part of the square. In this sense, working in the Paint layer is like sketching with a pencil or painting with a brush: you have areas of your paper or canvas that have been covered, and areas that haven't.

Bitmapped image in the Paint layer.　　　　　　Erasing the bitmapped image.

The images brought into SuperPaint from scanners, screen-capture utilities, or frame grabbers are bitmapped; they can be edited or "cleaned up" in the Paint layer.

The Draw Layer

Paint layer in front.

Draw layer in front.

The Draw layer is initially "behind" the Paint layer when you start SuperPaint, but you can bring it to the front simply by clicking the Paint/Draw Layer switch at the top of the Tools palette.

Items in the Draw layer are discrete objects (hence the term "object-oriented graphics"). Thus, if you draw a circle and a square in a Draw layer, SuperPaint recognizes them as individual, mathematically defined entities. This means, among other things, that you can move the circle without disturbing the square, and you can change the proportions or other attributes of either object at any time.

Two overlapping objects in the Draw layer.

The circle has been moved without disturbing the rectangle.

So, if working in the Paint layer is similar to sketching with pencil and paper, working in the Draw layer is similar to cutting out shapes and laying them out in a collage.

Working with Both Layers

Both layers have advantages and drawbacks. Fortunately, SuperPaint allows you to easily move graphics between the layers to take advantage of the strengths of each. Generally speaking, the Paint layer lets you be spontaneous and creative, while the Draw layer provides smooth precision.

As you work through this tutorial, you will experiment with fills and examine graphics resolution in both layers. We don't describe in detail how each individual tool works, particularly those that are relatively straightforward, such as the Paint Brush and the Pencil, because that is the function of Part 4. (Besides, you will grasp how they work after using them once or twice.)

We are more interested in helping you become aware of how all the features work together, and how they can be used to suit your needs. This understanding will remove SuperPaint from the category of "electronic doodle pad," placing it into the realm of an indispensable tool. And again, we want to encourage you to experiment with the program.

Note: This Tutorial does not concentrate on color features, and only a handful of the illustrations are in color. However, if you are using a color system, please feel free to use color options in place of the called-for blacks, whites and grays.

Let's Get Started

We assume that you've installed SuperPaint on your system, started the program, personalized it, and perhaps "played around" a little. If you haven't yet installed it, go back to the *Introduction* and follow the instructions on installing SuperPaint. You might also scan the *Tools & Menus* section of this manual for an introduction to the palettes and commands that are available.

Tutorial Scenario

The Ocean Tours newsletter is going electronic! In this tutorial, you are going to use SuperPaint to create an electronic version of the Ocean Tours logo, and produce a simple graphic for the next issue of the Ocean Tours newsletter, which for the first time is being produced with desktop publishing software.

The Ocean Tours newsletter.

Tools and Fills

SuperPaint 3.0

Begin the program by double-clicking the SuperPaint icon. If this is the first time you've used SuperPaint, you will be asked to personalize your copy of the program; enter your name in the first text field and, if you wish, press the Tab key to enter additional information in the second. Click *OK*, or press Return or Enter. (If you are already working in SuperPaint, close any open windows and choose **New** from the File menu to open a new, blank document.)

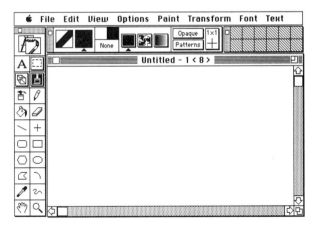

Personalization dialog box.

You'll see the menu bar, a new, untitled document window, the Tools palette to the left of the window, and the Line & Fill palette and the Frequent Fills palette above the window.

If your screen doesn't look like the illustration, you've probably used SuperPaint already and have changed some of its default settings. If the palettes are not in the same position as shown, it won't make any difference for this tutorial.

Note: The number between the angle brackets in the title bar of the document window indicates the bit depth of the document. A one indicates a 1-bit, or black-and-white, document, while an 8-bit document is a color document. Refer to Part 4, Chapter 5 for more information on document bit depth.

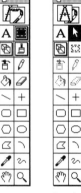

Paint-layer tools.   Draw-layer tools.

The two overlapping icons at the top of the Tools palette — the paint brush and the compass — represent SuperPaint's two layers. The icon that's on top is the layer in which you're working. Clicking the icon area switches layers (and the order of the icons). SuperPaint starts out in the Paint layer.

Click the Paint/Draw Layer icon to switch to the Draw layer. Notice the differences in the Tools palette and the menu bar. The tools that are dimmed are unavailable in the Draw layer.

Let's display the document rulers to ensure that the items you make on your screen approximate our illustrations. Choose **Grid & Rulers** from the Options menu to display the Grid & Rulers dialog box. Click the *Show rulers* check box and click *OK,* or press Return or Enter.

Grid & Rulers dialog box.

Rulers appear along the top and left sides of the window. Notice that there is a dotted line in each ruler that tracks the pointer. Press the space bar to "hot key" to the Grabber and drag the document down and to the right in the document window. This scrolls or repositions the document in the window so the upper left corner and the zero points on the rulers are visible. (Hot keys are described and listed in Part 4, Chapter 1.)

Drawing an Object

Select the Oval shape tool, move the pointer into the window so that the tracking lines in both rulers are at one inch, press the Shift key to restrict the tool to drawing circles, and drag out a circle that is approximately two inches in diameter (the tracking lines both end at three inches).

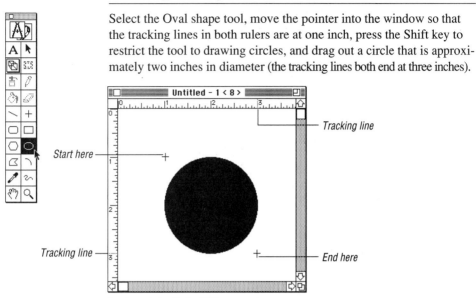

Drawing a circle with the Shift key pressed.

A selected object in the Draw layer.

When you release the mouse button, small black "handles" appear at the corners of what would be a square enclosing the circle. These appear when an object in the Draw layer is "selected" (or is "active"), and they define the *bounding box* of the active object. A bounding box is the smallest rectangle that completely encloses the object. The handles are used to change the size and shape of an object by changing the size and shape of the bounding box.

Note: There is an **Undo** command in the Edit menu that you can use to reverse the last action performed. You may find this very convenient as you work. Choose it now, twice, to remove and then restore the circle.

If you click anywhere in the document window (except on the object), the object is deselected and the handles disappear. To select the shape again, click anywhere inside it with the Selection Arrow.

The Selection Arrow is an important Draw-layer tool — with it you can activate objects and then move them, resize them, and change their attributes. As you progress through this tutorial, you will use it a number of times to perform various actions. So rather than saying "select the Selection Arrow from the Tools palette, click the object to select it," and then do something each time, we just say "use the Selection Arrow" to perform some action. The "hot key" for the Selection Arrow is the A on the keyboard; pressing the A will switch the currently selected tool to the Selection Arrow as long as the key is pressed.

Shapes and Patterns

In both layers, the two-dimensional shapes produced by dedicated shape tools (such as the Oval), consist of an outline and the enclosed area. The outline attributes are Line Width and Line Fill. The enclosed area has one attribute: Area Fill. These attributes are displayed and changed on the Line & Fill palette.

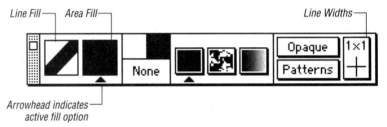

Line Fill — Area Fill — Line Widths —

Arrowhead indicates — active fill option

In the Draw layer, these shapes are objects whose attributes are easily changed. So, the circle on the screen consists of a thin black outline (Line Fill is set to black and Line Width is one pixel) and a black Area Fill. Let's change the fills so these components are apparent.

First, open the Patterns pop-up palette and select a checkerboard pattern for the Area Fill. To open the pop-up palette, position the pointer on the box on the Line & Fill palette that displays the word *Patterns* and press the mouse button. The palette opens and the current pattern is highlighted with a black border. Drag the pointer to the pattern you want and release the mouse button. Notice what happens to both the active object and the Area Fill display on the Line & Fill palette.

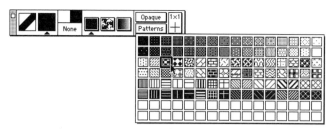

Patterns pop-up palette with checkerboard pattern selected.

You can "tear off" the Patterns (or any other) pop-up palette by dragging past the edge of the popped-up palette. You then can drag its "title" bar to position this floating palette anywhere you'd like on the screen. If you are working with a small monitor, leave the palette closed so it doesn't interfere with your work. (Subsequent illustrations show the Patterns palette positioned in the lower right corner of the screen; this is to aid you determining which patterns were selected.)

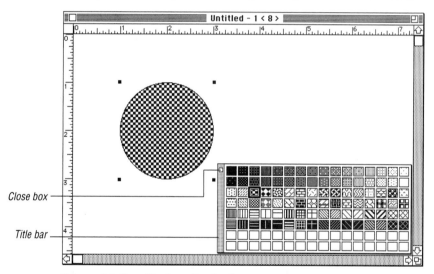

Patterns palette "torn off" and repositioned on the screen.

Next, select thicker line settings from the Line Widths pop-up palette on the Line & Fill palette — with thicker lines, changes to the Line Fill will be more readily visible. Open the Line Widths pop-up palette in the same manner as the Patterns pop-up palette, and select one of the thicker bars. Notice what happens to the Line Widths display and the outline of the circle.

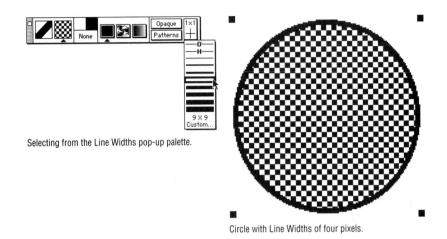

Selecting from the Line Widths pop-up palette.

Circle with Line Widths of four pixels.

Note: If you select one of the shape tools and move the pointer into the document window, it is displayed as a thick cross to reflect the changed line widths.

The Line Fill is similar to the Area Fill. Click the Line Fill display on the Line & Fill palette to activate it — the arrowhead switches from beneath the Area Fill display. (If necessary, use the Selection Arrow to reselect the circle.)

Select a pattern from the Patterns palette. Notice that the Line Fill display and the outline of the circle are updated. If you wish, try a few more patterns, changing both the Line Fill and the Area Fill.

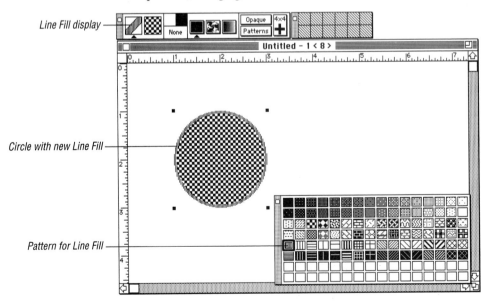

Line Fill display

Circle with new Line Fill

Pattern for Line Fill

Next, set the Line Widths to zero to remove the object outline. Set the Area Fill to a dark gray pattern.

We now have a gray circle about two inches in diameter, with no outline. If that isn't what appears on your screen, you can make any necessary adjustments to the object; or if you prefer, delete the object on the screen (by pressing the Delete key, or choosing **Clear** from the Edit menu), and use the Oval tool to draw another circle.

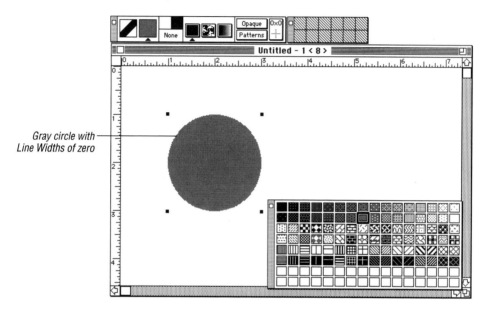

Gray circle with Line Widths of zero

More About Fills

Paint/Draw Layer switch

Click the Paint/Draw Layer switch to return to the Paint layer. In this layer, the Area Fill and Line Fill act like "paint," meaning that once applied, you can alter them only by painting over or erasing them. So you must define both fills before creating graphics — Paint-layer fills are not "attributes," as they are in the Draw layer.

All of the painting tools — the brushes, the Paint Bucket, and even the Pencil — use the current Area Fill as their primary "paint." (In black-and-white documents the Pencil writes in black regardless of the Area Fill.) The shape tools use both Line Fill and Area Fill, as in the Draw layer.

In both layers, the Line Fill and the Area Fill can be quite complex. You can apply a color, a texture, or a gradient to the black parts of a pattern (considered to be the pattern *foreground*), and you can assign a separate color to the white, or *background,* portions.

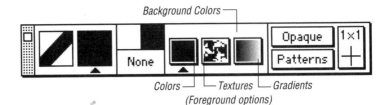

Background Colors ⌐

Colors ⌐ └ Textures └ Gradients
(Foreground options)

The black pixels of the pattern represent the foreground.

Note: In black-and-white (1-bit) documents, fills are almost as versatile: in the Draw layer, you can assign a foreground option and a background color to a pattern; in the Paint layer, the textures and gradients are black and white, and only one color assignment can be made; the color is applied to all the black pixels in the layer. These color assignments can be previewed on a color machine, or printed on a color printer.

A gradient assigned to the foreground; the background remains the same.

Let's try a few fill combinations. First select a bold checkerboard pattern for the Area Fill, and then experiment, applying different foreground options. (If you're working on a color machine, apply background colors too.) Notice that the current pattern remains selected as you change the foreground and background components. Similarly, if you change the pattern, the current foreground and background options are applied to the new pattern. (The Line Fill has the same components and can be just as complex as the Area Fill.)

Note: When SuperPaint is installed on a black-and-white machine, the textures provided are optimized for 1-bit documents and may not resemble those shown here.

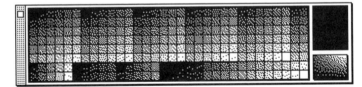

The Colors palette (in a color document).

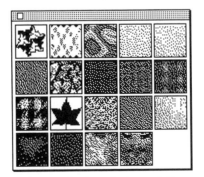

The Textures palette (in a color document). The appearance of this palette varies, according to the textures in the SP Pouch.

The Gradients palette (in a color document).

When a gradient is assigned to the pattern foreground and you use one of the tools, an "elastic band" appears when you release the mouse button, stretching from the center of the object to the pointer (this does not occur with Peaked gradients; see Part 4, Chapter 4). This band lets you define the direction or path of the gradient: position the end of the band and click to complete the application of the gradient. As an example, for a sunset effect, you would stretch the band vertically from the center point.

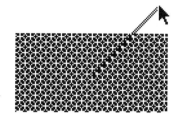

An "elastic band" lets you define the path of the gradient.

The gradient follows the specified path.

When printed, the blending of gradients applied in the Draw layer appears much smoother than it does on your screen. This is especially true in black-and-white documents.

Permanent Fills

As you may have realized while experimenting with patterns and the other fill components, to paint with a solid color, for example, it is necessary to first select a solid pattern. To quickly select a solid pattern for the Line Fill or Area Fill, just click the appropriate Permanent Fill cell on the Line & Fill palette. The three Permanent Fills are: solid foreground and black color; solid foreground and white color; and no pattern, or no fill (*None*).

Permanent Fills

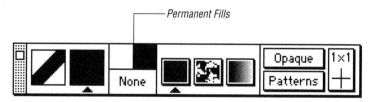

Creating a Texture

Water texture (8-bit).

A texture is simply an image or graphic that can be used as the foreground component of the Line Fill or the Area Fill. In addition to those provided with SuperPaint, you can create your own. Take a few moments now and use some of the Paint tools and different Area Fills to create a representation of water that you can save as a texture, for use as a fill for the word "Excursions" on the Ocean Tours newsletter. Be sure to use some of the tools on the Brush Tools pop-up palette. As an example, the black-and-white texture in the margin was created using the Airbrush, the Twister, the Paint Bucket, and the Smudge tool. (Double-click the Airbrush icon on the Tools palette to display the Airbrush Settings dialog box.)

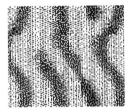

Black-and-white
water texture (1-bit).

The image you create does not have to be large — textures are repeated without breaks, as necessary — but you might give some thought to the edges of the texture so its repetition appears seamless.

When you are finished with the water representation, use the selection Rectangle from the Selection Tools pop-up palette to select the area to be saved as a texture. Choose **Selection to Texture** from the File menu. In the dialog box presented, type a name for the texture file (let's use *water-2*). The dialog box should display *SP Pouch* on the pop-up folder menu, as texture files must be saved in the SP Pouch folder to appear on the Textures palette. If there is a Paint Textures folder in the SP Pouch, you can save your texture in that folder if you wish. Click *Save*, or press Return or Enter, to close the dialog box; the texture is added to the Textures palette, and you can use it as a foreground fill component.

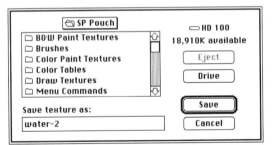

The Selection to Texture dialog box.

Frequent Fills

The Frequent Fills palette.

You may have noticed that each time you use a tool with a different fill combination selected, that fill is added to the Frequent Fills palette. If you want to re-use a fill combination, simply click the fill on the Frequent Fills palette. This is particularly helpful with complex fills — rather than resetting the pattern, the foreground and the background, you can simply select the original fill from the palette.

Another Circle

Now that you have a feel for some of the Paint-layer options, let's get back to the logo. Double-click the Eraser icon on the Tools palette to quickly erase the screen. Make the Area Fill the dark gray you used for the circle in the Draw layer, and make the Line Fill *None*, or be sure the Line Widths are zero. (If the Patterns palette is open, close by clicking the close box in the "title" bar.) Select the Oval shape tool and Shift-drag a circle, approximately two inches in diameter, to the right of the one in the Draw layer.

Circle in the Paint layer —

Circle in the Draw layer —

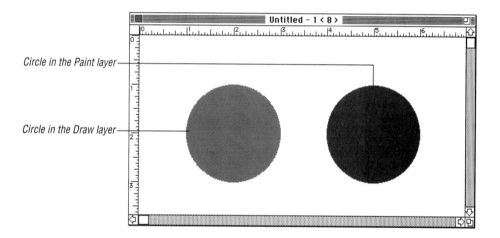

Resolution in Both Layers

The words and images on your screen and on the pages from most printers are formed by groups of tiny dots. Different devices have different sized dots — LaserWriter dots are smaller than ImageWriter dots, for example, while ImageWriter dots are approximately half the size of screen dots. (The screen dots are also called *pixels*, which is short for picture elements.)

The resolution of display and output devices, such as your Macintosh screen and your printer, is measured in dots per inch (usually abbreviated to dpi); that is, the number of its dots the device can fit into one inch. Often this number is the same in both the horizontal and vertical directions, in which case only one figure is given: the Macintosh screen is 72 dpi, while LaserWriter resolution is 300 dpi.

Paint-layer graphics are limited to 72 dpi because that is the resolution of the Macintosh screen. SuperPaint does not recognize the dots in the Paint layer as a circle, and so it cannot smooth the outline for you when transmitting the information to a printer. This is where the term *bitmapped* comes from: the dots are transmitted to the printer in a direct one-to-one mapping.

Draw-layer graphics on the other hand, are mathematically defined entities, and although they appear to be the same resolution as Paint-layer graphics (because the screen display is limited to 72 dpi), when the information is transmitted to the printer, the graphic is printed at the maximum resolution of the printer.

Let's print our document to actually compare the resolution of both layers. Later we'll look at SuperPaint features that allow you to convert Paint-layer graphics to Draw-layer objects and vice versa.

File	
New...	⌘N
Open...	⌘O
Close	⌘W
Save	⌘S
Save As...	
Selection to Texture...	
Revert to Saved	
Place	▶
Export...	
Document Info...	
Page Setup...	
Print... ⌘P	
Quit	⌘Q

Choose **Print** from the File menu to open the Print dialog box. The appropriate options should already be set: click *OK*, or press Return or Enter. When the page is printed, the differences in resolution between the two circles will be readily apparent.

The Draw-layer graphic (left) is resolution independent.
The Paint-layer graphic (right) will always be 72 dpi.

Masking and Magnification

As mentioned earlier, a few of the icons on the Tools palette were dimmed when you switched from the Paint to the Draw layer (tools that are dimmed are unavailable). The unavailable tools are the pixel-manipulation tools like the Paint Brush and the Eraser — tools that perform actions unrelated to the Draw layer. These tools and the nature of the Paint layer mean you can be a little more creative in the Paint layer. But you need not sacrifice the smoothness of the Draw layer. Let's create the stylized wave crest of the Ocean Tours logo in the Paint layer, and then trace it in the Draw layer.

Tools that are unavailable in the Draw layer are dimmed.

The Ocean Tours logo.

First we will mask all of the document except the circle, in effect creating a stencil. Then if too much of the boundary of the circle is erased, repairing the curve will be simple — we won't have to start over and re-create the circle.

Begin by selecting the circle we "painted" on the screen: use the Lasso from the Selection Tools pop-up and drag around the circle. When you release the mouse button, SuperPaint will close the shape and then "tighten" the selection area to exclude the white space around the circle.

In the Paint layer, a selection area is delineated by a moving-dash line, which is sometimes referred to as "marching ants." (Notice that the terms *select* and *selection* do not have quite the same meaning in the Paint layer as in the Draw layer.)

"Marching ants" define a Paint-layer selection area

Choose **New Mask** from the **Masking** submenu of the Paint menu. The selection area is filled with diagonal lines to indicate that it is protected from all paint operations. (If you like, use the Eraser and try to erase part of the circle.) Now choose **Invert Mask** from the **Masking** submenu of the Paint menu. The entire screen except the selection area is now masked (like a stencil).

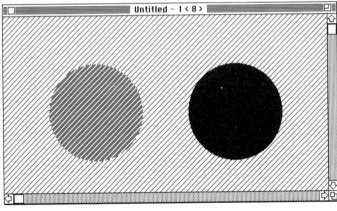

Inverted mask.

Choose the **Brush Shapes** command from the Options menu, or double-click the Paint Brush icon on the Tools Palette, to display the Custom Brushes dialog box. Select the smallest round brush shape and click *OK*, or press Return or Enter to close the dialog box.

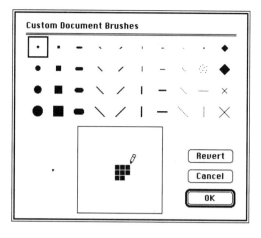

If you used the **Brush Shapes** command to open the dialog box, the last-selected tool is still active — select the Paint Brush. Set the Area Fill to white and begin painting the wave outline into the Paint-layer circle. Use the illustration of the logo in the margin as a guide. (You need not be too concerned about getting your image to match exactly the one in our illustrations; a close approximation is sufficient.)

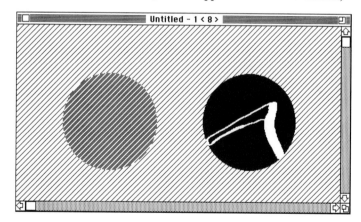

Continue to paint the white wave crest into the circle. Switch the Area Fill to the gray of the circle, conveniently on the Frequent Fills palette, to touch up as necessary. (Notice how the inverted mask is of benefit here.)

Zoom In

For a little more control over your work, you can magnify the image and work on a pixel-by-pixel basis. Position the Paint Brush over the area you want to work on, press E on the keyboard to "hot key" to the enlargement Magnifier, and click to zoom in one level of magnification.

The window splits into two sections or "panes." The left side is a portion of the image at normal magnification, while the right side is the magnified view. With E still pressed, click again to zoom to the 4x view. The area of the image that is displayed in the magnified view (on the right) is indicated in the normal view (on the left) by a rectangle of dotted lines. You can move around in the split-image document just as you would a normal document: the scroll bars on the bottom and right side of the window, or use the Grabber to drag the image around in the window. (You can "hot key" to the Grabber by pressing the space bar.) You can use the Grabber in either side of the split window, or you can use it to move the dotted-line rectangle.

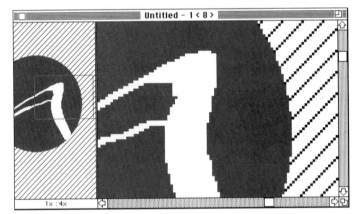

The 4x magnification view.

Click once more to zoom into the highest level of magnification (8x). Each black square in the magnified view represents a single dot or pixel in the circle. Use the Paint Brush or the Pencil to add and remove pixels until the outline of the wave crest is relatively smooth. (The Pencil works like a single-pixel eraser when you begin writing on a pixel that is the color of the current Area Fill, or black in black-and-white documents.)

When you are done editing at increased magnification, double-click the Pencil icon on the Tool palette to return to normal magnification. (Double-clicking the Pencil icon is a shortcut to and from normal and 8x magnification.)

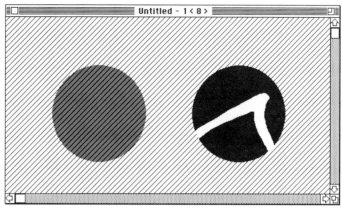

Normal view.

Note: Command-key shortcuts are listed with the commands in the menus. All of the hot keys and double-click shortcuts are listed on the Quick Reference Card.

 When you are satisfied with the Paint-layer logo, choose **Delete Mask** from the **Masking** submenu, and then switch to the Draw layer.

It's important to periodically save your work — if something goes wrong, you won't lose everything. Choose **Save** from the File menu (or use the Command-S shortcut). Since we've been working in a new, untitled document, the Save As dialog box is presented; type a document name (let's use *Ocean Tours Logo*) and click *Save*, or press Return or Enter.

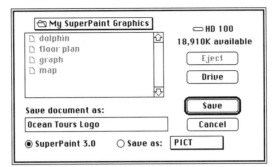

Introducing Bezier Curves

You can use the Freehand tool to draw free-form shapes and lines. In the Draw layer, the free-form shapes are defined by *Bezier paths* (also called *Bezier curves*). A Bezier path is an outline that is described mathematically and can be reshaped later.

Anatomy of a Bezier path in Reshape mode.

You can also use the controls in the Bezier Settings dialog box to influence the outline: a Bezier path will smooth itself out after you've drawn it, depending how you've defined the settings for the tool. We will use the default settings so the amount of smoothing is minimal. (If you want to see the Bezier Settings dialog box, choose **Bezier Settings** from the Draw menu, or double-click the Freehand tool icon on the Tools palette.)

Bezier Settings dialog box, default settings.

Tracing the outline of
the wave crest.

Be sure the Area Fill is solid white; make the Line Fill solid black and the Line Widths both one pixel. Select the Freehand tool and trace the outline of the wave crest in the Paint-layer logo as a single shape. Begin a little outside of the circle and extend the other "wing" beyond the circle, as shown. (You don't need to close the shape precisely; SuperPaint will close it for you.) This Draw object is like any other: you can move it, use the handles to resize it, and change its Area Fill, Line Fill, and Line Widths.

Note: You can use the Freehand tool to draw editable lines (rather than closed shapes) by setting the Area Fill to *None*; SuperPaint then does not close the shape drawn. However, in the Draw layer, the object is still treated as a shape; for example, if you changed the Area Fill to black, it would be filled as if there was a line joining the endpoints. (The tip of the Selection Arrow must be on the line defining the shape to select any Draw object, Bezier or otherwise, that has an Area Fill of *None*.)

Reshaping the Wave Outline

Bezier curves are a useful and powerful feature of SuperPaint. Becoming proficient at reshaping them requires a bit more time than does mastering the Paint Brush, for example. Thus, you may find it useful to manipulate a copy of the wave outline to get a feel for reshaping before working on the wave outline itself.

Choose the **Duplicate** command from the Edit menu (or use the Command-D shortcut) to duplicate the shape. The duplicated object is off-set slightly down and to the right of the original; the duplicate is active and the original deselected. Use the Selection Arrow to drag the duplicate below the circles.

Draw	
Bring to Front	⌘=
Send to Back	⌘-
Group	⌘G
Ungroup	⌘U
Lock	
✓**Unlock**	
Align Objects...	⌘M
Object Info...	⌘I
Reshape Bezier	⌘R
Convert to Bezier	▶
Bezier to Polygon	▶
Join Beziers	
Bezier Settings...	

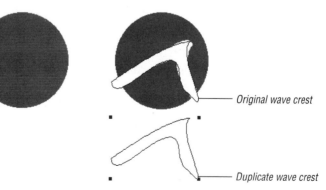

Original wave crest

Duplicate wave crest

Note: If you changed the default settings in the Preferences dialog box, your Bezier object may have switched to Reshape mode automatically, in which case you'll have filled circles and squares at intervals along the path.

Choose **Reshape Bezier** from the Draw menu (or use the Command-R shortcut) to place the object into Reshape mode.

Instead of the four handles at the corners of the object's bounding box, there are now filled circles and squares marking the line's anchor points. Also, the Draw menu has been replaced by the Reshape menu. (Depending how you drew the path, there may be more or fewer points along the curve, and in slightly different positions, than the ones illustrated here.)

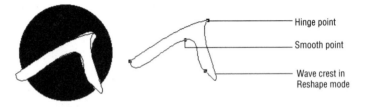

Hinge point

Smooth point

Wave crest in Reshape mode

A Bezier path is made up of *segments*. The spot where a segment joins another segment, or where a segment ends, is called an *anchor point*. When a Bezier object is in Reshape mode, you can move its segments and change the curves, add and delete anchor points, and even break the path.

There are two types of anchor points and two types of segments. An anchor point is either a *smooth* or a *hinge* point; a segment connects two anchor points, and is either *curved* or *straight*. Smooth points are represented by circles, and hinge points by squares.

Remember, the illustrations here will not exactly match what's on your screen, since the path you drew is slightly different and its anchor points probably appear in different spots.

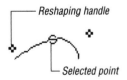

Reshaping handle

Selected point

Begin by clicking one of the anchor points to select it; the circle or square becomes hollow, and one or two special reshaping handles may appear. Drag the anchor point to reposition it, and drag any reshaping handle(s) to change the curve of the attached segment(s). Use the duplicate wave outline to familiarize yourself with reshaping a Bezier path: drag the anchor points and reshaping handles all over the screen.

Add anchor points, if necessary, by Option-clicking any spot on the path. Switch hinge to smooth points and straight segments to curved, as necessary, by double-clicking them. (Reshaping Bezier paths is fully described in Part 4, Chapter 8.)

Note: If you inadvertently click outside of the shape, use the Selection Arrow to reselect the object and choose **Reshape Bezier** again to re-enter Reshape mode.

When you are finished manipulating the duplicate outline, click outside the object to exit Reshape mode. The object is automatically deselected, so use the Selection Arrow to reselect the duplicate. Choose **Clear** from the Edit menu, or press the Delete key, to delete it.

Original wave crest in Reshape mode.

Use the Selection Arrow to select the original wave outline on top of the Paint-layer logo. Choose **Reshape Bezier** from the Draw menu (or use the Command-R shortcut) to place the object into Reshape mode.

Reshape the outline until it closely matches the wave crest in the Paint layer. Add and move points as needed, and switch hinge to smooth points and straight segments to curved, as necessary. Once the shape is approximately correct, you may find it helpful to move the outline away from the underlying Paint-layer logo for better viewing as you finish the reshaping.

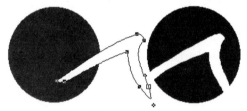

Move the outline away from the Paint-layer logo for better viewing.

Precise reshaping can be a delicate operation and can take a little time and effort. It will become easier as you become more familiar with the process. Also, don't forget your screen is 72 dpi — the curve is actually smoother than it appears.

When you are satisfied with the wave outline, click outside the shape to exit Reshape mode. Use the Selection Arrow to drag the object on top of the Draw-layer circle, as shown.

Stacking Order

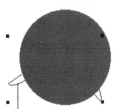

After choosing
Send to Back from
the Draw menu

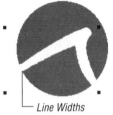

Line Widths
set to zero

Multiple objects are selected.

After grouping, there is one
set of handles.

Although the Draw layer is a single layer, the objects in the layer have a stacking order: later objects are always on top of earlier objects. This isn't always apparent when the objects don't come into contact with each other. However, when objects overlap, you can see the stacking order, as with the wave outline on top of the circle.

You can change the relative order of objects in the window by moving any object to the bottom or the top of the stack. Choose **Send to Back** from the Draw menu to move the wave crest behind the circle. Now choose **Bring to Front** to put it in front again.

Make any final adjustments to the positioning of the wave crest with the Selection Arrow. When you are satisfied with its position, set the Line Widths to zero.

Now we'll select the two objects at once and link them so they're treated as one object. Use the Selection Arrow to drag a rectangular frame that completely encloses the circle and the wave — this is a shortcut for selecting all objects within a given area. (Another method of selecting multiple objects is to Shift-click each object one by one.) Choose **Group** from the Draw menu. There is now one set of handles.

Switch to the Paint layer. Erase the contents of the Paint layer by double-clicking the Eraser icon on the Tools palette, or double-click the selection Rectangle icon to select the area in the document window and then press the Delete key.

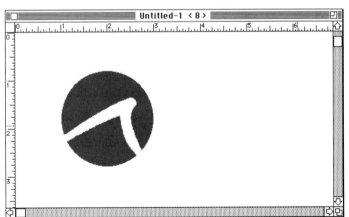

The contents of the Paint layer are erased.

Next, we will reduce the size of the document so large areas of empty space are not saved and transferred to the page-layout program. Choose **Document Info** from the File menu to display the Document Info dialog box. This dialog box can be used to check on and change the size and bit depth of the active document. (Bit depth is discussed in Part 4, Chapter 5.)

```
Document Info
─────────────────────────────────────────────────
┌─Document is...──────
│ ○ Black & White (1-bit)   Measure in: [ Inches    ]
│ ◉ Color: [ 8-bit ]

┌─Make the document...─┐   Width:     Height:
│ [ Narrower ] [ Wider ]   [ 2.5 ]    [ 2.5 ]   Pages: 1
│ [ Shorter  ] [ Taller ]  Orientation: ◉ Tall  ○ Wide

Chosen printer: LaserWriter
Printer page: 8.00 x 10.78        [ Cancel ]  [ OK ]
```

The *Width* text box is highlighted: type 2.5, press the Tab key to highlight the *Height* text box, and type 2.5 again. Click *OK*, or press Return or Enter to close the dialog box. The document is reduced to 2.5 x 2.5 inches. Switch to the Draw layer and use the Selection Arrow to center the logo in the document window.

Now, let's save our work: choose **Save** from the File menu, or use the Command-S shortcut; changes to the document *Ocean Tours Logo* are saved. Finally, choose **Print** from the File menu, or use the Command-P shortcut, to see how the logo actually looks.

You now have a smooth, high-resolution logo that can be imported into your desktop publishing program and scaled appropriately, or you can use the **Scale Selection** command in the Transform menu to change its size prior to placing it in the newsletter.

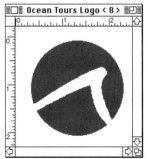

The document is reduced.

AutoTrace

Next, we will work on the dolphin that is leaping out of the table-of-contents block in the lower right corner of the newsletter. If you've taken a break, start SuperPaint; if you are already working in the program, close any open documents, and choose **New** from the File menu.

First, we'll import a clip-art dolphin that you happen to have in the Tutorial folder. (You could use the Paint tools to produce a dolphin yourself; we have provided one to save time.) Choose **Open** from the File menu; a standard dialog box opens so you can find and open the *dolphin* clip-art document. The clip-art document window opens on top of the untitled window in which you are currently working, but doesn't interfere with it at all. (You can have as many as ten separate documents open at once.)

```
┌─────────────────────────────────────────────┐
│          ┌──── Tutorial ────┐                │
│       ┌─────────────────────┬─┐    ▭ HD 100  │
│       │ D dolphin           │⬆│             │
│       │ D Sailing Ship      │ │   ┌─────────┐│
│       │                     │ │   │ Eject   ││
│       │                     │ │   └─────────┘│
│       │                     │ │   ┌─────────┐│
│       │                     │ │   │ Drive   ││
│       │                     │ │   └─────────┘│
│       │                     │ │              │
│       │                     │ │   ┌─────────┐│
│       │                     │ │   │ Open    ││
│       │                     │⬇│   └─────────┘│
│       └─────────────────────┴─┘   ┌─────────┐│
│                                   │ Cancel  ││
│       Selected type: SuperPaint 3.0└────────┘│
│       ┌──────────┐                           │
│       │ Formats... │                          │
│       └──────────┘                           │
└─────────────────────────────────────────────┘
```

Use the Selection Arrow to select the dolphin. Copy the selection to the Clipboard: either choose **Copy** from the Edit menu, or use the Command-C shortcut.

Choose **Close** from the File menu, use the Command-W shortcut, or click the close box in the left side of the document title bar to close the clip-art document.

The Close box ——

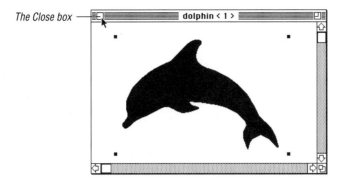

 Switch to the Draw layer of the untitled document. Paste the dolphin into the window: choose **Paste** from the Edit menu or use the Command-V shortcut. Pasted graphics are always placed into the center of the window.

Now, let's re-orient the dolphin so it appears to be leaping up and to the left. Choose **Rotate Right** from the Transform menu to rotate the object clockwise 90 degrees. The angle of the dolphin still isn't quite right, so we'll free rotate it a bit.

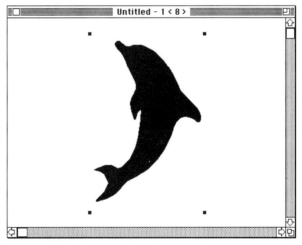

After Rotate Right.

First, let's display the Coordinates palette so the angle of rotation is available. Choose **Show Coordinates** from the **Floating Palettes** submenu of the View menu (the rotation readout will show 90 since the dolphin was rotated right ninety degrees).

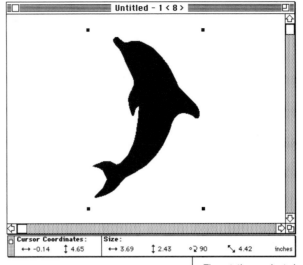

Cursor Coordinates :		Size :				
↔ -0.14	↕ 4.65	↔ 3.69	↕ 2.43	○↷ 90	↘ 4.42	inches

The rotation readout shows 90

✳ Next choose **Free Rotate** from the Transform menu; the pointer becomes a "starburst." Use this transformation pointer to drag the upper left handle down and left (the starburst becomes an arrow when on a handle), rotating the object counterclockwise. The bounding box of the object is filled with gray during transformation. Rotate the object until the angle of rotation displayed on the Coordinates palette is 35 degrees. The apparent distortion of the dolphin's outline is a display limitation; the Draw object maintains its smooth resolution. Click outside the bounding box to exit Transform mode.

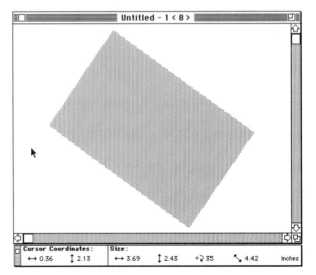

Cursor Coordinates :		Size :				
↔ 0.36	↕ 2.13	↔ 3.69	↕ 2.43	○↷ 35	↘ 4.42	inches

The bounding box of the object is filled with gray during transformation.

Now we'll copy the dolphin to the Paint layer so we can select the lower part of the tail. Use the Selection Arrow to reselect the object and choose **Copy to Painting** from the Edit menu to make a bitmapped copy of the dolphin in the Paint layer.

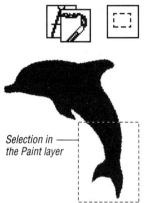

Switch to the Paint layer. The copy is exactly on top of the original in the Draw layer. Use the selection Rectangle to make a selection such that the top of the rectangle intersects the bitmapped dolphin below the dorsal fin, completely enclosing the tail of the dolphin, as shown. (This is an operation that you could not do in the Draw layer.)

AutoTracing Bitmapped Graphics

Selection in the Paint layer

Now we will trace the outline of the selected portion of the tail into the Draw layer (automatically rather than by hand, as we did for the wave crest). To *trace* the outline of a selected bitmapped graphic into the Draw layer, first choose **AutoTrace Settings** from Paint menu to open the AutoTrace Settings dialog box. Click the *Beziers* button for the *Trace to* option, and then drag the sliders in the *Beziers* section of the dialog box so all three are positioned one mark to the right of the left edge of the ruled control bar, as shown. Click *OK*, or press Return or Enter, to close the dialog box

AutoTrace Settings

Find objects at least:

5 pixels high

○ and
● or

5 pixels wide

Trace to:
● Beziers
○ Polygons

☐ Outline only

Beziers

More Points per Line — Less Points per Line

All Straight Lines — All Curves

Sharp Corners — No Corners

Revert   Cancel   OK

Next, choose **AutoTrace** from the Paint menu to cause SuperPaint to trace the outline of the tail into the Draw layer.

We won't need the Paint-layer dolphin again, so double-click the Eraser icon on the Tools palette to clear the Paint layer. The Draw-layer dolphin will still be visible.

Switch back to the Draw layer. The tracing of the lower part of the dolphin is selected, since it is the object most recently brought into the Draw layer. Give it an Area Fill of white (a tracing initially has no fill).

This tracing is an object that is on top of the original dolphin. If you were to drag it to one side and then print the document, you would see that the tracing is not quite as smooth as the original dolphin in the Draw layer, since AutoTrace followed the jagged contours of the Paint-layer shape.

The tracing has been assigned an Area Fill of white.

The Draw-layer dolphin is shown at left, and the tracing is shown at right.

Let's reshape the white tail to smooth the worst of the distortion. Choose **Reshape Bezier** from Draw menu, or use the Command-R shortcut.

The tail object is relatively small; to make the reshaping easier, choose **Scale Selection** from the Transform menu. In the dialog box presented, click the *400%* buttons for the horizontal and vertical percentages; click *OK*, or press Return or Enter to close the dialog box.

Scale Selection

Horizontal		Vertical	
○ 25%	○ 200%	○ 25%	○ 200%
○ 50%	○ 300%	○ 50%	○ 300%
○ 100%	◉ 400%	○ 100%	◉ 400%
○ Other: 400 %		○ Other: 400 %	

[Cancel] [OK]

At four times original size, the object is quite large; it will be necessary to reposition the object in the document window a few times as you reshape it. Also, the object may appear to be outside the boundaries of the document, but it will not be truncated or otherwise affected.

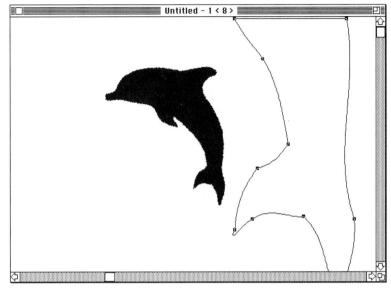

The tail has been scaled to 400%.

Now, reshape the outline as you did with the wave crest for the logo.

Note: If you accidentally click outside the object, deselecting it, simply reselect the object and re-enter Reshape mode.

Use the scroll bars or drag the object when you need to see another section of the outline.

When you are done, choose **Scale Selection** from the Transform menu to scale the object back to its original size; enter 25% for both factors. Use the Selection Arrow to align the white tail on top of the dolphin. You can use the commands in the **Nudge** submenu of the Edit menu, or the arrow keys on the keyboard, to move the tail one pixel at a time to position it precisely.

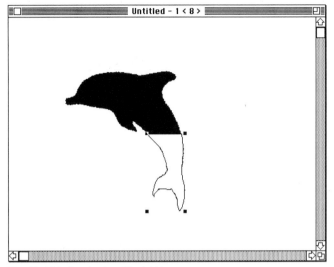

The white tail is aligned on top of the dolphin.

When you are satisfied with the position of the tail, set the Line Fill to white. There may be a few black pixels of the underlying black dolphin visible at the edges of the white tail, but these will not be not be visible when the dolphin is superimposed on the gray table-of-contents block.

(If more than a few black pixels are visible, you could set the Line Width to two pixels, but as the line becomes thicker, a size mismatch becomes evident at the junction of the white tail with the black body. Alternately, you could reshape the tail further, or you could select the black dolphin, choose **Edit SuperBits** from the Draw menu, and erase the lower portion of the dolphin. SuperBits objects and editing them are introduced in the next section.)

When the image is satisfactory (although you cannot see the tail), Shift-click the black dolphin so both objects are selected, and choose **Group** from the Draw menu.

As before, we will reduce the size of the document so large areas of empty space are not saved and transferred to the page-layout program. Choose **Document Info** from the File menu to display the Document Info dialog box.

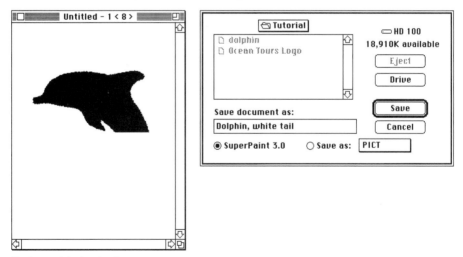

Document Info

┌─ Document is... ─────────
○ Black & White (1-bit)   Measure in: │ Inches │
◉ Color: │ 8-bit │

┌─ Make the document... ─┐   Width: Height:
│ Narrower │ │ Wider │   │ 3.5 │   │ 4.5 │   Pages: 1
│ Shorter │ │ Taller │   Orientation: ◉ Tall ○ Wide

Chosen printer: LaserWriter
Printer page: 8.00 × 10.78   │ Cancel │ │ OK │

Type 3.5 in the *Width* text box, press the Tab key and type 4.5 in the *Height* text box. Click *OK*, or press Return or Enter, to close the dialog box. Use the Selection Arrow to center the logo in the smaller document.

Choose **Close** from the File menu, use the Command-W shortcut, or click the close box in the document title bar. Since we've been working in a new, untitled document, you'll be asked if you want to save changes to the document. Click *Yes*, or press Return or Enter. The Save As dialog box opens; type a document name (let's use *Dolphin, white tail*) and click *Save*, or press Return or Enter.

Untitled - 1 < 8 >

🗁 **Tutorial**   ⊂ HD 100
☐ dolphin   18,910K available
☐ Ocean Tours Logo
                          │ Eject │
                          │ Drive │

Save document as: │ Save │
│ Dolphin, white tail │ │ Cancel │
◉ SuperPaint 3.0 ○ Save as: │ PICT │

The document size is reduced.

SuperBits Objects

Thus far in the Tutorial we have traced Paint-layer graphics into the Draw layer, both by hand and with AutoTrace, and we have copied a Draw-layer graphic to the Paint layer to alter it. You can also copy bitmapped graphics into the Draw layer and smooth them to take advantage of the precision of the layer. It was mentioned earlier that you could have created your own dolphin. If you would like to try this yourself, we will quickly go through the procedure.

If you've taken a break, start SuperPaint; if you are already working in the program, close any open documents, and choose **New** from the File menu. If you're restarting SuperPaint, you'll have to copy the dolphin in the Tutorial folder to the Clipboard again. If you're continuing from the previous section, the dolphin should still be on the Clipboard.

 Be sure you are in the Paint layer of the new, untitled document. Choose **Paste** from the Edit menu, or use the Command-V shortcut, to paste a copy of the dolphin into the Paint layer. (We are skipping the first step: using the Paint-layer tools, black and white fills, and increased magnification to produce a dolphin silhouette — the process is similar to the one you used to paint the wave crest into the circle.) Pasting a Draw object into the Paint layer causes it to be converted to a bitmapped graphic at 72 dpi.

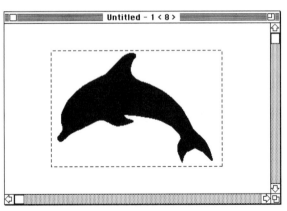

The dolphin is pasted into the center of the window.

 The dolphin is pasted into the center of the window as a rectangular selection. We don't want to convert the enclosed white space into a SuperBits object along with the dolphin, so select the dolphin with the Lasso (the rectangular area is deselected when you select the Lasso from the Selection Tools pop-up palette).

"Marching ants" define the Lassoed selection.

Choose **Create SuperBits** from the Paint menu to display the Create SuperBits dialog box. Set the horizontal and vertical resolution to 300 dpi (the resolution of most laser printers). Be sure the *Resize to match resolution* option is not selected. If you are working on a color machine, click the *Black & white* button to save processing time and memory, since this is not a color graphic.

```
Create SuperBits

┌─Horizontal ──────────┐  ┌─Vertical ──────────┐
│  ○ 72 (Screen)        │  │  ○ 72 (Screen)      │
│  ○ 144 (ImageWriter)  │  │  ○ 144 (ImageWriter) │
│  ○ 216 (ImageWriter LQ)│  │ ○ 216 (ImageWriter LQ)│
│  ◉ 300 (LaserWriter)  │  │  ◉ 300 (LaserWriter) │
│  ○ 360 (StyleWriter)  │  │  ○ 360 (StyleWriter) │
│  ○ Other: [300  ] dpi │  │  ○ Other: [300  ] dpi│
└───────────────────────┘  └──────────────────────┘

☐ Resize to match resolution
☐ Smooth (300 dpi, b & w only)
◉ Black & white  ○ Color        [ Cancel ]  [ OK ]
```

You can select the *Smooth (300 dpi, b & w only)* option to cause SuperPaint to smooth some of the jagged outline for you. We left the option unselected in the following illustrations so the differences between the unsmoothed and smoothed SuperBits object are more apparent. When you close the dialog box, the bitmapped shape is *copied* to the Draw layer becoming an editable *bitmapped object*. Delete the Paint-layer shape.

Note: A SuperBits object can be moved and resized with the Selection Arrow like a regular Draw-layer graphic, but you cannot, for example, change its fill by selecting it and then changing the Area Fill on the Line & Fill palette.

Switch to the Draw layer. The object is already selected; choose **Edit SuperBits** from the Draw menu, or use the Command-R shortcut. (If there is not enough memory available to edit the entire object at once, it can be edited in sections. You will be asked to frame the portion to be edited.)

The SuperBits window opens on top of the untitled window in which you are working. The object is in the SuperBits Paint layer, and appears larger than it did since the resolution of the SuperBits object is higher than the screen resolution (300 dpi versus 72 dpi), and each dot in the object is represented by a screen dot in the SuperBits editing window. The Paint menu has replaced the Draw menu, and all of the tools are available on the Tools palette. (If you were working with the rotated dolphin from the previous section, you would notice that the SuperBits object is displayed in its original orientation, i.e., before rotation.)

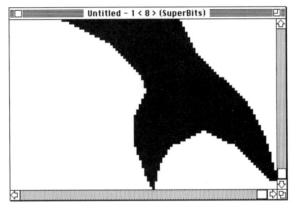

The SuperBits window.

The jagged outline resulting from the resolution of the Paint layer is apparent; it is even more apparent at higher magnifications. Double-click the Pencil to zoom to 8x magnification. Press the space bar to "hot key" to the Grabber; drag the magnification frame in the left pane so an edge of the dolphin is magnified.

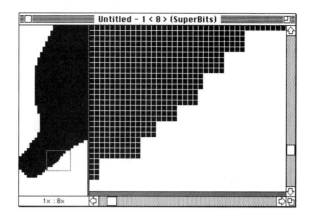

Use the Pencil to fill in the "steps" between the jagged peaks, smoothing the outline. (All of the Paint tools are available for SuperBits editing.) Use the scroll bars or the Grabber to move the image in the panes to continue working. After smoothing a section of the dolphin, close the SuperBits window: choose **Close SuperBits** from the File menu (Command-W), or click the close box in the title bar.

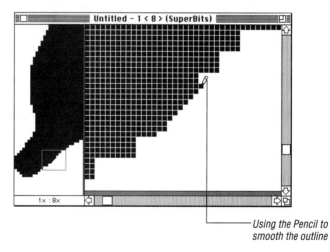

Using the Pencil to smooth the outline

You will be asked if you want to save the changes made to the Super-Bits object. Click *Yes*, or press Return or Enter, to close the dialog box and update the SuperBits object.

Print the document and examine the difference between the edited and unedited portions of the SuperBits object.

The Paint-layer dolphin.

The dolphin edited as a SuperBits object.

This exercise was an introduction to editing SuperBits objects; this document need not be saved.

Another SuperBits Object

Another method of creating a SuperBits object is with the **Place** command. The **Place** command can be used, for example, to place a scanned image saved as a TIFF document; the image is placed into the Draw layer as a SuperBits object. The document in the Tutorial folder named *Sailing Ship* is an image that was scanned at 300 dpi and saved as a TIFF document. From an open document, you can choose **TIFF** from the **Place** submenu of the File menu, select *Sailing Ship* in the Place TIFF dialog box, and examine the object placed into the Draw layer of the open document. You can also use **Edit SuperBits** to repair the image (there are some gaps and splotches in the image that are a result of the scanning process), or to color it, paint on it, add to it, or otherwise alter the image in any way you wish.

When you're done, choose **Quit** from the File menu. This document need not be saved.

What's Next?

Now that you've completed the tutorial, you should feel comfortable using SuperPaint on your own. Continue to experiment with the features and options (especially combinations of them) — we have touched on only a very few. For some more advanced exercises, turn to Part 5, *Tips and Techniques*, and go through those step-by-step procedures. You also can open the examples provided in the Samples folder to examine some of the ways others have used SuperPaint. Examine the images in detail and take them apart to determine how the effects are achieved — just don't save the changes when you close the documents.

Also, don't think that SuperPaint is limited to creating just "art" or images: with a few lines and circles and the Text tool, you can quickly produce some very useful documents such as maps and office forms. In addition, as we mentioned, the program is also very useful for "cleaning up" scanned images.

Use the Quick Reference Card and Part Three, *Tools and Menus*, for quick reference. Turn to Part Four, *Using SuperPaint*, to learn about any of SuperPaint's features in depth.

Part 3: Guide to Tools & Menus

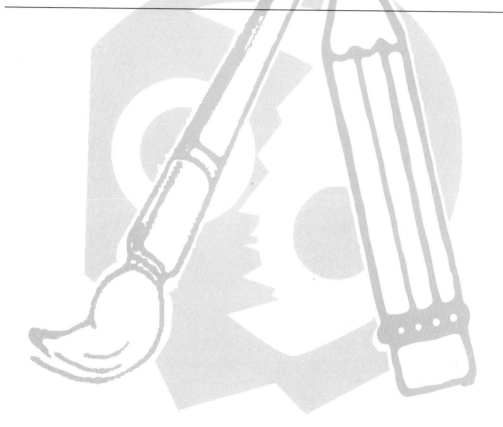

Guide to Tools & Menus

This section briefly describes each of SuperPaint's tools and its menu commands.

SuperPaint Palettes   *3-3*

SuperPaint Menus   *3-13*

SuperPaint Palettes

When you begin SuperPaint, three palettes are open. The Tools palette provides access to all of the specialized Paint and Draw tools. The Line & Fill palette contains the fill, line, color, texture, gradient, pattern, and transfer mode controls. The Frequent Fills palette holds the twelve fill combinations most recently used. You can reposition or close these palettes at any time.

All SuperPaint palettes are "floating," meaning they can be moved. Each floating palette has a gray "title" bar on its top or left side, which includes a close box. Drag the title bar to reposition the palette; click the close box to close the palette.

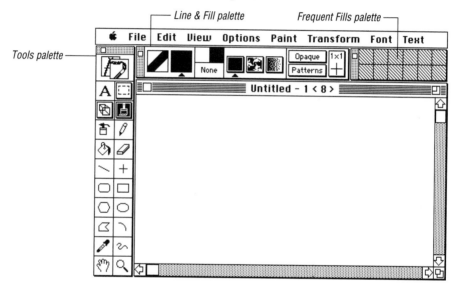

Note: This section of the manual is an introduction to and summary of the primary tools and controls for the program — secondary "pop-up" palettes are not described, nor are all of the "hot keys" and keyboard modifiers. Part 4, *Using SuperPaint*, describes every feature in detail, and the Quick Reference Card summarizes options and shortcuts.

The Tools
palette.

The Tools Palette

The Tools palette consists of a series of boxes, each of which displays an icon that represents a specific tool or effect. Three of these boxes represent pop-up palettes (to save space and provide easy access, sets of related tools have been grouped together and placed on pop-up palettes). These pop-up palettes are indicated by drop-shadowed boxes, and the last-selected tool is displayed; you can click the icon to select that tool again without opening the pop-up palette.

To open a pop-up palette, position the pointer on the drop-shadowed box and press the mouse button; the pop-up palette appears to one side of the box. Drag the pointer to highlight the desired tool and release the mouse button. Each pop-up palette can be "torn off" to form a floating palette by dragging past the edge of the pop-up palette.

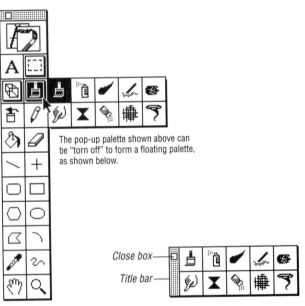

The pop-up palette shown above can be "torn off" to form a floating palette, as shown below.

Close box

Title bar

A few of the tools change when you switch from the Paint layer to the Draw layer, or vice versa. For example, the Paint Bucket and the Eraser are dimmed in the Draw layer, indicating that they are unavailable. Two of the tools are actually transformed: the Draw layer's Selection Arrow replaces the Paint layer's area Selection Tools pop-up palette, and the Draw layer's Two-Layer Selection tool replaces the Paint layer's Brush Tools pop-up palette.

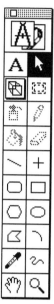
The Tools palette when the Draw layer is active.

The Tools palette when the Paint layer is active.

The Tools palette consists of the following:

 Paint/Draw Layer switch – Switches the layers; the icon representing the active layer is in front. Tools unavailable in the Draw layer are dimmed.

 The **Text** tool allows you to enter text in the Paint or Draw layer. The text attributes are defined with the Font and Text menus.

Selection Tools (Paint Layer): The **Selection Tools** pop-up palette is to the right of the Text tool. Six area Selection Tools are available on this pop-up palette; the last-selected tool is displayed.

The Paint-layer area Selection Tools are:

Rectangle – Selects a rectangular area. (Double-click to select the area displayed in the document window.)

Lasso – Defines an irregularly shaped area that tightens to exclude surrounding empty space. (Double-click to Lasso the area displayed in the document window.)

Oval – Selects an oval area. (Double-click to define an oval that fills the document window.)

Polygon – Defines a selection area by enclosing it with straight-line segments.

Freehand Selection tool – Defines an irregularly shaped area.

Two-Layer Selection tool – Defines a rectangular area that simultaneously selects graphics in both layers. (Double-click to select the area displayed in the document window.)

Selection Tools (Draw Layer): The **Selection Arrow** replaces the Selection Tools pop-up palette; the Selection Arrow selects, or activates, an object.

The **Two-Layer Selection** tool defines a rectangular selection area; all paint and draw objects within this rectangle are selected for cutting and pasting. (The same tool appears on the Selection Tools pop-up palette in the Paint layer.) Double-click to select the entire area displayed in the document window.

*Selection Arrow
in the Draw layer*

*Two-Layer Selection
tool in the Draw layer*

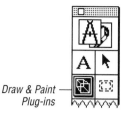

Draw & Paint Plug-ins

Draw & Paint Plug-ins: Any plug-in tools found in the SP Pouch that work in both the Paint and Draw layers are added to this pop-up palette (the last-selected tool is displayed). These tools may use the current Area Fill, Line Fill and Line Widths, and they work within the limitations imposed by each layer (i.e., bitmapped versus objects). Choose **About SuperPaint** from the Apple menu and click the *Plug-ins* button for information about the plug-in tools. Some of the plug-in tools provided with SuperPaint are:

 3-D Box – Produces a three-dimensional box that can be wire frame, solid (press Option key), or shaded (press Command key). Uses current Area Fill, Line Fill, and Line Widths.

 AllGon – Produces a specific grouping of symmetric polygons, including "multigons" and starbursts; the properties are defined in the All-Gon Settings dialog box (double-click to display). Uses current Area Fill, Line Fill and Line Widths.

 Bubbles – Produces a stream of bubbles that vary in size and shape according to the speed of the mouse. Press the Shift key to produce only round bubbles; press the Option key to produce rectangles; Option-Shift produces squares. Uses current Area Fill, Line Fill and Line Widths.

 Cycloid – Generates a geometric shape based on rolling circles (remember that old Spirograph?). The cycloid parameters are defined in the Cycloid Settings dialog box (double-click to display). Uses the current Line Fill and Line Widths.

QuickShadow – Produces a symmetric shape (box, triangle, etc.) with a drop shadow; the shape, shadow thickness and orientation are set in the QuickShadow Settings dialog box (double-click to display). Uses current Area Fill, Line Fill and Line Widths.

Spiral – Produces a spiral with the current line attributes. You control the spacing of the spiral and the existence of spokes. (Double-click to display the Spiral Shapes dialog box.) Uses the current Line Fill and Line Widths.

Paint Layer: The Brush Tools pop-up palette is to the right of the Draw & Paint Plug-ins; the last selected tool is displayed. These tools work only in the Paint layer; the "paint" is the current Area Fill, usually with the property of the selected Transfer Mode. Any Paint-only plug-in tools found in the SP Pouch are added to this palette. The Brush Tools provided with SuperPaint are:

In the Paint layer, the Brush Tools pop-up palette replaces the Two-Layer Selection tool

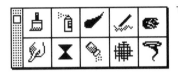

The Brush Tools floating palette.

 Paint Brush – Paints with the current brush shape; the brush shape can be defined in the Custom Brushes dialog box (double-click to display).

 Spray Can – Sprays the Area Fill in a round pattern; press the Option key to use the current brush shape. Double-click to display the Custom Brushes dialog box.

 Calligraphy Brush – Width of brushstroke varies with the speed of the mouse, or pressure on the stylus (with a graphics tablet). Double-click to display the Calligraphy Brush Settings dialog box, where different brush styles are available, as is continuous or discontinuous paint.

 Charcoal – Uses the Area Fill to produce a charcoal-on-paper effect.

 Dry Brush – Paints with current brush shape; the paint "runs out" as you move the mouse.

 Smudge tool – Smudges the area under the tip of the tool; the effect is most apparent in areas of high contrast. Uses current brush shape; the brush shape can be defined in the Custom Brushes dialog box (double-click to display).

 Spin tool – Produces an effect based on two lines of equal length spinning about a center. Direction of spin is controlled from a menu appended to the menu bar; line length and spin speed are set in the Spin Tool Settings dialog box (double-click to display).

 Sprinkler – Stamps a series of shapes into the document; a shape category, such as stars, musical notes, or suns, is selected from a menu appended to the menu bar. (Double-click to display Custom Plug-in Brushes dialog box, where you can edit the selected shapes.) Sprinkler menu commands also let you create and edit shapes.

Texture Brush – Combines an Area-Fill effect and a Line-Fill effect around the center of the pointer. The result can range from a multi-colored airbrush to a "tinsel garland." Double-click to display a dialog box in which you can change both effects and test the results.

Twister – Scatters the pixels under the tip of the tool, providing a diffused or blurred effect; this is most apparent at edges or other areas of sharp transition.

 The **Airbrush** sprays the current Area Fill; you can adjust flow rate, spray area, dot size, spray distribution, and nozzle shape, and preview the changes in the Airbrush Settings dialog box (double-click to display). Available only in the Paint layer.

The **Pencil** writes a single-pixel line of current Area Fill (black in black-and-white documents). If you begin writing on the current Area Fill, the pencil erases the pixels. Double-click to switch between normal magnification and 8x zoom; the zoom view is centered on the middle of the window. (Available only in the Paint layer.)

The Airbrush, Pencil, Paint Bucket, and Eraser are available only in the Paint layer.

 The **Paint Bucket** pours current Area Fill over all contiguous pixels of the color under the spout when the mouse button is pressed. (Available only in the Paint layer.)

The **Eraser** erases the area under the tool. Double-click to erase the entire window; press the Option key to halve the size of the eraser. (Available only in the Paint layer.)

The **Line** produces a straight line at any angle, using the current line attributes (Line Fill, Transfer Mode, Line Widths, arrows, and dashes). Double-click to display the Custom Arrows dialog box. Press the Shift key to cause the tool to behave like the Perpendicular Line tool.

The **Perpendicular Line** produces a straight line (current attributes) that can be only vertical, horizontal, or diagonal (45 degrees). Press the Option key to allow diagonal lines at 30 degrees and 60 degrees; double-click to display the Custom Document Dashes dialog box.

The **Rounded Rectangle** produces a rectangle with rounded corners, using current Area Fill, Line Fill and Line Widths. Double-click to display the Round Corners dialog box, in which you can define the rounding of the corners.

The **Rectangle** produces a rectangle using current Area Fill, Line Fill and Line Widths. Double-click to switch between Paint/Draw-from-Center and Paint/Draw-from-Corner modes. Press the Shift key to produce a square.

 The **Multigon** generates an equilateral polygon of a specified number of sides, using current Area Fill, Line Fill and Line Widths. You can choose from five common polygon shapes, or you can enter a custom number of sides in the Multigon Sides dialog box (double-click to display).

 The **Oval** produces an oval using current Area Fill, Line Fill and Line Widths. Double-click to switch between Paint/Draw-from-Center and Paint/Draw-from-Corner modes. Press the Shift key to produce a circle.

 The **Polygon** allows you to produce an irregular shape defined by straight lines (the current Area Fill, Line Fill and Line Widths are used). Define each point with a single click, and double-click to signal the last point; SuperPaint will close the polygon for you, unless the Area Fill is *None*.

 The **Arc** produces a one-quarter oval of the current Area Fill; the arc is bounded by a line of the current Line Fill and Line Widths. Press the Shift key to produce a one-quarter circle.

In the Paint layer, the **Eyedropper** picks up the color beneath the tip of the tool. In the Draw layer, the Eyedropper picks up the Area Fill or the Line Fill (depending on the active display) of the selected object.

In the Paint layer, the **Freehand** tool defines a free-form shape. In the Draw layer, this tool draws a free-form object; the object is defined by editable Bezier curves. Current Area Fill, Line Fill and Line Widths are used.

The **Grabber** moves the document in the window, and the frame in the left pane of the reduced and magnified views. The effect is the same as using the scroll bars. (Double-clicking toggles between normal magnification and the reduced view, which is one-quarter normal size.)

The **Magnifier** increases the magnification of the image, centered on the area around the pointer. Option-clicking decreases the magnification. A plus or minus sign in the pointer indicates enlarge or reduce.

The Line & Fill Palette

A *fill*, either line or area, is a pattern with a foreground and a background, where the background or white portions of the pattern can be a color, and the foreground or black portions can be a color, a gradient, or a texture. Thus a fill can range from simple black or white, to complex and very colorful. In addition, there is a Transfer Mode associated with the fill.

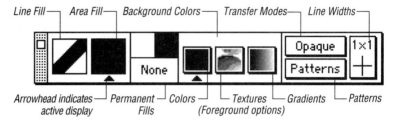

Line Fill — Area Fill — Background Colors — Transfer Modes — Line Widths —

Arrowhead indicates — Permanent — Colors — Textures — Gradients — Patterns
active display — Fills — (Foreground options)

Line & Area Fills – The current line and area fills are displayed: the left box displays the Line Fill as a diagonal bar; the box to the right represents the Area Fill. The arrow below indicates the active display.

Permanent Fills – Provide rapid access to the three unique and most frequently used fills: white (solid pattern, white color), black (solid pattern, black color), and *None* (no pattern, no color).

Foreground/Background Elements – There are three foreground options: Colors, Textures, and Gradients. The arrow indicates the active option. The three foreground pop-up palettes can be torn off. The area of the Line & Fill palette immediately surrounding the three foreground boxes represents the background color. (On a black-and-white machine, you can assign basic spot colors: a palette appears containing color names.)

Transfer Modes – The Transfer Mode is a property of the fills applied with SuperPaint's tools; the modes include *Opaque*, *Translucent*, *Paint on Darker*, and *Invert* (on color machines, *Transparent Bkgnd.*, *Transparent* and *Set Transparent %* are added). Select a mode from the pop-up palette; the current mode is displayed.

Patterns – This pop-up palette contains a large selection of patterns and room for you to add your own. Double-click a pattern cell on the tornoff palette to display the Custom Patterns dialog box (or choose **Patterns** from the Options menu).

Line Widths – Choose one of the standard line-width options from the pop-up palette, or select *Custom* to display the Custom Line Width dialog box. In the dialog box, thickness can be defined separately for both horizontal and vertical lines, to a maximum line thickness in both directions of 99 pixels. The current numeric settings are displayed; for lines up to eight-by-eight pixels, a physical representation is displayed also.

The Frequent Fills Palette

This palette allows you to quickly re-select any of the last twelve fills that you used — a fill is placed on this palette when you draw or paint with it. This is particularly useful with complex fill combinations.

Frequent Fills palette.

The Coordinates Palette

The Coordinates palette is closed initially; to open it, choose **Show Coordinates** from the **Floating Palettes** submenu of the View menu. The palette opens at the bottom of your screen; as with all floating palettes, you can reposition it by dragging the gray "title" bar on the left side of the palette.

Cursor Coordinates:		Size:				
↔ 2.07	↕ 0.90	↔ 0.00	↕ 0.00	°↻	↖ 0.00	inches

The palette provides the location of the pointer as a horizontal and a vertical distance from the zero point of the rulers, in the current units of measurement; the coordinates are updated continuously. The palette also provides the width, height, degree of rotation, and diagonal measure for the *bounding box* of the current selection. When you use most of the tools, or move a selection, the dimensions are replaced with *delta* measurements, which indicate how far the selection or tool has been dragged from its starting point.

SuperPaint Menus

SuperPaint provides a standard menu bar with pull-down menus. The menu bar changes as you work: when you switch from the Paint layer to the Draw layer, the Draw menu replaces the Paint menu (and vice versa); when you choose the **Reshape Bezier** command from the Draw menu, the Reshape menu replaces the Draw menu until you deselect the object being reshaped. Certain plug-in modules also cause menus to be added to the menu bar.

| ✦ | File | Edit | View | Options | Paint | Transform | Font | Text |

| ✦ | File | Edit | View | Options | Draw | Transform | Font | Text |

| ✦ | File | Edit | View | Options | Reshape | Transform | Font | Text |

From top to bottom: The menu bar with the Paint layer active, with the Draw layer active, and in Reshape mode.

The Apple Menu

About SuperPaint presents a dialog box that contains important information (including the program version number and the estimate of memory available), and provides access to About boxes for the installed plug-in modules.

Help presents the Help dialog box; you can receive on-line assistance for a variety of topics.

The File Menu

New creates a new, blank SuperPaint document using the current default settings (size, orientation and bit depth).

Open opens a previously created document. You can have up to ten documents open at once.

Close closes the current document (pressing the Option key prior to opening the File menu makes the command **Close All**, which closes all open documents).

Save saves the active document to disk (pressing the Option key prior to opening the File menu makes the command **Save All**, which saves all open documents). Previously saved documents are updated; the Save As dialog box appears for untitled documents.

Save As lets you name and save an untitled document, or save a copy of an existing document under a new name; you also can select the format in which the document is saved.

Selection to Texture lets you save the selected graphics to the SP Pouch as an image that is added to the Textures pop-up palette.

Revert to Saved replaces the current document with the version that was last saved to disk.

Place lets you import an image, placing it into the Draw layer. A sub-menu lets you select an existing TIFF, MacPaint,® StartupScreen, or EPS file, or directly access an image-acquisition device by means of its plug-in module.

Export lets you save all or part of an image as a TIFF document or an EPS document.

Document Info allows you to define attributes for the current document, including size, bit depth, and orientation.

Page Setup presents a dialog box of printing options, such as paper size and orientation; the contents of the dialog box depend on the currently chosen printer.

Print causes a Print dialog box to appear, allowing you to print the active document.

Quit closes SuperPaint and returns to the Finder.

The Edit Menu

Edit	
Undo	⌘Z
Cut	⌘H
Copy	⌘C
Paste	⌘U
Clear	
Select All	⌘A
Duplicate	⌘D
Replicate...	
Cut to Painting	⌘Y
Copy to Painting	
Align to Grid	
Nudge	▶

Undo reverses the last action performed in the document.

Cut removes the selected graphics from the document and places them on the Clipboard.

Copy places a copy of the selected graphics on the Clipboard.

Paste pastes the contents of the Clipboard into the current layer.

Clear deletes the selected graphics from the document without placing them on the Clipboard.

Select All selects the entire working area of the Paint layer, or all objects in the Draw layer.

Duplicate creates a copy of the selected object or objects. (Available in the Draw layer only.)

Replicate presents a dialog box that lets you make multiple copies of the selected object or objects; you can define attributes such as relative position, scaling and rotation for each copy. (Available in the Draw layer only.)

Cut to Drawing (Painting) transfers a Paint (Draw) layer selection to the Draw (Paint) layer.

Copy to Drawing (Painting) copies a Paint (Draw) layer selection to the Draw (Paint) layer; the original remains in the Paint (Draw) layer.

Align to Grid aligns the selected area or object to the grid defined in the Grid & Rulers dialog box.

Nudge moves the selection one pixel in the direction chosen in the submenu: **Up**, **Down**, **Left**, **Right**. (You can use the arrow keys to achieve the same movements.)

```
 Nudge           ▶   Up
                     Down
                     Left
                     Right
```

The View Menu

Floating Palettes presents a submenu: **Hide (Show) Tools**, **Hide (Show) Line & Fill**, **Hide (Show) Frequent Fills**, and **Show (Hide) Coordinates**. The Tools palette, the Line & Fill palette, and the Frequent Fills palette initially are open. The Coordinates palette initially is closed.

```
 View
 Floating Palettes        ▶         Floating Palettes    ▶    Hide Tools
 Hide Floating Palettes  ⌘H                                   Hide Line & Fill
                                                              Hide Frequent Fills
 Tile                                                         Show Coordinates
 Stack
 Overlap
 Full Screen             ⌘F

 Hide Draw Layer         ⌘L
 Hide Page Breaks

 Color Preview
 Show Page               ⌘K

 Zoom In                 ⌘[
 Zoom Out                ⌘]

 Untitled – 1            ⌘1
 Untitled – 2            ⌘2
```

Hide Floating Palettes hides any visible floating palettes and becomes **Show Floating Palettes,** which will re-open them in the positions they held when hidden. These commands apply to all floating palettes, not just the four listed in the **Floating Palettes** submenu.

Tile sizes and arranges all open documents such that they are all visible and do not overlap.

Stack makes all open documents a standard size and stacks them so only the one on top is visible. To make a hidden document active, choose its name from the View menu (or use the Command key shortcut), close the documents on top of it, or resize the documents on top of it so that you can click some part of its window.

Overlap sizes and staggers all open documents such that the title bar of each is visible behind the active window.

Full Screen is a toggle command that hides or shows the title bar and scroll bars of the open documents. The menu bar may be hidden also — refer to the Preferences dialog box (if the menu bar is hidden, press Command-F to bring back the menu, title, and scroll bars).

Hide (Show) Draw Layer/Hide (Show) Paint Layer alternately hides or shows the layer currently inactive, or "in back." The command switches between Hide and Show, and Paint and Draw, as appropriate.

Hide (Show) Page Breaks alternately hides or shows the page-break marks in multi-page documents.

Color Preview allows you to view the color assignments made in a black-and-white document; this command is available only when working with a black-and-white document on a color machine.

Show Page presents a reduced view of the entire document; you can also redefine the working area of a virtual document.

Zoom In enlarges the current display; displays can be one-quarter normal, normal, and 2x, 4x, and 8x magnifications. In any magnified view, the document window is split into two panes: the right is the magnified image, the left is a portion of the document window with a frame indicating the magnified area. (Similar to using the Magnifier.)

Zoom Out reduces the magnification of the current display. In one-quarter normal view, the document window is split into two panes: the right is a portion of the document at normal magnification, the left is the reduced view with a frame indicating the area shown in the right pane. (Similar to using the Magnifier with the Option key pressed.)

[Document Titles] – The titles of all open documents are appended to the menu; you can select any open document by choosing its title (or by using the associated Command-key shortcut).

The Options Menu

Options
Colors...
Arrows ▶
Dashes ▶
Patterns...
Gradients...
Brush Shapes...
Round Corners...
Multigon Sides...

Grid & Rulers...

✓ Paint from Corner
Paint from Center

Preferences...
Capture Defaults...

Colors appears only on a color machine. The Custom Color Table dialog box is displayed, in which you can choose, customize, and save color tables.

Arrows lets you specify whether lines have arrowheads on either or both ends. A submenu is presented with: **No Arrows, Arrow on Start, Arrow on End, Arrows on Both**, and **Custom Arrows**. The Custom Arrows dialog box lets you choose and customize an arrowhead design (this dialog box also can be displayed by double-clicking the Line tool icon).

Arrows
✓ No Arrows
Arrow on Start
Arrow on End
Arrows on Both

Custom Arrows...

Dashes lets you specify whether lines are dashed. A submenu is presented with: **Not Dashed, Dashed**, and **Custom Dashes**. The Custom Dashes dialog box lets you choose and customize a dashed-line scheme (this dialog box also can be displayed by double-clicking the Perpendicular Line tool).

Dashes
✓ Not Dashed
Dashed

Custom Dashes...

Patterns presents the Custom Patterns dialog box; you can choose and customize pattern designs, saving them on the Patterns palette for the active document. (This dialog box also can be displayed by double-clicking any pattern on the Patterns palette after it has been torn from the Line & Fill palette.)

Gradients appears only on a color machine. The Custom Gradients dialog box is displayed; you can choose and customize a gradient. (This dialog box also can be displayed by double-clicking any gradient on the Gradients palette after it has been torn from the Line & Fill palette.)

Brush Shapes presents the Custom Brushes dialog box; you can choose and customize a brush shape. (This dialog box also can be displayed by double-clicking the Paint Brush, Spray Can, or Smudge tool icons.)

Round Corners presents the Round Corners dialog box; you can customize the degree of roundness for the corners of rounded rectangles. (This dialog box also can be displayed by double-clicking the Rounded Rectangle tool icon.)

Multigon Sides presents the Multigon Sides dialog box in which you set the number of sides for polygons drawn with the Multigon tool. (This dialog box also can be displayed by double-clicking the Multigon tool icon.)

Grid & Rulers presents the Grid & Rulers dialog box in which you can set the units of measurement for the active document, define a grid spacing, turn on and off grid snap, and show or hide the grid and rulers.

Paint (Draw) from Corner and **Paint (Draw) from Center** let you choose the starting point for the tools that produce symmetric shapes. A check before the first command indicates the shape is begun at a corner, while a check before the second indicates the shape is begun at its center. This applies only to the tools that produce symmetric shapes: Rounded Rectangle, Rectangle, Multigon, and Oval (a cross in the center of those icons indicates begin-from-center mode). Double-clicking the Rectangle or Oval shape tool icons on the Tools palette switches between the two modes.

Preferences presents the Preferences dialog box in which you can change various program settings to suit the way you use SuperPaint.

Capture Defaults presents the Capture Defaults dialog box in which you specify the information to be saved as defaults for the next time you use SuperPaint. This includes which palettes are open and their positions, the Line & Fill palette settings, the current text settings, and the currently selected tool.

The Paint Menu

Masking presents the Masking submenu:

New Mask establishes a selection area as a mask, protecting it from being painted on or erased.

Add to Mask combines the current selection area with the existing mask.

Remove from Mask deletes any intersection of the current selection area with the existing mask.

Hide Mask (Show Mask) allows you to turn off and on the moving diagonal lines that indicate a masked area.

Invert Mask creates a stencil (you can work only within the original selection area).

Turn Off Mask removes the protection from the selected area or areas, without deleting the mask (the command then becomes **Turn On Mask**, which re-establishes the protection).

Convert to Selection converts the mask back into a selection area.

Delete Mask deletes the mask.

Fill Modes lets you specify the quality of the fill applied to the document or a selection area when the **Fill** command is chosen. (Fill Modes also affect certain plug-in-module commands, such as **Spatter**.) A submenu is presented with: **Opaque, Translucent, Paint on Darker, Invert, Transparent Bkgnd., Transparent** (as a percentage), and **Set Transparent %** (**Transparent Bkgnd., Transparent**, and **Set Transparent %** appear only on color machines). **Set Transparent %** presents a dialog box that lets you specify the transparency of the fill as a percentage. These modes are similar to the Transfer Modes found on the Line & Fill palette; the two affect different methods of fill application.

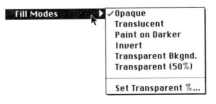

Paint Multiple controls whether intermediate lines and shape outlines remain on the screen as you drag the line or shape to the size you want — the effect is comparable to a rapid freeze-frame action that is controlled by the speed of the mouse. The command is checked when the option is on, and it works with all the line and shape tools except the Polygon and Freehand tools.

Brush Symmetry presents the Brush Symmetry dialog box which lets you produce mirror effects, or up to nine radially related strokes simultaneously, using the brushes and associated painting tools. (Both effects are centered in the document window.)

Airbrush Settings presents the Airbrush Settings dialog box in which you set the flow rate, spray-area diameter, nozzle shape, spray pattern, and dot size for the Airbrush.

AutoTrace traces a Paint-layer selection, creating line-art objects in the Draw layer.

AutoTrace Settings presents the AutoTrace Settings dialog box in which you set the parameters for the AutoTrace operation.

Create SuperBits presents the Create SuperBits dialog box, in which you specify the resolution of the new object, and then copies the Paint-layer selection into the Draw layer as a SuperBits object. (The **Copy to Drawing** command also produces a SuperBits object; you specify its resolution in the Object Info dialog box.)

Repeat Effect repeats the command last chosen from the commands that follow.

Invert reverses the image, or selected area, changing black to white, white to black, and colors to contrasting colors.

Fill fills the document, or selected area, with the current Area Fill, according to the mode specified with the **Fill Modes** command.

Spatter fills the image, or selected area, with a fine spray of the current Area Fill (assigned the current Fill Mode).

Trace Edges outlines all contiguous pixels of any color within the image or selected area.

Note: Certain paint plug-in modules are accessed by commands, which are appended to the Paint menu when the modules are placed in the SP Pouch. The following six commands are plug-ins supplied with SuperPaint.

Brightness & Contrast presents the Brightness & Contrast control window which lets you change the brightness and contrast of a selection or the entire image.

Color Balance presents the Color Balance control window which lets you adjust the mixture of hues in a selection or the entire image.

Darken overlays the image, or selected area, of a color document with a translucent gray wash; in a black-and-white document, a random spray of black pixels is added.

Diffuse softens or defocuses the image, or selected area, blurring lines and edges (similar to a single pass over the area with the Twister).

Lighten overlays the image, or selected area, of a color document with a translucent white wash; in a black-and-white document, a random spray of white pixels is added.

Pickup allows you to replace the contents of a selection area with a copy of whatever is beneath the selection in the Paint layer (contrast this with pasting down a selection).

The Draw Menu

```
Draw
Bring to Front    ⌘=
Send to Back      ⌘-

Group             ⌘G
Ungroup           ⌘U
Lock
✓Unlock

Align Objects...  ⌘M
Object Info...    ⌘I

Reshape           ⌘R
Convert to Bezier  ▶
Bezier to Polygon  ▶
Join Beziers
Bezier Settings...
```

Bring to Front puts the selected object(s) in front of all other objects.

Send to Back puts the selected object(s) behind all other objects.

Group combines a set of selected objects into a group that behaves as one object.

Ungroup separates a group into its original component objects.

Lock locks the selected object(s); locked objects cannot be moved or edited. A check before the command indicates the selected object is locked.

Unlock unlocks the selected locked object(s). A check before the command indicates the selected object is unlocked.

Align Objects presents the Align Objects dialog box, in which you set horizontal and vertical alignment options; the selected objects are then aligned accordingly.

Object Info presents the Object Info dialog box, which allows you to check or set the location, size, and rotation of the selected object. The resolution of a SuperBits object can also be changed in this dialog box.

Reshape allows you to reshape a polygon, arc, a Bezier object, or edit a SuperBits object. Depending on the type of object selected, the command appears as **Reshape Polygon**, **Reshape Arc**, **Reshape Bezier**, or **Edit SuperBits**.

Convert to Bezier converts the selected polygon to a Bezier object according to the selected submenu command. Choosing **Point-to-Point** converts every point in the polygon to a hinge point, and the polygon lines become straight segments; the shape of the object does not change. Choosing **Curve Fit** applies the current Bezier Settings during conversion; the shape of the object may change.

Bezier to Polygon converts a selected Bezier object to a polygon according to the selected submenu command. Choosing **Point-to-Point** converts every point on the Bezier path to a polygon point, and the segments become straight lines; the shape of the object probably will change. Choose **Polygon Fit** to maintain the shape of the object with the addition of points.

Join Beziers links two open Bezier objects into a single object.

Bezier Settings presents the Bezier Settings dialog box in which you set parameters for the definition of Bezier objects (drawn with the Freehand tool, or produced by the **Curve Fit** command).

The Reshape Menu

Reshape	
Bring to Front	⌘=
Send to Back	⌘−
Straight Segment	
Curve Segment	
Hinge Point	
Smooth Point	
Close Curve	
Break Curve	
Delete Point	
Add Point	

This menu replaces the Draw menu when you choose the **Reshape Bezier** command. The Draw menu returns when you deselect the object. For a complete discussion of Bezier curves, straight and curved segments, and smooth and hinge points, refer to Part 4, Chapter 8, *Paint and Draw Commands.*

Bring to Front puts the selected object in front of all other objects.

Send to Back puts the selected object behind all other objects.

Straight Segment changes the segment(s) between the selected points to straight segment(s).

Curve Segment changes the segment(s) between the selected points to curved segment(s).

Hinge Point changes the selected point(s) in the Bezier object to hinge point(s).

Smooth Point changes the selected point(s) in the Bezier object to smooth point(s).

Close Curve closes the ends of the Bezier object by creating a segment between them.

Break Curve breaks the Bezier curve at the selected point(s).

Delete Point deletes the selected point(s) from the Bezier curve.

Add Point adds a point to the Bezier curve between two selected points.

The Transform Menu

```
Transform
Scale Selection...
Rotate Selection...

Flip Horizontal
Flip Vertical
Rotate Left
Rotate Right

Free Rotate
Slant
Stretch
Distort
Perspective

Remove Transformations
```

Scale Selection presents the Scale Selection dialog box, which allows you to reduce or enlarge a selection by specified horizontal and vertical factors.

Rotate Selection presents the Rotate Selection dialog box, in which you specify a clockwise or counterclockwise rotation in degrees for the selection.

Flip Horizontal flips the selection horizontally about its vertical centerline.

Flip Vertical flips the selection vertically about its horizontal centerline.

Rotate Left rotates the selection counterclockwise ninety degrees.

Rotate Right rotates the selection clockwise ninety degrees.

Free Rotate lets you interactively rotate a selection in either direction to any angle. (The degree of rotation is indicated on the Co-ordinates palette.)

Slant lets you interactively slant a selection to any angle.

Stretch lets you interactively stretch or shrink a selection horizontally, vertically, or both.

Distort lets you distort a selection by dragging any of its corners in any direction. (Available in the Paint layer only.)

Perspective lets you "tilt" a selection to add perspective. (Available in the Paint layer only.)

Remove Transformation removes any transformations made to the selected object(s). (Available in the Draw layer only.)

The Font Menu

The Font menu displays the typefaces available from your System; choosing one affects any selected and subsequent text.

Font

Chicago
Courier
✓Geneva
Helvetica
Monaco
Symbol
Times

Text

Text Setting...   ⌘T
Style   ▶
Justify   ▶
Spacing   ▶

9 point
10
✓12
14
18
24
36
48
72
Other (6)...
Smaller
Larger

The Text Menu

Text Settings presents the Text Settings dialog box, in which you can choose a typeface (font), style, size, spacing, and justification for the selected and subsequent text. The results of changing any of the settings are previewed in the dialog box.

Style applies style options to the selected and subsequent text. The options are presented as a submenu: **Plain**, **Bold**, **Italic**, **Underline**, **Outline**, and **Shadow**. More than one option can be selected.

Justify presents justification options for the selected and subsequent text as a submenu: **Left**, **Center**, and **Right**.

Spacing defines a line spacing for the selected and subsequent text by

Style
✓Plain
Bold
Italic
Underline
Outline
Shadow

Justify
✓Left
Center
Right

means of a submenu: **Single**, **1-1/2**, **Double**, and **Custom**. Choosing **Custom** presents a dialog box in which you can specify a custom line spacing in single-point increments; the current setting is displayed.

	Spacing
✓Single	
1 - 1/2	
Double	
Custom (2 pt)...	

[Size list] – Choose one of the listed point sizes for the selected and subsequent text. The point sizes installed in your system are the outlined numbers.

Other presents the Other Size dialog box, allowing you to specify a point size not listed in the menu.

Smaller makes the selected and subsequent text one point smaller.

Larger makes the selected and subsequent text one point larger.

Part 4: Using SuperPaint

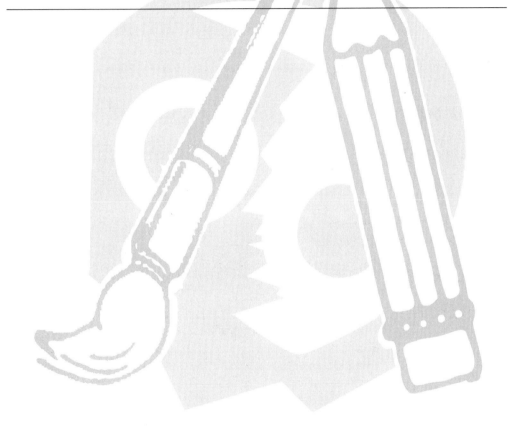

Using SuperPaint

This is the part of the manual that describes in detail all of SuperPaint's features. This part of the manual is divided into chapters, which are arranged in conceptual order, rather than alphabetical order.

Chapter 1: SuperPaint Basics

Before you start creating graphics with SuperPaint, you should know some of the basics of working with the program, beginning with how to take advantage of having paint and draw capabilities in one program, and how to use the shortcuts provided by the program's "hot keys."

This chapter also introduces the concept of plug-in tools and commands, which let you customize SuperPaint. In addition, using the on-line Help feature is described in this chapter.

SuperPaint's Layers

SuperPaint combines paint, draw, and basic image-processing capabilities in one easy-to-use graphics program. With the Paint features of the program, you can create and edit images on a pixel-by-pixel basis, while the Draw functions let you produce precise objects that are printed at maximum resolution.

The Paint and Draw capabilities operate in two separate layers that are superimposed to form a single image. Both layers have some common tools and commands; there are also a few tools and commands that are specific to each. In addition, you can easily move graphics between layers, you can change the order of the layers, and you can hide the back layer.

In addition, SuperPaint includes some image-enhancement capabilities. For example, you can lighten, darken, smudge, and change the brightness, contrast and color balance of all or part of your image.

The Paint Layer

Graphics created in the Paint layer are simply collections of dots or pixels, and they are referred to as *bitmapped* graphics. The dots have no special relationship to each other, as "part of a circle," for example, and so bitmapped graphics are edited dot by dot. If you have a "rectangle" that intersects a "circle" in the Paint layer, you can't just move them apart, you have to "edit" them apart by changing the pixels. If you drag aside what appears to be a shape overlapping another, you'll find that the portion "obscured" does not exist. The dot-by-dot nature of the layer provides a great deal of artistic control; however, large-scale editing in the Paint layer can be difficult, particularly if you are working with many colors and textures.

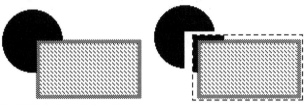

The Paint layer is a collection of dots.

Normally, Paint-layer graphics print at 72 dots per inch (dpi), regardless of the printer's capabilities. However, SuperPaint's SuperBits feature provides a means to edit and print bitmapped graphics at higher resolutions. (For an introduction to the concept of dots and resolution, refer to Part 2, *Tutorial*.)

Note: Scanned images are bitmapped, and as such can be edited and "cleaned up" in the Paint layer.

The Draw Layer

Items in the Draw layer are discrete objects, and thus called *object-oriented* graphics. They are also often called *vector* graphics because they are defined mathematically as lines and curves.

Because it is an individual entity, you can easily change an existing object's fill, size, location, and so on. For example, a circle and rectangle in the Draw layer are individual objects. You can move the rectangle without affecting the circle, and you can easily change its proportions or orientation.

Because they are described mathematically, objects are displayed or printed at the resolution of the output device. In other words, although the circle is displayed on your monitor screen at 72 dpi, it will be printed on your LaserWriter at 300 dpi.

The Draw layer contains individual objects.

Paint and Draw Together

Although the Paint and Draw layers are superimposed to form a single image, you work in one layer at a time. You can switch freely between the layers, and you can move or copy text and graphics from one layer to the other. You also can hide the back layer at any time, for viewing, editing, or printing.

The image on the left is the Draw layer with the Paint layer hidden; the center image is the Paint layer with the Draw layer hidden; the image on the right shows both layers superimposed.

Switching Layers

Paint/Draw Layer switch; Draw layer is active (in front).

The Paint/Draw Layer switch is at the top of the Tools palette; the overlapping icons represent the Paint (paint brush) and Draw (compass) layers. The icon on top represents the active layer.

To change layers:

- Click anywhere in the switch box (you don't have to click either icon directly), or press Command-/ (slash).

Hiding the Paint or Draw Layer

Paint/Draw Layer switch; Paint layer hidden.

Although you can work in only one layer at a time, both layers are usually displayed together. However, you can hide the inactive layer (the one in back) so it is not displayed or printed. The icon for the hidden layer is dimmed in the Paint/Draw Layer switch.

To hide the inactive layer:

- Choose **Hide Paint** (or **Draw**) **Layer** from the View menu.

- Use the Command-L shortcut.

or

- Option-click the Paint/Draw Layer switch.

Note: The command will be **Hide Paint Layer** or **Hide Draw Layer**, depending on the layer in which you are working.

To display both layers again:

- Choose **Show Paint** (or **Draw**) **Layer** from the View menu.

- Use the Command-L shortcut.

or

- Option-click the Paint/Draw Layer switch.

Note: The command will be **Show Paint Layer** or **Show Draw Layer**, depending on the layer in which you are working.

You can switch layers even when one layer is hidden; the previously active layer becomes the hidden layer. If you choose the **Print** command, only the active layer is printed. Choosing **Save** or **Save As** when a layer is hidden will save both layers.

Moving Graphics Between the Paint and Draw Layers

You can move graphics from one layer to the other. An object created in the Draw layer and moved to the Paint layer is converted to a 72-dpi bitmapped version of the object. When a bitmapped graphic is moved from the Paint layer to the Draw layer, it becomes a *bitmapped object* (a SuperBits object), which can be edited at any resolution. This feature combines the advantages of both layers, providing pixel-by-pixel control and maximum output resolution.

The dolphin on the left is an edited 300-dpi SuperBits object in the Draw layer. The dolphin on the right is a 72-dpi bitmapped graphic in the Paint layer.

You can move graphics from one layer to another with the usual Macintosh Edit-menu commands **Cut**, **Copy**, and **Paste** (described in Part 4, Chapter 7). In addition, SuperPaint provides four special commands in the Edit menu to move graphics between the Paint and Draw layers: **Copy to Drawing, Cut to Drawing, Copy to Painting**, and **Cut to Painting.** (Also, graphics are copied to the Draw layer from the Paint layer by the **Create SuperBits** command.)

Note: SuperBits objects are described in detail in Part 4, Chapter 9.

To move selected graphics from one layer to the other:

- Choose **Copy to Drawing** (or **Copy to Painting**) from the Edit menu.

  This puts a copy of the graphic into the other layer, leaving the original intact in its layer.

or

- Choose **Cut to Drawing** (or **Cut to Painting**) from the Edit menu, or use the Command-Y shortcut.

  This moves the graphic out of one layer into the other.

Note: The commands are **Copy to Painting** and **Cut to Painting**, or **Copy to Drawing** and **Cut to Drawing**, depending on the layer in which you are working.

Graphics put into the Draw layer are converted into SuperBits objects. Graphics put into the Paint layer are converted into bitmapped images.

SuperPaint's Menu Bar

SuperPaint's menu bar contains eight items, some of which change according to what you're doing in the program. The menu bar includes:

- the Paint menu when you're in the Paint layer.

- the Draw menu when you're in the Draw layer.

- the Reshape menu when you've chosen the **Reshape Bezier** command from the Draw menu.

🍎 File	Edit	View	Options	Paint	Transform	Font	Text

🍎 File	Edit	View	Options	Draw	Transform	Font	Text

🍎 File	Edit	View	Options	Reshape	Transform	Font	Text

SuperPaint's menu bar changes according to what you are doing in the program.

In addition, some plug-in modules add menus to the menu bar (for example, when you select the Sprinkler tool, a Sprinkler menu appears in the menu bar). Part 3, *Guide to Tools & Menus,* lists all of SuperPaint's primary menu commands (their keyboard equivalents are found next to the commands in the menus). The commands are described in detail in Part 4.

Plug-in Modules

SuperPaint can be customized with plug-in modules. These modules "plug in" to the program to add to or enhance its features. Existing plug-ins include Paint and Draw tools, artistic effects (for example, Aldus Gallery Effects™), textures, color tables, Paint commands, and image-acquisition and file-import modules. Some plug-ins are created by third-party software developers, while others, such as color tables and textures, can be created within SuperPaint.

The nature of the plug-ins makes them appear integral to the program, but they actually are contained in SuperPaint's Pouch folder. You can remove or add plug-in modules at any time.

Note: Plug-in modules provided with SuperPaint are described in more detail in Part 4, Chapters 5, 6, and 7.

Getting Current Plug-in Information

Most of the plug-in modules provided with SuperPaint are described in this manual. Information about other plug-ins (such as those written by third parties) is available from the About SuperPaint dialog box, provided the plug-ins are installed in the SP Pouch, and provided the information was included with the plug-in. Plug-ins come from a variety of sources, and the information provided may not be consistent or complete.

To get information about a plug-in module:

1. Choose **About SuperPaint** from the Apple menu.

    The About SuperPaint dialog box appears.

2. Click the *Plug-ins* button.

    The Credits display in the dialog box becomes a scrolling list of plug-in modules.

3. Select a module name from the list and click *About* (or double-click the module name in the list).

Aldus SuperPaint 3.0

Licensed to: John Marlatt
Aldus Consumer Division
US 12-1234-123456789

Preferences file 'SuperPaint Prefs'
in folder 'SP Pouch'
on volume 'HD 100'

Plug-in Modules:

Paint Tools
Spray Can
Calligraphy Brush
Charcoal
Dry Brush
Smudge
Sprinkler
Texture Brush

About...

Credits

Done

Select a plug-in and click the *About* button for information.

Plug-ins from SuperPaint 2.0

All of the plug-ins provided with SuperPaint 2.0 have been rewritten for this version of SuperPaint. If you are upgrading from Version 2.0, you should use the Version 3.0 plug-ins, since they utilize the new features, and many provide additional options.

Note: SuperPaint 3.0 will recognize and load earlier versions of the plug-in modules, but they probably will not work with all of SuperPaint's new features (for example, most will not work in color). Also, SuperPaint 2.0 does not recognize plug-ins created for later versions of SuperPaint. If these plug-ins are put into the Version 2.0 Pouch folder, they will not be loaded when SuperPaint 2.0 is run.

Hot Keys

"Hot keys" let you access tools and palettes by pressing a single key. The current tool switches to the hot-key tool, or the palette appears under the pointer, as long as the hot key is pressed. You can use the hot-key tool or make selections from the palette normally. When you release the hot key, the tool you were using returns, or the palette closes. This feature provides quick access to the palettes and tools, and is very useful when working in full-screen mode with all palettes hidden.

Note: Hot keys are not available while the Text tool is selected. Hot keys are disabled when the Caps Lock key is engaged.

Listed in order of appearance on the keyboard, left to right and top to bottom, the hot keys are:

Continuous Color palette	Q*
Line Widths palette	W
Magnifier	E or R **
Tools palette	T
Selection Arrow (Draw layer)	A
Selection Tools palette (Paint layer)	S
Eyedropper	D
Line & Fill palette	F
Gradients palette	G

Textures palette	H
Draw & Paint Plug-ins palette	Z
Patterns palette	X
Colors palette	C
Frequent Fills palette	V
Brush Tools palette (Paint layer)	B
Transfer Modes palette	M
Grabber	Space bar

* Color machines only
** E hot keys to the Magnifier with the "+" to enlarge. R hot keys to the Magnifier with the "-" to reduce.

On-Line Help

Information about using SuperPaint is available from within the program at any time. Just choose **Help** from the Apple menu to display the Help dialog box. The dialog box contains a scrolling list of topics in alphabetical order. Select a topic and click the *Help* button (or double-click the topic) to display information about the topic.

```
┌─────────────────────────────────────────────────────────────┐
│ SuperPaint Help                                      Topics   │
│                                                               │
│ Click a topic in the list, then click the Help               │
│ button to show information on that topic (or    │About SuperPaint│⬆│
│ double-click the topic).                        │Airbrush       │ │
│                                                 │Aligning Objects│ │
│ Button Functions :                              │Arc tool       │ │
│ Previous : go to the previous Help page.        │AutoTrace      │ │
│ Next : go to the next Help page.                │Bezier Objects │ │
│ Done : closes SuperPaint 3.0 Help.              │Bezier Settings│ │
│ Help : shows information on the selected topic. │Bezier to Polygon│ │
│ Topics : returns to this page.                  │Bit Depth      │ │
│                                                 │Brightness & Contrast│ │
│ You can use the left and right arrow keys       │Calligraphy Brush│ │
│ to go to the previous or next page.             │Capture Defaults│ │
│                                                 │Charcoal tool  │⬇│
│                                                               │
│                        [Previous] [Next] [Done] ( Help )      │
└─────────────────────────────────────────────────────────────┘
```

Click *Next* to go to the next topic in the list; click *Previous* to go to the previous topic in the list. Click *Topics* (or press Return or Enter) to return to the Help dialog box and the list of topics. When you are finished, click *Done* to return to the active document.

Chapter 2: SuperPaint Environment

This chapter describes SuperPaint's working environment, focusing on the use of "palettes" to provide access to the tools and related controls that you'll use to create graphics. This chapter also describes working at different levels of magnification, and using SuperPaint's measurement aids.

In addition, you can use the Preferences and Capture Defaults functions described at the end of this chapter to customize SuperPaint to suit the way you work.

Palettes

Palettes provide access to related items such as tools and fill components. SuperPaint's primary palettes are the Tools palette, the Line & Fill palette, the Frequent Fills palette, and the Coordinates palette. (The Coordinates palette is described in this chapter; the other three primary palettes are described in subsequent chapters.)

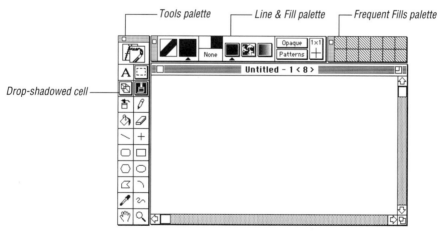

Three primary palettes and a new document window open when you start SuperPaint.

There are two types of palettes: floating palettes and pop-up palettes. To reduce screen and palette clutter, sets of related tools and controls have been grouped on pop-up palettes. These palettes "pop" out of drop-shadowed boxes or cells on two of the primary palettes, and they can be "torn off" to become floating palettes. Floating palettes can be positioned anywhere on your monitor screen.

In addition, all of the palettes can be displayed under the pointer by pressing a hot key. (These hot keys are listed in Part 4, Chapter 1.)

Working with Palettes

You can make selections from palettes, show or hide them, and position them conveniently on the screen. Each floating palette has a gray "title" bar on its top or left side, which includes a close box. You can drag the title bar to reposition the palette, and click its close box to close the palette. As you drag, you'll see just the outline of the palette until you release the mouse button. To use a palette that is behind another palette, just click any visible part. (If a palette is completely obscured by another, you'll have to move the top palette.)

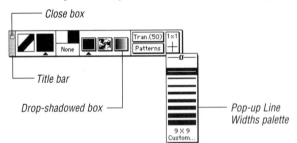

Pop-up palettes are found on the Tools palette and the Line & Fill palette, and are represented by drop-shadowed boxes:

- On the Tools palette – Draw & Paint Plug-in tools, Selection Tools, and Brush Tools.

- On the Line & Fill palette – Colors, Textures, Gradients, Patterns, Line Widths, and Transfer Modes.

To change which of the primary floating palettes are open, and their specific locations, when you start your SuperPaint sessions, use the **Capture Defaults** command, described at the end of this chapter.

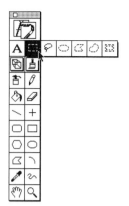

Selecting from Palettes

To select an item from a floating palette, just click the desired item.

To make a selection from a pop-up palette, position the pointer on its drop-shadowed box and press the mouse button to open the pop-up palette. Drag the pointer to the desired selection and release the mouse button. The pop-up palette closes and the selected item is displayed on the drop-shadowed box.

Pop-up palettes can be "torn off" of the primary palettes and positioned anywhere on the screen as floating palettes. Simply drag past any edge of the open pop-up. As you drag past the edge, a dotted frame representing the palette appears. Drag to any location on the screen and release the mouse button.

The pop-up palette shown above can be "torn off" to create the floating palette shown below.

Showing & Hiding Floating Palettes

When SuperPaint first starts, the Tools, Line & Fill, and Frequent Fills palettes are open. The other primary palette, the Coordinates palette, initially is closed.

The **Floating Palettes** submenu in the View menu lets you open and close these primary palettes individually: simply choose the appropriate command from the submenu. If the primary palette is open, the command is "Hide primary" palette; if the palette is closed, "Show" replaces "Hide."

In addition, you can hide all open floating palettes at once with the **Hide Floating Palettes** command. All primary and torn-off pop-up palettes are closed, leaving only the document window. The command becomes **Show Floating Palettes**, which re-opens the palettes in the locations they held when closed (only those closed by the **Hide Floating Palettes** command are re-opened). Command-H is the Command key shortcut for hiding and showing the floating palettes.

Reduced and Magnified Views

SuperPaint lets you view and work on your document at five levels of magnification: 0.25x, 1x, 2x, 4x, and 8x. At any magnification other than normal (1x), the document window is split vertically to display two views of the document, one at normal magnification and one at the lower or higher magnification. These left and right displays are referred to as window "panes."

The left pane always displays the lower of the two magnifications. If you are working at increased magnification, the left pane is the normal view. If you are working at reduced magnification, the left pane is the reduced view. The left pane also contains a gray rectangle that frames the portion of the document displayed in the right pane.

Rectangle indicates the area displayed in the right pane —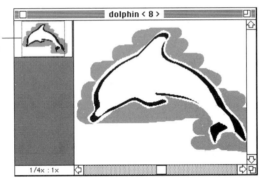

Split window in reduced view.

The effects of all tools at all levels of magnification correspond to their effects at normal size. For example, the Pencil always writes a line that would be one-pixel wide at normal magnification, although at 8x magnification it may appear much larger.

When you use the scroll bars or the Grabber to move the document, it shifts in both views. In addition, you can use the Grabber to move the frame in the left pane. Select the Grabber from the Tools palette, or "hot key" to it by pressing the space bar, and drag the frame until it encloses the area you want displayed in the right pane.

Increasing and Decreasing Magnification

The three levels of enlargement allow you draw and paint precisely, while the reduced view lets you see and work in an area larger than the document window. (This is especially convenient when you want to paint or draw large, simple items such as a frame for the entire page.) The current level of magnification is indicated below the left pane, next to the horizontal scrolling arrow.

Increasing Magnification

There are two methods of increasing the current level of magnification:

- Choose **Zoom In** from the View menu, or use the Command-[(left square bracket) shortcut.

   SuperPaint zooms in on the center of the document window, or the center of the right pane.

- Select the Magnifier from the Tools palette, or "hot key" to it by pressing E (for enlarge), and click anywhere in the document window.

   SuperPaint zooms on the location of the Magnifier. A plus sign in the Magnifier pointer indicates it is in enlarge mode.

Normal view.

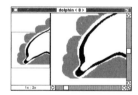

2x magnification.

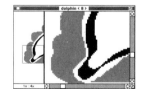

4x magnification.

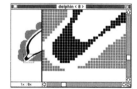

8x magnification.

To zoom directly to the highest magnification (8x), press the Option key before choosing **Zoom In** (this will not work with the Command-[shortcut), or press the Command key before using the Magnifier (this will not work with the hot-key Magnifier).

Decreasing Magnification

There are three methods of decreasing the current level of magnification:

- Choose **Zoom Out** from the View menu, or use the Command-] (right square bracket) shortcut.

  SuperPaint zooms out on the center of the document window, or the center of the right pane.

- Select the Magnifier from the Tools palette, press the Option key, and click anywhere in the document window.

  SuperPaint zooms on the location of the Magnifier. A minus sign in the Magnifier pointer indicates it is in reduce mode.

  You can also switch to the reduction Magnifier by pressing the R hot key.

- Double-click the Grabber icon on the Tools palette to go to one-quarter view from any other magnification, and from one-quarter magnification to normal view.

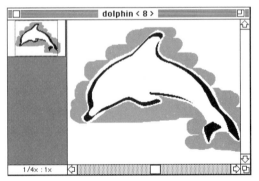

1/4x magnification.

To zoom directly from a higher magnification to normal view, press the Option key before choosing **Zoom Out** (this will not work with the Command-] shortcut), or press the Command and Option keys before using the Magnifier (this will not work with the hot-key Magnifier). To return to normal or "regular" magnification from any higher or lower level of magnification, press Command-Option-R.

Zooming in the Paint Layer

In the Paint layer you have two additional methods of quickly zooming from any level of magnification to 8x, and from 8x to normal magnification:

- Double-click the Pencil icon on the Tools palette.

    SuperPaint zooms on the center of the document window, or the center of the right pane.

- With the Pencil selected, Command-click anywhere in either pane.

    The zoom is centered on the point clicked.

Using the Rulers

SuperPaint can display rulers across the top and down the left side of your document. You can also specify the units of measurement and change the location of the rulers' zero point.

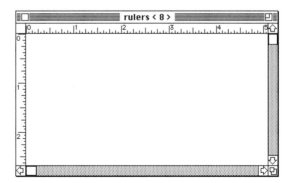

To display the rulers:

1. Choose **Grid & Rulers** from the Options menu to display the Grid & Rulers dialog box.

```
Grid & Rulers

Measure in: [ Inches ]

Grid spacing: [0.50] inches

☐ Grid snap on (⌘-shift-G)        [ Cancel ]
☐ Show grid    (⌘-shift-U)
☐ Show rulers  (⌘-shift-M)        [   OK   ]
```

2. Click the *Show rulers* checkbox.

   You can also change the units of measurement for the active document — select from the *Measure in* pop-up menu: *Inches, Centimeters, Points, Pixels, Picas,* or *Millimeters.*

3. Click *OK,* or press Return or Enter to close the dialog box.

You can change the document units of measurement at any time without affecting the size of anything in the document. The units can be changed in the Document Info, Object Info, Grid & Rulers, Round Corners, Replicate, and Custom Dashes dialog boxes. In addition, the current units of measurement are displayed on the Coordinates palette.

Note: The rulers can be displayed (and hidden) without opening the dialog box by pressing Command-Shift-M.

Tracking lines displayed in each ruler are aligned with the cursor hot point.

When the rulers are displayed, a dotted line in each ruler tracks the pointer's position; the lines track the cursor's *hot point* (the tip of the arrow, the center of the crosshair, and so on).

To hide the rulers, choose the **Grid & Rulers** command again, click *Show Rulers* to deselect the option, and click *OK*, or press Return or Enter to close the dialog box. (Or use the Command-Shift-M shortcut.)

Pressing the Option key while choosing **Grid & Rulers** from the Options menu suppresses the dialog box and turns off all settings in the dialog box. If you Option-choose the command again, the settings are restored to their status prior to the first Option-command. If none were originally checked, all will be checked.

Setting the Rulers' Zero Point

The set zero point box

You can change the location of the zero point for either or both of the rulers. Position the pointer in the box formed by the intersection of the two rulers (the *set zero point* box) and then drag to the new zero point. The rulers are redrawn to reflect the new zero position. To reset the rulers to their original zero points, click inside the set zero point box.

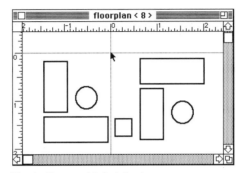

Changing the zero points for both rulers.

Using the Grid

SuperPaint's grid system lets you create and align objects at consistent increments. You can set the size of the grid to suit your purposes, using any of the standard units of measure; you can show the grid on the screen, or keep it hidden; and you can turn on a "snap" option that keeps tool and selection movements aligned to the grid points. The grid does not print.

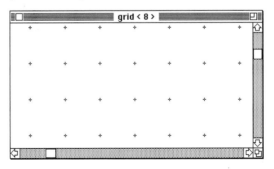

To use the grid:

1. Choose **Grid & Rulers** from the Options menu to display the Grid & Rulers dialog box.

```
┌─────────────────────────────────────────┐
│ Grid & Rulers                            │
│ ─────────────────────────────────────── │
│                                          │
│ Measure in: [ Inches        ]            │
│                                          │
│ Grid spacing: [0.50] inches              │
│                                          │
│  ⊠ Grid snap on (⌘-shift-G)  ┌────────┐  │
│  ⊠ Show grid    (⌘-shift-V)  │ Cancel │  │
│  ☐ Show rulers  (⌘-shift-M)  └────────┘  │
│                              ┌────────┐  │
│                              ║   OK   ║  │
│                              └────────┘  │
└─────────────────────────────────────────┘
```

2. Enter a spacing increment for the grid in the *Grid spacing* text box.

   Beginning from the upper left corner of the document, grid points are this distance apart horizontally and vertically.

   You can also change the units of measurement for the active document — select from the *Measure in* pop-up menu: *Inches, Centimeters, Points, Pixels, Picas,* or *Millimeters.*

3. Select either or both grid options.

   Grid snap on turns on the snap option so that tools and selections automatically "snap" to the nearest grid point (displayed or not). Refer to the following section, "Grid Snap," for more information.

   Show grid displays the grid points on your screen.

4. Click *OK*, or press Return or Enter, to close the dialog box.

You can change the document units of measurement at any time without affecting the size of anything in the document. The units can be changed in the Document Info, Object Info, Grid & Rulers, Round Corners, Replicate, and Custom Dashes dialog boxes. In addition, the current units of measurement are displayed on the Coordinates palette.

Note: The grid can be displayed (and hidden) without opening the dialog box by pressing Command-Shift-V. Grid snap can be turned on (and off) by pressing Command-Shift-G.

Minimum and maximum grid spacing values are:

Units	Minimum	Maximum
Inches	0.03	2.00
Centimeters	0.08	5.08
Points	2.00	144.00
Pixels	2.00	144.00
Picas	0.17	12.00
Millimeters	0.71	50.80

When grid spacing is set to 0.75 inches or more, the grid-point representation changes from dots to small crosses.

Pressing the Option key while choosing **Grid & Rulers** from the Options menu suppresses the dialog box and turns off all settings in the dialog box. If you Option-choose the command again, the settings are restored to their status prior to the first Option-command. If none were originally selected, all will be selected.

Grid Snap

When grid snap is on (regardless of whether the grid points are visible), it affects most Paint and Draw tools, as well as some other SuperPaint operations, by causing graphics and tool movements to align to grid points. Grid snap only affects newly created graphics; existing graphics are not repositioned when grid snap is turned on.

Grid snap affects:

- All tools in the Paint layer except the Paint Bucket, Freehand Selection tool, Eyedropper, Magnifier, Grabber, and Lasso.

- All tools in the Draw layer except the Eyedropper, Magnifier, Grabber, and Selection Arrow.

- Paste operations: a pasted item is aligned to the grid.

- Dragging operations: a dragged item jumps to the next grid point as you move it.

- The results produced by the **Duplicate**, **Replicate**, and **Paint Multiple** commands.

The Align to Grid Command

Grid snap automatically aligns items with the grid as they are created, moved or pasted. You can also use the **Align to Grid** command to align an existing selection area or existing objects to the grid.

To align selections to the grid:

1. Select an object or objects in the Draw layer, or select an area of the Paint layer.

2. Choose **Align to Grid** from the Edit menu.

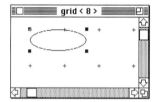

An object's *bounding box* aligned with the grid.

The selection is aligned with the grid such that the upper left corner of its *bounding box* – the smallest rectangle that can enclose the selection – is on a grid point. (In the Draw layer, the bounding box is indicated by the object's handles; in the Paint layer, there is no such indication.)

Using **Align to Grid** in the Paint layer aligns the upper left corner of the entire selection to the grid, without changing the relative spacing of the items, even if you've lassoed items that seem to be separate.

In the Draw layer, using **Align to Grid** with multiple selected objects aligns each object with the grid individually. This alters the spacing between objects. However, if the objects are grouped before choosing **Align to Grid**, the grouped object is aligned with the grid at the upper left corner of the grouped object's bounding box, and the spacing between the group's objects remains the same.

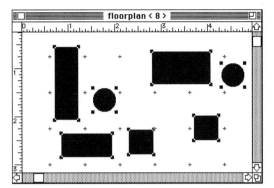

Selected objects in the Draw layer (not grouped).

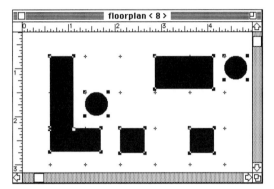

Each selected object is aligned to the grid individually.

The Coordinates Palette

The Coordinates palette constantly provides the location of the on-screen pointer (or cursor), as well as selection dimensions and delta (movement) measurements, to help you create and position graphics accurately. When the program is first started, the floating Coordinates palette is not visible. To display it, choose **Show Coordinates** from the **Floating Palettes** submenu of the View menu. As with other floating palettes, you can reposition it by dragging its title bar, close it by clicking its close box, and capture its position with the **Capture Defaults** command so that it always opens in the same location.

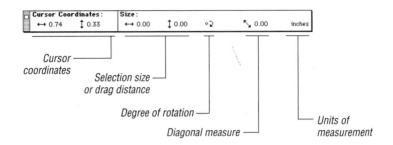

Cursor coordinates

Selection size or drag distance

Degree of rotation

Diagonal measure

Units of measurement

The Coordinates palette is divided into two sections. The first section, *Cursor Coordinates*, provides a constant readout of the pointer's position. The second section changes according to your actions; this section, labeled *Size* or *Delta* depending on what you're doing, displays a series of measurements that indicate:

- The horizontal and vertical dimensions for the bounding box of a selection or group, *or*, the distance a selection or tool has been moved from its starting point.

- The number of degrees an item has been rotated.

- The diagonal measurement for the selection's bounding box.

The information on the Coordinates palette is displayed in the current units of measurement (rotation is always measured in degrees). The current units are indicated on the palette.

Cursor Coordinates

The location of the pointer (or cursor) is measured from the zero points of both rulers to the cursor's hot point; it is displayed as a horizontal distance and a vertical distance.

Size Measurements

When an area or object is selected, or a shape is being created (with one of the shape tools), the first two figures in the second section of the Coordinates palette are the width and height of the bounding box of the selection or shape. These dimensions remain on the palette until you use another tool or move the selection. (Selection handles are not included in the measurement.)

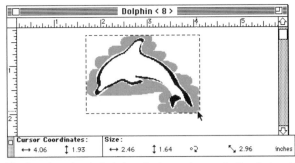

The dimensions of a selection's *bounding box* are shown on the Coordinates palette.

Size measurements are always given in terms of the item's *bounding box*. No matter what you paint, draw, or select, rectangular bounding-box dimensions are the measurements given. If you select multiple objects in the Draw layer, the size of the rectangle that encloses all of the objects is displayed.

Delta Measurements

When you move a selection or work with certain tools, the first two figures in the second section of the Coordinates palette are the horizontal and vertical distances the selection or tool has been moved from its starting point (the *Size* label changes to *Delta* also). Delta measurements are made from the point at which you pressed the mouse button to begin using a tool (or the original location of the upper left corner of a selection's bounding box) to its current location.

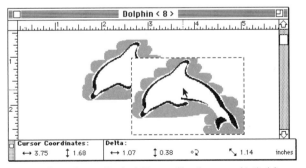

Delta coordinates down and to the right are positive; those up and to the left are negative.

Delta measurements are given in the current units of measurement, and follow a standard coordinate system. Movements down and to the right are positive, while movements up and to the left are negative. The zero/zero (0,0) point is always the point at which you began using the tool, or the upper left corner of the selection's bounding box.

Rotation

The *Rotation* readout on the Coordinates palette displays the rotation of a selected area or object, or the angle of an arc, in degrees. Clockwise rotation is displayed as a positive number, and counterclockwise as negative.

When you choose the **Free Rotate** command from the Transform menu, the rotation is displayed constantly in the Coordinates palette as you rotate the selection. It remains displayed until you create or select something else.

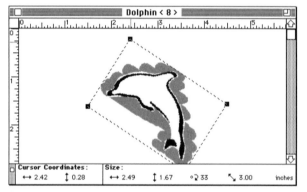

Clockwise rotation is indicated by positive numbers; counterclockwise rotation is indicated by negative numbers.

When a Draw object is selected that was rotated previously with the **Free Rotate**, **Rotate Selection**, **Replicate**, or **Object Info** commands, its degree of rotation is displayed on the Coordinates palette. (Objects transformed with the **Slant** command have no rotation.)

The shape produced with the Arc tool is a portion of a circle (even with an Area Fill of *None*), and the angle of the arc is defined by the edges that meet at the center of the circle. In the Draw layer, this angle is dis-played on the Coordinates palette whenever an arc is selected. A basic arc drawn with the Arc tool always has an angle of ninety de-grees, but you can reshape it (with the **Reshape Arc** command from the Draw menu) and change the angle. The angle in degrees is dis-played as you reshape the arc, and later whenever it is reselected. If you rotate an arc using the **Free Rotate** command, the angle of rotation is displayed on the Coordinates palette only while the arc is being rotated.

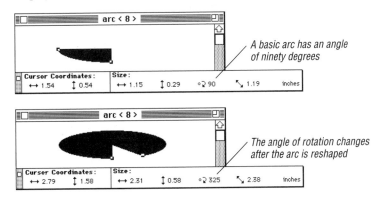

Diagonal Measurement

The final numeric display on the Coordinates palette is the diagonal measurement. The *Size* diagonal measurement is the distance from the upper left to the lower right corners of the bounding box for the se-lected area or object, or the shape being drawn. The *Delta* diagonal measurement is the distance the tool or selection has moved diagonally from its starting point.

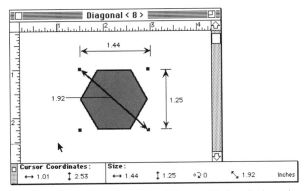

Diagonal measurement begins at the upper left corner of the bounding box and ends at its lower right corner.

Preferences and Defaults

The **Preferences** and **Capture Defaults** commands let you configure the program to suit the way you work. Options set in the Preferences dialog box, and the default settings captured with **Capture Defaults**, are stored in the SP Pouch folder in a file named "SuperPaint Prefs" (described later in this chapter).

Setting Preferences

Choosing the **Preferences** command from the Options menu displays the three-page Preferences dialog box, in which you can set a number of options for start-up and work sessions. Use the *Next* and *Prev* buttons to move from one page of the dialog box to another.

```
┌──────────────────────────────────────────────────┐
│  ┌────────────────────────────────────────────┐  │
│  │ Preferences: Draw Layer Settings           │  │
│  │ ─────────────────────────────────────────  │  │
│  │    After using a Shape Tool:               │  │
│  │                                            │  │
│  │      ◉ Tool remains selected               │  │
│  │      ○ Arrow becomes selected              │  │
│  │                                            │  │
│  │    ☐ Go into Reshape mode after drawing a Bezier │
│  │                                            │  │
│  │    Objects are dragged as:                 │  │
│  │                                            │  │
│  │      ◉ Objects                             │  │
│  │      ○ Outlines                            │  │
│  │                                            │  │
│  │   ┌──────┐ ┌──────┐ ┌────────┐ ┌────────┐ │  │
│  │   │ Prev │ │ Next │ │ Cancel │ │   OK   │ │  │
│  │   └──────┘ └──────┘ └────────┘ └────────┘ │  │
│  └────────────────────────────────────────────┘  │
└──────────────────────────────────────────────────┘
```

Default settings for the *Draw Layer Settings* page.

The first page, *Draw Layer Settings*, offers the following options:

- *After using a Shape Tool* – You can elect to have the current creation tool (line, shape, or Draw & Paint Plug-in tool) remain selected when drawing is complete, or switch automatically to the Selection Arrow so you can move and resize the object just drawn. (Refer to Part 4, Chapters 6 and 7 for more information on these tools.)

- *Go into Reshape mode after drawing a Bezier* – If this option is selected, a Bezier object drawn in the Draw layer with the Freehand tool is automatically put into reshape mode. (Refer to Part 4, Chapter 8 for more information on reshaping Bezier objects.)

- *Objects are dragged as* – You can elect to have objects in the Draw layer displayed as they are moved, or a simple dotted outline can be displayed while moving an object; the object snaps to the outline when you release the mouse button. (This option is described in detail in Part 4, Chapter 7.)

The second page of the Preferences dialog box, *Window Settings,* contains options for documents and the document window.

```
┌─────────────────────────────────────────────────────┐
│  ┌────────────────────────────────────────────────┐  │
│  │                                                │  │
│  │  Preferences: Window Settings                  │  │
│  │  ───────────────────────────────────────────   │  │
│  │                                                │  │
│  │  Window at start up:                           │  │
│  │    ◉ New         ○ Open dialog      ○ None     │  │
│  │                                                │  │
│  │  Document default bitdepth (color machine)     │  │
│  │    ○ 1-bit   ◉ 8-bit   ○ 16-bit   ○ 32-bit    │  │
│  │                                                │  │
│  │  New document size:                            │  │
│  │    ◉ Default size      ○ Set using dialog      │  │
│  │                                                │  │
│  │  □ Hide menu bar in Full Screen mode           │  │
│  │                                                │  │
│  │  ┌──────┐  ┌──────┐  ┌────────┐  ┌──────────┐ │  │
│  │  │ Prev │  │ Next │  │ Cancel │  │    OK    │ │  │
│  │  └──────┘  └──────┘  └────────┘  └──────────┘ │  │
│  └────────────────────────────────────────────────┘  │
└─────────────────────────────────────────────────────┘
```

Default settings for the *Window Settings* page.

- *Window at start up* – When SuperPaint starts a new session, you can be presented with a new, untitled document, the Open dialog box, or you can be left to choose between the **New** and **Open** commands. (This option is described more fully in Part 4, Chapter 3.)

- *Document default bit depth* – Sets the default bit depth for new documents on color machines. Black-and-white machines always default to black-and-white (1-bit) documents. (Refer to Part 4, Chapter 3 for more information on this option, and Part 4, Chapter 5 for more on bit depth.)

- *New document size* – Whenever a new document is opened, it can be the default size (8 x 10.78 inches), or the Document Info dialog box can be presented, in which you specify dimensions before the document is opened. (This option is described in Part 4, Chapter 3.)

- *Hide menu bar in Full Screen mode* – When this option is selected, the menu bar is hidden when the **Full Screen** command is chosen from the View menu. When this option is not selected, only the title bars and scroll bars of the open documents are hidden by **Full Screen**. (This option is described more fully in Part 4, Chapter 3.)

The third page of the Preferences dialog box, *Miscellaneous Settings*, contains four additional options.

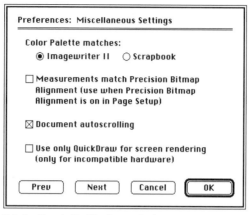

Default settings for the *Miscellaneous Settings* page.

- *Color Palette matches* – Defines which of the two available spot-color palettes is used for color assignments and color previewing; applies to black-and-white documents only. (The two palettes are described in Part 4, Chapter 5.)

- *Measurements match Precision Bitmap Alignment* – Select this option when *Precision Bitmap Alignment* is selected in the Laser-Writer Options dialog box (displayed from the Page Setup dialog box) to ensure that items are the same size on the screen and the printed page. (Refer to Part 4, Chapter 11 for more information.)

- *Document autoscrolling* – When this option is selected, the document is scrolled automatically when you drag past the edge of the window. (This is described in Part 4, Chapter 3.)

- *Use only QuickDraw for screen rendering* – Select this option only if you have a non-Apple monitor or graphics card and the program fails to render images properly.

Capturing Defaults

The **Capture Defaults** command in the Options menu lets you change the appearance of SuperPaint when the program starts. You can change palette locations and the items selected on them, as well as various menu-item and dialog-box settings that are used as default values each time SuperPaint starts, and then capture the new settings with this command. Default settings are stored in the SuperPaint Prefs file (described in a following section).

```
┌─────────────────────────────────────────────┐
│  Capture Defaults                            │
│  ─────────────────────────────────────────── │
│     ⊠ Palette Positions    ⊠ View Menu       │
│                                              │
│     ⊠ Tools Palette        ⊠ Dialog Boxes    │
│                                              │
│     ⊠ Line & Fill Palette  ⊠ Text            │
│                        ┌────────┐ ┌────────┐ │
│                        │ Cancel │ │   OK   │ │
│                        └────────┘ └────────┘ │
└─────────────────────────────────────────────┘
```

The **Capture Defaults** command displays a dialog box containing six checkboxes that allow you to change the current default settings for the following:

- *Palette Positions* – The positions of the four primary palettes and whether they are visible (Tools, Line & Fill, Frequent Fills, Coordinates).

- *Tools Palette* – The currently selected tool, the current active layer, and the current Paint Brush shape.

- *Line & Fill Palette* – The current Line Fill and Area Fill pattern, which fill display is active, and the current Line Widths settings.

- *View Menu* – Whether full-screen mode is in effect, and Hide/ Show Page Breaks status (whether page breaks are visible) when a new document is opened.

- *Dialog Boxes* – All current settings in the Bezier Settings, Auto-Trace Settings, Round Corners, Scale Selection, Rotate Selection, Replicate, Grid & Rulers and Capture Defaults dialog boxes, the document orientation, the number of sides for the Multigon, whether arrows are used, whether dashes are used, as well as the formats currently selected in the Open dialog box.

- *Text* – The current selections for font, style, size, justification, and spacing.

To capture new start-up settings, make any changes to the items listed, and then choose **Capture Defaults** from the Options menu. Select or deselect categories in the Capture Defaults dialog box, and click *OK*, or press Return or Enter. The next time you start SuperPaint, the new settings will take effect.

The Preferences File

The options and settings that you can change with the **Preferences** and the **Capture Defaults** commands are stored in a file named "SuperPaint Prefs." This file is usually stored in the SP Pouch folder, although you can move it or rename if you wish. If SuperPaint cannot find the preferences file, it will prompt you to locate the file or create a new one.

The SP Pouch is where SuperPaint looks for all of its textures, tools, color palettes, and plug-ins modules. If you save the preferences file in another folder that does not include these files, the plug-ins, textures, and so on will not be available in the program.

To restore SuperPaint's initial default settings, throw away the SuperPaint Prefs file. The next time you start the program, SuperPaint will create a new preferences file using the default settings used the first time you started the program.

To create a new SP Prefs file:

1. Throw away the current preferences file.

2. Start SuperPaint.

   The Specify Preferences File dialog box appears.

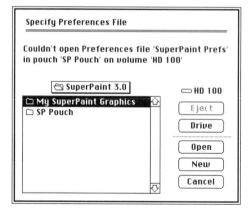

3. Click the *New* button to create a new preferences file.

    The Create New Preferences File dialog box appears.

```
┌─────────────────────────────────────────────────┐
│ Create New Preferences File                      │
│  ─────────────────────────────                   │
│                                                  │
│          ▔▔▔▔▔▔▔▔▔▔▔                             │
│         │ 🖰 SP Pouch │                           │
│          ▔▔▔▔▔▔▔▔▔▔▔                             │
│    🗀 B&W Paint Textures    ⬆      ⊂⊃ HD 100     │
│    🗀 Brushes                                     │
│    🗀 Color Paint Textures                        │
│    🗀 Color Tables                   ┌────────┐   │
│    🗀 Draw Textures                  │ Eject  │   │
│    🗀 Menu Commands         ⬇       └────────┘   │
│                                     ┌────────┐   │
│    Save Preferences File as:        │ Drive  │   │
│    ┌──────────────────────────┐     └────────┘   │
│    │ SuperPaint Prefs         │     ┌────────┐   │
│    └──────────────────────────┘     │  Save  │   │
│                                     └────────┘   │
│                                     ┌────────┐   │
│                                     │ Cancel │   │
│                                     └────────┘   │
└─────────────────────────────────────────────────┘
```

4. If you want to change the name of the file from SuperPaint Prefs, enter a name for the file.

5. Open the SP Pouch folder.

    If you want the preferences file stored in a location other than the SP Pouch, specify that location. (This is not recommended, as the folder in which the SuperPaint Prefs file is stored becomes SuperPaint's Pouch folder.)

6. Click *Save*.

    A new preferences file is created with the same default settings used the first time you started SuperPaint.

Note: To reduce clutter, the SP Pouch folder can contain folders. This means you can organize your textures, plug-in modules, and so on. SuperPaint looks first in the SP Pouch folder and then in any folders within it for those items. The program will not look further, however; in other words, do not put folders within folders within the SP Pouch.

Chapter 3: SuperPaint Documents

This chapter describes working with documents (or image files) in SuperPaint. The chapter explains opening, defining, saving, and closing documents. In addition, document formats, display options, and placing and exporting images are also discussed.

Working with Documents

SuperPaint works with *documents*, which other applications sometimes refer to as *files*. The terms are interchangeable, but for consistency we use the term *document* throughout this manual.

To work with an document, you must first *open* it. When you are finished, you can *save* the changes, and then *close* the document.

Document Preferences

When you start SuperPaint, a new blank document (of the default size) is created; the Open dialog box is presented so you can open an existing document; or you are left to choose **Open** or **New** from the File menu. Similarly, whenever you choose **New** from the File menu, either a new, default-sized document is created automatically, or the Document Info dialog box is presented in which you define a size for the new document.

These responses are controlled by settings in the Preferences dialog box. To change what happens when you start SuperPaint, or to change SuperPaint's response to the **New** command:

1. Choose **Preferences** from the Options menu to display the Preferences dialog box.

```
Preferences:  Draw Layer Settings
─────────────────────────────────────

  After using a Shape Tool:
      ● Tool remains selected
      ○ Arrow becomes selected

  ☐ Go into Reshape mode after drawing a Bezier

  Objects are dragged as:
      ● Objects
      ○ Outlines


   ( Prev )   ( Next )   ( Cancel )   【  OK  】
```

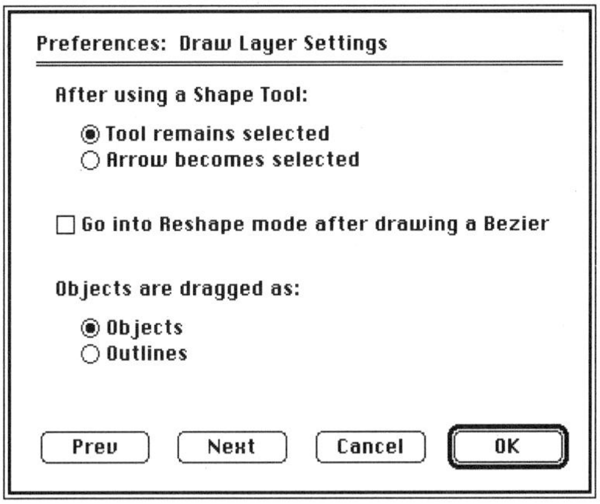

This dialog box has three pages of preferences.

2. Click *Next* to move to the *Window Settings* page.

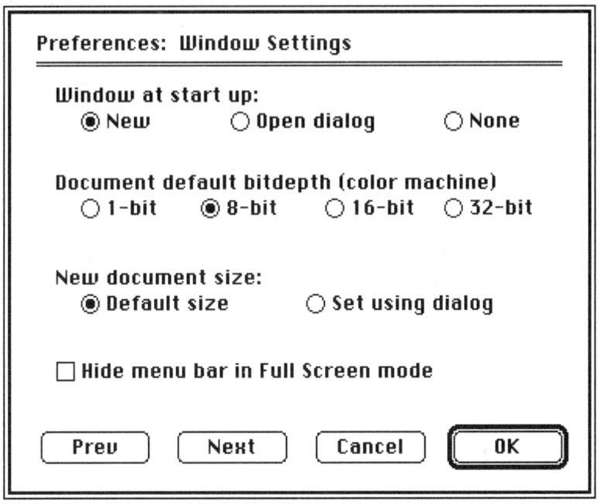

```
Preferences:  Window Settings
─────────────────────────────────────

  Window at start up:
      ● New          ○ Open dialog       ○ None

  Document default bitdepth (color machine)
      ○ 1-bit    ● 8-bit    ○ 16-bit    ○ 32-bit

  New document size:
      ● Default size          ○ Set using dialog

  ☐ Hide menu bar in Full Screen mode

   ( Prev )   ( Next )   ( Cancel )   【  OK  】
```

3. Select a *Window at start up* option.

   If *New* is selected, SuperPaint will automatically open a new, default-sized document whenever you start the program. If you select *Open dialog*, SuperPaint will display the Open dialog box when you start the program. Or select *None* so you can choose **New** or **Open** from the File menu depending on your needs.

4. Select a *Default document bit depth.*

   Bit depth defines the number of colors available in a document. Select a default bit depth for new documents; these selections are dimmed on black-and-white machines. SuperPaint will run faster if the document bit depth matches the bit depth of the monitor. (Bit depth is discussed in detail in Part 4, Chapter 5.)

   On color machines, the document bit depth is displayed inside angle brackets next to the name in the title bar of the document window.

5. Select a *New document size* option.

   If *Default size* is selected, new documents are sized according to the normal capabilities of the currently chosen printer (with the **Chooser** command in the Apple menu), and the paper size selected in the Page Setup dialog box.

Select *Set using dialog* if you want the Document Info dialog box to appear each time you choose the **New** command. This dialog box includes options that let you define document size and bit depth.

The default document size represents the dimensions of the maximum possible print area, given the page size currently selected in the Page Setup dialog box, and the printer currently selected in the Chooser. Thus, the default document size changes when you change printers or paper size, and when you select or deselect the *Larger Print Area* option in the LaserWriter Options dialog box. Refer to Part 4, Chapter 11 for more on printing and the Page Setup and LaserWriter Options dialog boxes.

The type of printer currently chosen and the dimensions of the printable area for the current page size (i.e., the default document size) are displayed in the Document Info dialog box.

Note: Information on the other options in the Preferences dialog box is available in Part 4, Chapter 2.

Opening a New Document

To open a new, blank document, choose **New** from the File menu, or press Command-N. Depending on the *New document size* Preferences setting, either a new document is created automatically using the current defaults, or the Document Info dialog box is displayed, allowing you to specify size, orientation, and bit depth of the new document.

You can temporarily reverse the *New document size* setting by pressing the Option key while choosing **New**. In other words, if you have *Set using dialog* selected, Option-**New** gives you a default-sized document. If you have *Default size* selected, Option-**New** presents the Document Info dialog box. On a color machine, you also can override the default bit depth by pressing the Shift key while choosing **New**. The new document will be a 1-bit document.

The first new document created in a SuperPaint session is called "Untitled-1." Subsequent new documents are sequentially numbered, untitled documents: Untitled-2, Untitled-3, and so on.

You can open a new document at any time (up to ten documents may be open at once). As you open additional documents, available system memory is reduced and the working area of each subsequent document may also be reduced. If the amount of memory available to SuperPaint is insufficient to open another document, an *Unable to open* message is displayed. Refer to the discussion of virtual documents later in this chapter for additional information.

```
┌──────────────────────────────────┐
│  ✋   Unable to open.             │
│                                  │
│      You need to close a file     │
│      before opening another.      │
│         ┌──────────────┐          │
│         │      OK      │          │
│         └──────────────┘          │
└──────────────────────────────────┘
```

Opening an Existing Document

You can open a document that is in a format recognized by SuperPaint at any time, with up to ten documents open at once. (The caveat of the previous paragraph is applicable here as well.)

To open a previously created document:

1. Choose **Open** from the File menu, or press Command-O to display the Open dialog box.

```
┌──────────────────────────────────────────────────────┐
│                                                        │
│     ┌──── My SuperPaint Graphics ────┐                 │
│     │ □ dolphin                      │↑│  ⊂ HD 100     │
│     │ □ floor plan                   │ │               │
│     │ □ graph                        │ │  ┌─────────┐  │
│     │ □ map                          │ │  │ Eject   │  │
│     │                                │ │  └─────────┘  │
│     │                                │ │  ┌─────────┐  │
│     │                                │ │  │ Drive   │  │
│     │                                │ │  └─────────┘  │
│     │                                │ │               │
│     │                                │ │  ┌─────────┐  │
│     │                                │ │  │ Open    │  │
│     │                                │↓│  └─────────┘  │
│     └────────────────────────────────┘  ┌─────────┐  │
│                                          │ Cancel  │  │
│     Selected type: PICT                  └─────────┘  │
│     ┌──────────┐                                       │
│     │ Formats… │                                       │
│     └──────────┘                                       │
└──────────────────────────────────────────────────────┘
```

All documents recognized in the current folder or disk are listed, and the first document in the list is highlighted. The format of the highlighted document is displayed above the *Formats* button.

To check or change the formats currently selected, click the *Formats* button to display the Formats dialog box.

```
┌──────────────────────────────────────────────────────┐
│                                                        │
│   Formats                                              │
│   ────────────────────────────────────────────        │
│                                                        │
│   ⊠ SuperPaint 3.0          ⊠ MacPaint                 │
│                                                        │
│   ⊠ PICT (SuperPaint 2.0)   ⊠ Stationery              │
│                                                        │
│   ⊠ SuperPaint 1.0 / 1.1    ⊠ StartupScreen           │
│                                                        │
│   □ Paint Texture           □ Draw Texture            │
│                                                        │
│                        ┌────────┐  ┌────────┐          │
│                        │ Cancel │  │   OK   │          │
│                        └────────┘  └────────┘          │
└──────────────────────────────────────────────────────┘
```

Click the appropriate checkboxes to select or deselect any of the formats. Only those documents in the selected formats appear in the Open dialog box scrolling list. Initially all formats are selected; deselect the formats you want to exclude from the list. The changes you make in this dialog box are retained for the rest of the current SuperPaint session; use the **Capture Defaults** command to change the default format selections (refer to Part 4, Chapter 2).

To close the Formats dialog box and return to the Open dialog box, click *OK*, or press Return or Enter to accept the settings, or click *Cancel*.

2. Find and select the document you want to open, then click *Open* (or simply double-click the document name).

Defining a Document

You can check and change the height, width, measurement units, orientation, and bit depth for an existing document at any time in the Document Info dialog box. Choose **Document Info** from the File menu to display the dialog box.

```
┌─────────────────────────────────────────────────────────────┐
│  Document Info                                               │
│  ┌─Document is...────────┐                                  │
│  │ ○ Black & White (1-bit) │  Measure in: [ Inches      ]   │
│  │ ● Color:  [ 8-bit ]     │                                │
│  └─────────────────────────┘                                │
│  ┌─Make the document...─┐   Width:    Height:               │
│  │ [Narrower] [ Wider ] │   [8.00]   [10.78]   Pages: 1     │
│  │ [Shorter]  [ Taller ]│   Orientation: ● Tall  ○ Wide     │
│  └──────────────────────┘                                   │
│  Chosen printer: LaserWriter                                │
│  Printer page: 8.00 н 10.78        [ Cancel ]   [  OK  ]    │
└─────────────────────────────────────────────────────────────┘
```

Note: The Document Info dialog box opens automatically for new documents if *Set using dialog* is selected for the *New document size* option in the Preferences dialog box.

The dialog box also indicates the currently selected printer and the dimensions of its print area on the currently selected page size. The *Printer page* dimensions displayed depend on the page size selected in the Page Setup dialog box, as well as the capabilities of the printer. For example, laser printers are physically incapable of printing on a strip approximately one-quarter inch wide around the edges of any page. Thus, with a LaserWriter chosen and *Larger Print Area* selected in the LaserWriter Options dialog box (displayed by clicking the *Options* button in the Page Setup dialog box), the printable area on a standard US Letter-sized page is 8.00 by 10.78 inches. (Without *Larger Print Area* selected, the printable area is 7.67 x 10.14 inches.) Refer to Part 4, Chapter 11 for more on printing and print options.

To check or change the bit depth, size, orientation, or units of measurement for a document:

1. Choose **Document Info** from the File menu to display the Document Info dialog box.

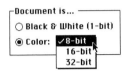

2. If you are working on a color machine, you can change the document bit depth.

   A document can be either black and white (1 bit) or color — click the appropriate button. For a color document, select a bit depth from the pop-up menu next to the *Color* button. Color documents can be either 8, 16, or 32 bits.

3. The units of measurement for the document can be changed with the *Measure in* pop-up menu.

   Available units are *Inches, Centimeters, Points, Pixels, Picas* and *Millimeters*. Changing the units of measure in an existing document does not change its size or the size of anything in it.

4. The size of the document can be changed by typing new measurements in the *Width* and *Height* text boxes, or by clicking the *Narrower, Wider, Shorter,* or *Taller* buttons.

   If you create a document larger than the printer page, SuperPaint divides it into pages and prints it on several pieces of paper. See the discussion of page breaks later in this chapter for more information.

   Each time you click the *Narrower, Wider, Shorter,* or *Taller* buttons, the document size increases or decreases by the height or width of the printer page shown at the bottom of the dialog box. As you change the dimensions of the document, the number of pages required to print it, based on the printer selected, is displayed.

5. The orientation of the document can be changed by clicking the *Tall* (portrait) or *Wide* (landscape) buttons.

Changing the orientation reverses the dimensions of the document; you may also want to change the page orientation in the Page Setup dialog box (see Part 4, Chapter 11).

Note: The default settings for document units of measure and orientation can be changed with the **Capture Defaults** command; refer to Part 4, Chapter 2 for more information.

Document bit depth determines the number of colors available in the document, and is independent of monitor bit depth. In other words, it's possible to work in a 32-bit document on an 8-bit system. Lowering the document bit depth reduces the memory required to process and store the document, while raising it provides more colors for more realistic images. On color systems, the default document bit depth is eight, unless you have changed the default setting in the Preferences dialog box. Part 4, Chapter 5 discusses the issues related to working in color, including bit depth and dithering.

Note: If you open a black-and-white SuperPaint 2.0 document on a color system, you can change its bit depth and add color to it.

The units of measurement for the active document can be changed at any time in the Document Info dialog box, or in the Grid & Rulers, Replicate, Custom Dashes, Round Corners, or Object Info dialog boxes.

Documents are resized from the upper left corner: if you make an existing document smaller, the areas of the document beyond the new measurements are truncated. The program will alert you if graphics will be lost as a result of the resizing, and you can either continue with the operation or cancel it. Any portion of a Paint-layer graphic that extends beyond the edges of the new document is lost. Objects in the Draw layer are lost only if they are completely beyond the edges of the new document. In other words, objects partially within the new document are saved, and you can recover the parts "hanging off" by dragging them completely into the document. (The portions of an object outside the boundaries of a document will not be printed.)

Page Breaks

When you're working with a document that's larger than the page size set in the Page Setup dialog box, SuperPaint automatically displays broken lines in the document window to indicate page breaks. You cannot manually enter or change the location of page breaks; however, changing document size or orientation in the Document Info dialog box, or changing the page size or orientation in the Page Setup dialog box, will affect the location of page breaks.

The broken line indicates a page break.

You can make page-break lines invisible by choosing **Hide Page Breaks** from the View menu. The command then becomes **Show Page Breaks**, which makes them visible again. (You can use the **Capture Defaults** command to change the default setting so page breaks are normally invisible. Refer to Part 4, Chapter 2.)

View	
Floating Palettes	▶
Hide Floating Palettes	⌘H
Tile	
Stack	
Overlap	
Full Screen	⌘F
Hide Draw Layer	⌘L
Hide Page Breaks	

Automatic Scrolling

When a document is larger than the document window, SuperPaint automatically scrolls the document as you work past the edge of the window. In other words, if you are dragging with a tool or selection and reach the edge of the window, you can keep going and the document will scroll automatically in the appropriate directions. The autoscrolling feature can be turned off and on by deselecting or selecting *Document autoscrolling* on the Miscellaneous Settings page of the Preferences dialog box.

Note: In virtual documents, autoscrolling stops when the edge of the working area is reached. You must use the Show Page dialog box, the Grabber, or the scroll bars at the bottom and right sides of the document window to continue scrolling.

Virtual Documents

SuperPaint keeps as much of a document in system memory (random access memory or RAM) as possible; if the entire image does not fit into the available system memory, the "left-over" portion is kept on your hard disk and accessed when needed. In this situation, the document is known as a *virtual document*. The "working area" of the document is that portion in RAM; the rest is the "virtual area." If the document window is larger than the working area, visible portions of the virtual area are indicated on the screen by diagonal lines.

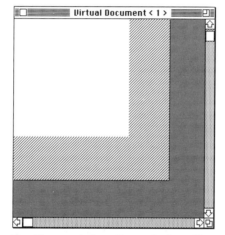

The white represents the working area; the diagonal lines represent the virtual area. The gray area is outside of the document.

As noted in the previous section, autoscrolling stops at the edge of the working area. Use the scroll bars, the Show Page dialog box, or the Grabber to move the document in the window, thereby also redefining the working area — portions of the virtual area are moved into RAM, and portions of the original working area are sent to the hard disk.

Note: Increasing the memory partition (allocating more RAM) for SuperPaint will reduce the virtual area of large documents.

To move or redefine the working area of a virtual document with the Show Page dialog box:

1. Choose **Show Page** from the View menu (or press Command-K) to open the Show Page dialog box.

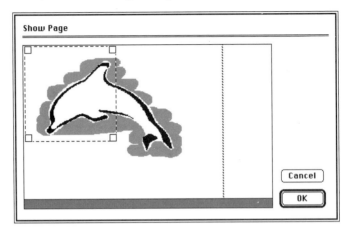

A reduced view of the entire document (including page breaks if they are visible) is displayed in the dialog box. The current working area is indicated by a frame of moving dashes with handles at the corners.

2. Move and resize the frame to redefine the working area of the document.

Drag anywhere within the frame to reposition it. Drag any handle to reshape the frame, making the rectangle wider and shorter, or taller and narrower; the total area enclosed remains the same.

3. Click *OK*, or press Return or Enter, to close the dialog box.

The new working area, or a portion of it, is displayed in the document window.

In general, the fact that part of a virtual document is on disk will not affect your work. You may notice a short delay while SuperPaint updates the document window when you scroll into the virtual area. Also, SuperPaint will not scroll into the virtual area while a Paint-layer selection area is active.

Low Memory

If the amount of system memory available is insufficient to perform some action or open another document, SuperPaint will alert you. (As you open successive documents, the amount of system memory available is reduced, and subsequent working areas are smaller.)

If you encounter a low- or out-of-memory alert message while working in SuperPaint, try some of these tips:

- *Close open documents.* If you have multiple documents open, close those you are not working in frequently.

- *Reduce the size of the Clipboard after pasting.* After copying and pasting a large amount of text or a large graphic, select a word or small graphic and choose **Copy** from the Edit menu to reduce the amount of memory consumed by the Clipboard.

- *Reduce the bit depth of the document.* Choose **Document Info** from the File menu to open the Document Info dialog box. If you aren't using any color in the document, set the document bit depth to 1 bit. If you are working in a 16-bit or 32-bit document, reduce the bit depth to 8 bits. (Some previously true colors may become dithered.)

If the alert appears frequently, save your document(s) and quit Super-Paint, and then try these memory-conservation tips:

- *Increase the application memory size.* When working under MultiFinder or System 7.0, click the SuperPaint icon to highlight it. Choose **Get Info** from the File menu to open the Info control window. Double-click the *Application Memory Size* text box to highlight it and enter a larger number.

- *Work under Finder instead of MultiFinder.* Choose **Set Startup** from the Special menu to open the Start up dialog box. Click the *Finder* button and click *OK*. Restart your Macintosh. (This is not applicable with System 7.0 and later.)

- *Minimize the number of memory-resident programs.* You may want to remove INITs (start-up applications) or CDEVs (control panel devices) from your System folder to increase available memory.

Working with Multiple Documents

It is possible to have up to ten documents open at once; however, only the document in which you are working is active. Each open document is listed in the View menu, with a Command key shortcut, so you can activate a document that may not be visible. The active document is checked in the menu, and its title bar includes horizontal lines. Each open document maintains its own status information, such as which tool is selected, current Line & Fill palette settings, and so on.

To switch from one document to another:

- Click any exposed area of the document you want to activate.

- Choose the document's title from the View menu.

- Press Command and the number assigned to the document in the View menu.

The selected document becomes the active document and its window is moved in front of all others.

Arranging Multiple Documents for Viewing

You can move a document window to any position on the screen by dragging its title bar. Press the Command key before beginning to drag an inactive document to prevent it becoming active and moving to the front.

There are three commands in the View menu for arranging multiple documents: **Tile**, **Stack** and **Overlap**. When you choose **Tile**, the document windows are sized and arranged so they are all visible and do not overlap. **Tile** normally creates rows and columns of windows.

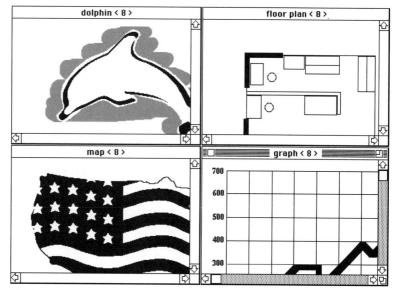

Tiled documents.

Press the Option key before opening the View menu to choose **Tile** to arrange up to three document windows in rows and make them as wide as the screen.

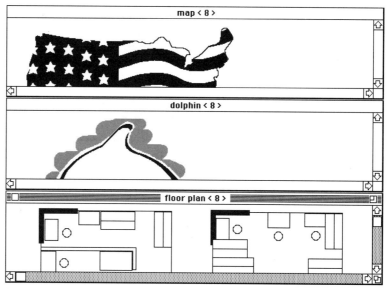

Three documents Option-Tiled.

The **Stack** command makes each document window as large as possible for the display (excluding the Tools and Line & Fill palettes), and stacks them on top of each other. To activate a document hidden in the stack, choose its name from the View menu, use the Command key shortcut, or resize and move the documents on top so you can click some part of its window.

When you choose **Overlap**, the open documents are made the same size and arranged so the title bar and left edge of each window is visible; that is, the windows are staggered down the screen.

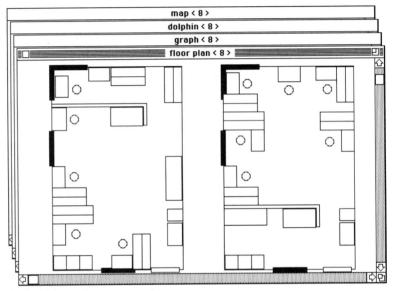

Overlapped documents.

Full-Screen Mode

Hot Key:

The space bar is the Grabber hot key.

The **Full Screen** command in the View menu hides the title bars and scroll bars of the open documents, and optionally, the menu bar. The displayed area of the document is maximized, filling as much of the screen as possible; any open palettes remain open. The menu bar is hidden in full-screen mode if *Hide menu bar in Full Screen mode* is selected on the Window Settings page of the Preferences dialog box.

Since there are no scroll bars in full-screen mode, use the Grabber to scroll your documents (the hot keys are particularly useful in full-screen mode). To restore the title bars and scroll bars, choose **Full Screen** again. If the menu bar is hidden, you can cancel full-screen mode by pressing Command-F.

Document window before **Full Screen** was chosen.

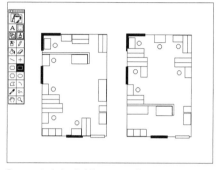

Document window in full-screen mode (notice that the menu bar is hidden).

Placing Images

The **Place** command lets you import images in various formats directly into the Draw layer. When no document is open, the **Place** command is dimmed. You can place image documents produced by SuperPaint or other programs, and documents containing scanned images. In addition, with the plug-in module for your scanner in the SP Pouch, images can be scanned directly into SuperPaint.

If you've installed the menu commands, the **Place** submenu of the File menu will contain the entries: **EPS**, **Apple Scanner**, **ThunderScan TIFF**, **MacPaint**, and **TIFF**. Image-acquisition plug-in modules in the SP Pouch may not be listed in the **Place** submenu, depending on the machine you're using. For example, the ThunderScan TIFF and Apple Scanner modules will not appear in the **Place** submenu of black-and-white systems.

The extent to which you can edit a placed graphic depends on its format. For example, an EPS document is placed as a high-resolution object; it can be moved, resized and transformed, but it cannot be edited as a Draw object. (It can be moved to the Paint layer, with the attendant loss of resolution, and edited.)

Note: Placing an EPS document and then choosing **Selection to Texture** is a method of creating high-resolution textures. Placing an EPS document and then saving the image in a different format (or copying it to the Clipboard), is a method of transporting an EPS image into a program that cannot open EPS documents directly.

A bitmapped image, such as a scanned image or a MacPaint image, is placed into the Draw layer as a single SuperBits object, which can be edited using the **Edit SuperBits** command. The resolution of the SuperBits object is that of the original image. For example, an image scanned at 300 dpi and saved as a TIFF document produces a 300-dpi SuperBits object, while a MacPaint image produces a 72-dpi SuperBits object. Refer to Part 4, Chapter 9 for information about editing SuperBits objects.

To place an existing MacPaint, TIFF, EPS, or StartupScreen image into the active document:

1. Choose the appropriate command from the **Place** submenu of the File menu to display the Place dialog box.

2. Use the *Drive* button, the pop-up folder menu, and the scrolling list to select the document to be placed.

3. Click *Place*, or press Return or Enter, to close the dialog box.

The Draw layer is activated and the image in the selected document is placed, becoming the active object.

Note: The dialog box presented when you choose an image-acquisition command from the Place submenu depends on the particular module in the import folder in the SP Pouch; refer to the information provided by its developer for details. In general, you capture an image from an attached device (such as a scanner) by following prompts in the dialog box. The new image is placed in the Draw layer of the active Super-Paint document as a SuperBits object.

Saving Documents

You can save the contents of the active document at any time without closing the document. It is good practice to save periodically as you work to insure against accidental loss.

Save

To save a document while you're working, choose **Save** from the File menu or press Command-S. If you are working in a previously saved (titled) document, regardless of its format, the document is updated and you can continue working. If it is a new, untitled document, the Save As dialog box is presented so you can enter a document name and specify a format.

Save All

To save multiple documents at once, press the Option key before opening the File menu; the **Save** command becomes **Save All**, which saves all open documents. (The keyboard shortcut Option-Command-S is available also.)

Save As

Use the **Save As** command to save a previously untitled document, and to save a new copy of an existing document. The Save As dialog box is presented in which you can specify a document name, format, and location. When using **Save As** with an existing document, the original document is left as it was when last saved, and a new document with the specified name, format, and location is created; this becomes the active document.

To save the active document with a new name, format, or location:

1. Choose **Save As** from the File menu to display the Save As dialog box.

```
┌─────────────────────────────────────────────────┐
│  ┌──────────────────────┐                        │
│  │ ⬧ My SuperPaint Graphics │        ⬥ HD 100     │
│  │ ▭ dolphin          ⬆ │    19,230K available   │
│  │ ▭ floor plan         │                        │
│  │ ▭ graph              │      ┌─────────────┐   │
│  │ ▭ map                │      │    Eject     │  │
│  │                      │      └─────────────┘   │
│  │                      │      ┌─────────────┐   │
│  │                   ⬇ │      │    Drive     │  │
│  └──────────────────────┘      └─────────────┘   │
│  Save document as:             ┌─────────────┐   │
│  ┌──────────────────────┐      │    Save      │  │
│  │ chart                │      └─────────────┘   │
│  └──────────────────────┘      ┌─────────────┐   │
│  ● SuperPaint 3.0  ○ Save as:  │   Cancel     │  │
│                      │ PICT │  └─────────────┘   │
└─────────────────────────────────────────────────┘
```

2. Enter a name for the document in the *Save document as* text box.

   Optionally, select a format for the document from the *Save as* pop-up menu. (Refer to the next section for more about document formats.)

   Optionally, select a drive and folder in which the document is to be located.

3. Click *Save*, or press Return or Enter, to close the dialog box.

   The active document is saved under the specified name, format and location; the document is not closed.

Saving in Other Formats

A document can be saved in any of the following formats:

- SuperPaint 3.0
- Texture
- PICT

- MacPaint
- Stationery
- StartupScreen

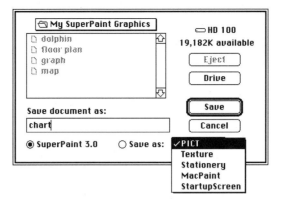

A document would be saved in a different format if, for example, you intend to open it in a program that does not recognize SuperPaint's native format. Each format available in the Save As dialog box is described in the following paragraphs. (You can also export EPS and TIFF documents, as described later in this chapter.)

SuperPaint 3.0

This is the native format for documents created by SuperPaint 3.0. It is not a standard format recognized by other applications, since current tool, fill, and line information, as well as other settings are saved with each document. Therefore, if you plan to open an image in another application, it should be saved in a format such as PICT that is recognized by other programs. If you open a document created in Super-Paint 2.0, you may want to use **Save As** to change its format to SuperPaint 3.0 — in addition to saving current information, the resulting document may require less disk space.

PICT

SuperPaint documents saved in PICT2 format are recognized and can be opened by other programs. The image quality is maintained, as are special effects such as gradient and texture fills. (This is SuperPaint 2.0's native format.)

Texture

There are two ways to add images to the Textures palette: the **Selection to Texture** command, and the **Save As** command with *Texture* selected for the format. (The Textures palette and the **Selection to Texture** command are described in more detail in Part 4, Chapter 4.) Once created, texture documents can be opened, edited and saved normally.

Note: As the size of a texture increase, so does the amount of disk space required to store the texture document and the amount of RAM required to work with it, so smaller textures are to be preferred. Use of the **Selection to Texture** command to create texture documents is recommended.

To save the active document as a texture:

1. Choose **Save As** from the File menu to display the Save As dialog box.

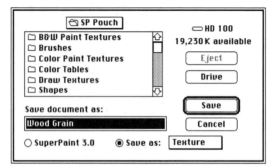

2. Select *Texture* from the *Save as* pop-up menu.

3. Enter a name for the texture document.

4. Use the *Drive* button and the folder pop-up menu to find the SP Pouch folder.

   To appear on the Textures palette, the texture document must be located in the SP Pouch folder. Optionally, it can be located in a folder within the SP Pouch.

5. Click *Save*, or press Return or Enter, to close the dialog box.

   The entire document is saved as a texture document — as a high-resolution Draw texture if the Draw layer is active, and as a bit-mapped texture if the Paint layer is active. The texture document must be located in the SP Pouch, or in a folder in the SP Pouch; the image then is available as a texture from the Textures palette.

Stationery

When a document is saved as Stationery, it is saved as a template that can be used over and over (an electronic version of personal stationery, office letterhead, and so forth). When you open a Stationery document, SuperPaint makes an untitled copy of the original; you can make changes and additions, and then save in another format under a different name, all without altering the original. To edit an existing Stationery template, open and make changes to the untitled copy, and then save it as Stationery, in the location of the original and under the same name.

MacPaint

SuperPaint documents can be saved in MacPaint format; these documents will be recognized by programs that read MacPaint documents. However, there are some limitations associated with converting to MacPaint format:

- Any graphics that extend beyond the boundaries of a standard 8.5 x 11-inch page are truncated.

- The document is one bit; that is, the image is converted to black and white.

- The document is bitmapped, with a resolution of 72 dpi (Draw-layer and SuperBits objects are merged into the Paint layer).

If you use SuperPaint to re-open a document saved in MacPaint format, you will find a black-and-white image in the Paint layer.

StartupScreen

The StartupScreen is the image that first appears when you turn on your Macintosh. You can replace the usual "Welcome" screen with a black-and-white or color SuperPaint graphic. Use **Save As** to save the active document in *StartupScreen* format; the document must be named "StartupScreen" (the document name should have no spaces or other punctuation), and it must be located in the System folder on your start-up disk.

If a color image saved as a StartupScreen is larger than the display area of the monitor, the screen is filled, with the upper left corner of the image aligned with the upper left corner of the screen. If a color image is smaller than the monitor's display area, it is centered in the screen. (Consult your monitor reference manual for screen size. You can reset the document's measurement units to pixels to verify the size of your graphic.)

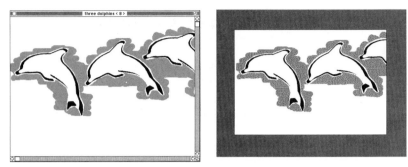

The original document.   The StartUp Screen as it appears on a Macintosh II.

Black-and-white StartupScreen images are always 342 pixels (4.75 inches) tall and 512 pixels (7.11 inches) wide — the dimensions of the Macintosh SE-sized screen. Larger images are truncated (the measurements are made from the upper left corner of the image), while smaller documents are increased in size, and the added area filled with white space.

Note: For the Macintosh to find and use the startup image, it must be titled *StartupScreen* and put in your System folder. The image will be displayed next time you start your system.

Revert to Saved

The **Revert to Saved** command in the File menu replaces the contents of the active document with the most recently saved version of that document. This lets you discard any changes made since the document was last saved.

Note: The command is unavailable if the active document is untitled. Also, you cannot undo a **Revert to Saved** command.

Exporting SuperPaint Documents

You can export all or part of an image as a TIFF document or as an Encapsulated PostScript (EPS) document. These documents maintain the special effects of the graphics (e.g., texture and gradient fills), and the high resolution of the Draw layer in formats usable by other programs. For example, you would export an image to an EPS document for use in a color-separation program such as Aldus PrePrint,™ and to a TIFF or an EPS document for placement by page-layout applications such as Aldus Personal Press™ and Aldus PageMaker.®

The options available in the Export dialog box vary slightly according to the layer in which you are working and whether any graphics are selected. Basically, you can:

- Export the entire SuperPaint document to a TIFF or an EPS document. The resolution of the Draw-layer is maintained when exported as EPS. The resolution of an exported TIFF image is always 72 dpi, unless there is a single selected SuperBits object in the Draw layer; in such a case, the resolution of the exported TIFF file will be the same as that specified for the SuperBits object.

- Export a selected area of the Paint layer; the bitmapped image is 72 dpi.

- Export a single selected SuperBits object in the Draw layer to a TIFF document at the resolution defined for the object. (Only one SuperBits object can be exported; creating and editing SuperBits objects are described in Part 4, Chapter 9.)

- Export the selected objects in the Draw layer to an EPS document.

Note: If there is a combination of bitmapped graphics and object-oriented graphics contained within an EPS texture when it is exported, the resulting EPS file will print as a bitmapped image.

To export all or part of an image from either layer:

1. Choose **Export** from the File menu to display the Export dialog box.

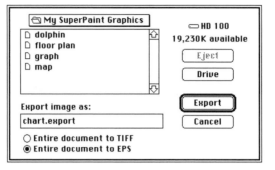

2. Click the "to TIFF" or the "to EPS" button to specify a format.

3. Enter a name for the document in the *Export image as* text field.

4. Use the *Drive* button and the pop-up folder menu to specify a location for the document.

5. Click *Export*, or press Return or Enter.

   The graphics are exported to the new EPS or TIFF document; the document in which you are working is not affected. Once exported, you will not be able to open the new document directly with SuperPaint; however, you could use the **Place** command to place the document into the Draw layer of the active document (as described earlier in this chapter).

Closing Documents

To close a document, choose **Close** from the File menu, use the Command-W shortcut, or click the close box on the left side of the title bar. If changes made to the document have not yet been saved, you'll be asked if you want to save the changes before the document is closed.

If more than one document is open, you can close them all at once by pressing the Option key before opening the File menu and choosing the **Close All** command. (The keyboard shortcut Option-Command-W also is available.)

Chapter 4: Lines and Fills

Floating and pop-up palettes were introduced in Chapter 2. This chapter describes most of the Line & Fill palette: the Line Fill and Area Fill displays, the Permanent Fills, and the Textures, Gradients, Patterns, Line Widths, and Transfer Modes pop-up palettes. (The Colors pop-up palette is discussed in the following chapter.) In addition, the Frequent Fills palette, and arrows and dashes are explained in this chapter.

What is a Fill?

A fill is simply a *pattern* composed of *foreground* and *background* elements. In most situations, the foreground element can be a color, a texture, or a gradient, and the background can be a color. (There is also a Transfer Mode associated with the fill; these are discussed later in this chapter.)

There are two types of fill — Line Fill and Area Fill — and all of the creation tools (those that paint or draw) use one or both. This integration of tools and fills is one of the most powerful features of SuperPaint: you can define a fill and then use it, with any tool.

Solid black Line Fill; patterned Area Fill.

Solid black Line Fill; patterned Area Fill, with color assigned to the foreground.

Solid black Line Fill; patterned Area Fill, and a gradient assigned to the foreground.

Patterned Line Fill and patterned Area Fill.

The Line & Fill palette is the focus of fill composition and display. To define a fill, you first select a pattern, and then select the foreground and background elements. You can change the pattern, the foreground, or the background at any time, without affecting the other two components of the fill.

The Line & Fill Palette

The Line & Fill palette is at the top of the screen when you start Super-Paint. This palette displays the current Line Fill and the current Area Fill, provides rapid access to three unique, frequently used fills, and includes pop-up palettes for all of the fill elements, as well as for line widths. (Opening and selecting from pop-up palettes is described in Part 4, Chapter 2.)

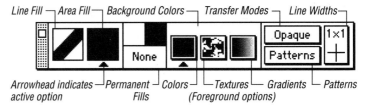

Line Fill — Area Fill — Background Colors — Transfer Modes — Line Widths —

Arrowhead indicates — Permanent — Colors — Textures — Gradients — Patterns
active option   Fills   (Foreground options)

Line Fill and Area Fill

A number of the creation tools produce *shapes* (rectangles, ovals, and so on) that are composed of an outline and an enclosed area. The attributes of this outline, and of the lines produced by the line tools, are Line Fill, its associated Transfer Mode, and Line Width. The attributes of the enclosed area are Area Fill and its associated Transfer Mode. In addition, most of the painting tools use the current Area Fill as their "paint."

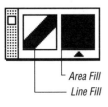

— Area Fill
— Line Fill

The Line Fill and Area Fill displays represent the currently selected fill combinations for both fills. There is an arrow under the active display; click the other to make it active. Define a fill for the active display as follows (each step is optional; each is described in subsequent sections of the chapter):

- Select a pattern from the Patterns pop-up palette.

- Select a pattern foreground from the Colors, Gradients, or Textures pop-up palettes.

- Select a background color from the background Colors pop-up.

- Select a Transfer Mode from the Transfer Modes pop-up.

Exceptions

The following are exceptions to the basic pattern/foreground/background definition of a fill:

- A texture or a gradient can be applied to only one of the fills at a time. For example, you cannot apply a texture to the Line Fill, and also have a texture or a gradient on the foreground of the Area Fill.

- In the Draw layer of color documents, text can be filled with a solid, opaque foreground (color, texture or gradient); that is, a pattern and a background color cannot be applied.

- In the Paint layer of a black-and-white (1-bit) document, a foreground color assignment is applied to all black pixels in the document, both Line Fill and Area Fill. A background color assignment cannot be made.

Permanent Fills

Permanent Fills.

The Permanent Fills are three unique fills that you will use often. The black cell represents a solid foreground pattern and black color, and the white cell represents a solid foreground pattern and white color. The *None* cell represents a fill of no pattern (no foreground or background), and thus, no fill.

As solid patterns, the black and white Permanent Fills are most often used to quickly replace a previously selected pattern. For example, if you have a Line Fill that is a checkerboard pattern with a red foreground and yellow background, and you want a solid blue Line Fill next, you would first select the black or white Permanent Fill to replace the checkerboard pattern (you could also select the solid black or solid white pattern from the Patterns palette), and then select a blue from the foreground Colors palette. If you simply select the blue without replacing the pattern, your Line Fill will be a checkerboard with a blue foreground and a yellow background.

With a Line Fill of *None*, the shapes you create will have no outlines. With an Area Fill of *None*, shapes will consist of only outlines. If you set both Line Fill and Area Fill to *None*, nothing will be created with any of the tools.

Note: Selecting one of the Permanent Fills automatically switches the Transfer Mode to Opaque.

Patterns

Hot Key:

X is the hot key for the Patterns palette.

Patterns are the principal component of the Line Fill and Area Fill. Patterns are found on the Patterns pop-up palette, which is available from the Line & Fill palette. These patterns are black and white; black is the foreground and white is the background. You can edit any of the basic patterns on the palette, or define your own, in the Custom Patterns dialog box.

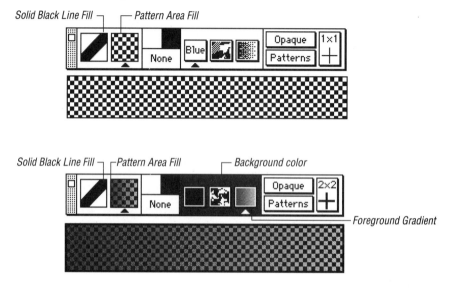

To select a pattern:

1. Open the Patterns pop-up palette from the Line & Fill palette.

   The pop-up can be "torn off" to form a floating palette.

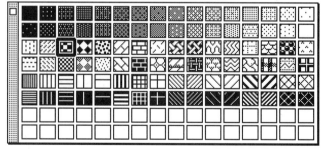

Patterns floating palette.

2. Drag the cursor to the desired pattern and release the mouse button.

   The pop-up palette closes and the selected pattern replaces the current Line Fill or Area Fill pattern, depending on the active display.

Creating and Editing Patterns

To create a new pattern, or edit an existing pattern:

1. Choose **Patterns** from the Options menu, or double-click a pattern on the torn-off Patterns palette.

   The Custom Patterns dialog box appears, displaying 32 of the patterns available on the palette. The currently selected pattern is also displayed in the editing area below the 32 pattern cells, at normal magnification and at 8x magnification.

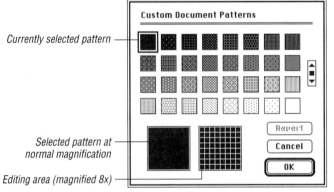

Currently selected pattern ——

Selected pattern at normal magnification ——

Editing area (magnified 8x) ——

Custom Patterns dialog box.

Use the scrolling arrows to the right of the 32 cells to display more patterns. The button between the two arrows displays the patterns at the top of the Patterns palette (the LaserWriter grays).

2. Click the pattern you wish to edit; to create a new pattern, select a blank cell.

   You can also fill the editing displays with an area eight pixels by eight pixels picked up from anywhere on the screen. Click or drag to pick up the area around the tip of the pointer.

3. Edit the pattern in the 8x editing box — when you move the pointer into the editing box, it becomes a Pencil.

Each black pixel of the selected pattern is represented as a black square. Clicking or dragging over black pixels makes them white; clicking or dragging over white pixels makes them black. As you edit the pattern in the magnified view, it is displayed at normal magnification.

Command-click anywhere inside the 8x editing area to reverse all black and white pixels.

Click the *Revert* button to discard changes to the edited pattern.

4. Click *OK*, or press Return or Enter, or double-click any pattern cell to close the dialog box.

The pattern you edited is added to the Patterns palette. If you clicked *OK*, or pressed Return or Enter, the new pattern also replaces the current Area Fill or Line Fill pattern. If you double-clicked a pattern other than the one you edited, the new pattern is still added to the palette, but the one double-clicked replaces the current Area Fill or Line Fill pattern.

Note: Patterns created or edited when a document is open are stored with that document. If you want to change SuperPaint's default patterns, edit them with no documents open. If you have done so, the original default patterns can be restored by discarding the SuperPaint Prefs file in the SP Pouch. (Refer to Part 4, Chapter 2 for more information on the SuperPaint Prefs file.)

Foreground and Background

Colors, gradients, and textures are the elements that can be applied to the pattern foreground (the black parts of the pattern). Three foreground pop-up palettes, one for each element, are found on the Line & Fill palette. The Gradients and Textures pop-up palettes are described in following sections; the Colors palette is described in the next chapter.

The background element of a pattern can be a color (including black or white). Background colors are selected from the background Colors pop-up palette, which is opened by positioning the pointer anywhere in the area surrounding the three foreground pop-up boxes, and pressing the mouse button.

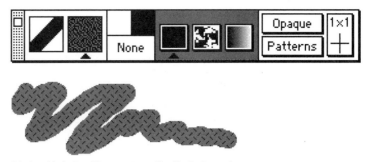

Painting with the Area Fill — a pattern with a blue background.

Note: In the Paint layer of black-and-white (1-bit) documents, you cannot assign a background color — one color can be assigned in the Paint layer and it is applied to all the black dots in the layer.

Textures

A texture is an image or portion of an image that has been saved as a texture document and placed in the SP Pouch. This image is added automatically to the Textures palette, and can be used on the foreground of either the Line Fill or Area Fill — in this way you could use a scanned image to "paint with a fish." A texture can be virtually any size, and it is repeated as necessary, seamlessly, during painting and drawing.

Dolphin filled with texture.

Note: The Line Fill and the Area Fill cannot both include textures, or a texture and a gradient, at the same time.

Using Textures

Hot Key:

H is the hot key for the Textures palette.

The Textures pop-up palette is opened and a texture selected in the same manner as selections are made from the other pop-up palettes. It also can be torn off, repositioned, and closed. (Refer to Part 4, Chapter 2 for more information about pop-up palettes.)

Textures can be bitmapped, object-oriented, SuperBits, or EPS images. All can be used in either layer, but object-oriented, SuperBits, and EPS textures in the Draw layer print at the resolution of your output device.

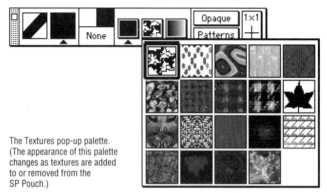

The Textures pop-up palette. (The appearance of this palette changes as textures are added to or removed from the SP Pouch.)

Creating a textured shape in the Draw layer.

In the Draw layer, when you use a texture fill, the fill is represented in the object by the mesh pattern shown at left until the object is completed. In the Paint layer, the texture is displayed as you work.

Creating and Storing Textures

Texture documents are stored in the SP Pouch, often in Textures folders. You can add textures to and remove them from the Textures palette by adding or removing texture documents from the SP Pouch.

The Textures palette is dynamic: it expands or contracts to accommodate the textures. Each cell on the palette is 32 x 32 pixels; thus, only a portion of textures larger than the cell is displayed. (This portion is not a composite of the image, and may not be representative of the entire texture image.)

Texture documents can be created with the **Save As** command and with the **Selection to Texture** command. Once created, texture documents can be opened, edited and saved like any other SuperPaint document.

To create a texture with the **Selection to Texture** command:

1. Select all or part of the active document.

    In the Paint layer, use any of the Selection Tools. In the Draw layer, use the Selection Arrow to activate objects. (The Two-Layer Selection tool cannot be used in the texture-creation process.)

2. Choose **Selection to Texture** from the File menu to display the Selection to Texture dialog box.

```
File
  New...           ⌘N
  Open...          ⌘O
  Close            ⌘W

  Save             ⌘S
  Save As...
  Selection to Texture...
  Revert to Saved

  Place            ▶

  Document Info...
  Page Setup...
  Print...         ⌘P

  Quit             ⌘Q
```

```
        📁 SP Pouch                    ⊂ HD 100
  ☐ B&W File Import          ⇧    15,996K available
  ☐ B&W Import
  ☐ Brushes                            [ Eject ]
  ☐ Color Tables
  ☐ Draw Textures                      [ Drive ]
  ☐ Shapes                   ⇩

  Save texture as:                    [  Save  ]
  Wood Grain                          [ Cancel ]
```

3. Enter a name for the texture document, and specify where it is to be saved.

    Texture documents found in the SP Pouch, or in any folder within the SP Pouch, are added to the Textures palette.

4. Click *Save*, or press Return or Enter, to close the dialog box.

    If you are working in the Paint layer, the selection is saved as a bitmapped texture; objects selected in the Draw layer (including SuperBits objects and placed EPS illustrations) are saved as a high-resolution texture.

Note: Saving a high-resolution texture as another texture is not recommended. That is, if you draw an object that is filled with an object-oriented texture, and then attempt to save that object as part of another texture, the resulting texture document can require a large amount of memory, and will slow SuperPaint considerably.

You can place an EPS illustration created in an application such as Aldus FreeHand and save it as a high-resolution Draw texture. Refer to Part 4, Chapter 3 for a description of the **Place** command. Also described in Part 4, Chapter 3 is use of the **Save As** command to create a texture document.

Gradients

A gradient, or more correctly, a graduated fill, is the blending of two or more shades of gray or colors to provide a smooth transition from one to another. (In black-and-white documents, shades of gray are simulated by pixel density.) A gradient can be used as the foreground fill component in both the Paint and Draw layers.

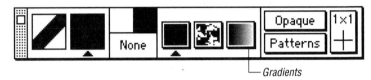

— Gradients

Note: The Line Fill and the Area Fill cannot both include gradients, or a gradient and a texture, at the same time.

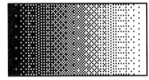

A 1-bit gradient in the Paint layer.

An 8-bit gradient in the Paint layer.

A 1-bit gradient in the Draw layer.

An 8-bit gradient in the Draw layer.

Hot Key:
G is the hot key for the Gradients palette.

When printed, there may be some banding evident in the blending (or transition between hues) of Paint-layer gradients in color documents. With Draw-layer gradients in both black-and-white and color documents, the blending of hues is smoother as the resolution of the output device increases.

You can select one of the gradients provided on the Gradients pop-up palette, or you can define your own in the Custom Gradients dialog box, using up to 256 grays or colors in a single gradient. (You cannot define custom gradients in black-and-white documents.)

Natura

Gradients can be applied with any tool, including the Text tool, in both the Paint and Draw layers.

Selecting a Gradient

There are four gradient types (methods of applying the gradient effect): Linear, Rectangular, Circular, and Peaked. With *Linear*, the blend is applied to any shape linearly, as it appears in the bar on the palette; you specify the direction of application. *Rectangular* produces an "X" effect in any shape; you specify the location of the center of the X. *Circular* produces a circular effect in shape; you specify the location of the center of the circle. *Peaked* produces a ridged effect that is based on the shape of the object — the gradient is applied from the boundaries (or the tangents of curved boundaries) of the shape toward its center.

To select a gradient effect for the foreground of the Line Fill or Area Fill:

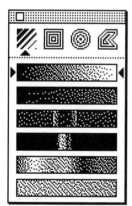

Gradients floating palette.

1. Open the Gradients pop-up palette.

The type and gradient currently selected are indicated by a pointer beneath the type icon and at each end of the appropriate gradient bar (the first time you open and begin to drag into the palette, Linear and the top gradient are selected).

2. Drag to change the type, or to select another gradient bar.

The pointer(s) move to indicate your selection.

3. Release the mouse button.

The palette closes and the selected gradient or type is assigned to the foreground of the active fill.

On the popped-up palette, you can make only one selection at a time (i.e., type or gradient); to change the other, re-open the palette and drag to make the selection. Of course, if you tear the Gradient palette from the Line & Fill palette, you will not have to re-open the palette to make a second selection: simply click the appropriate gradient-type icon or gradient bar.

When you use a tool and apply a fill that includes a gradient, the fill is represented by the mesh pattern shown below until gradient processing is completed. If the gradient type is *Linear*, *Rectangular*, or *Circular*, when you release the mouse button, an "elastic band" stretches from the center of the shape to the cursor. For linear effects, this band is used to specify the direction of the gradient blend. For rectangular and circular effects, the end of the band is used to specify the location of the center of the effect. Position the cursor and click the mouse button to complete the gradient effect.

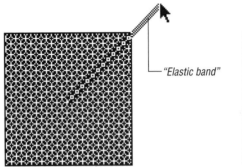

"Elastic band"

Linear gradient

Customizing Gradients

In color documents, you can define new gradients, and delete or replace existing gradients, in the Custom Gradients dialog box.

Rectangular gradient

To display the Custom Gradients dialog box:

- Choose **Gradients** from the Options menu.

Circular gradient

or

- Double-click one of the gradients on the Gradients palette.

Peaked gradient

The gradient currently selected on the Gradients palette is displayed in the gradient bar in the dialog box.

Polygon with a Peaked gradient fill.

Custom Document Gradients

New   Delete

Cancel   OK

To change the gradient displayed:

- Use the scroll arrows to the right of the gradient bar to cycle through the gradients.

  The gradients are displayed in the same sequence as on the palette. The button between the two arrows displays the gradient at the top of the palette.

or

- Click the *New* button to display a new white-to-white gradient.

To delete the displayed gradient from the palette:

- Click the *Delete* button.

Three components are used to alter an existing gradient, or fill a new one: the Start Color, the End Color, and Color Bulbs. The simplest gradient effect is a blending of Start Color to End Color.

To define a Start Color or an End Color:

1. Click the Start Color box or the End Color box to select it.

   The box is highlighted.

2. Select a color from the Continuous Color space, or pick up a color with the Eyedropper.

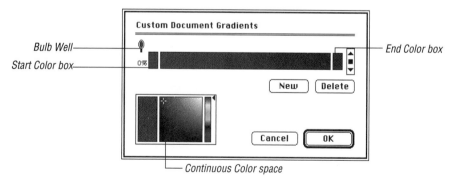

The selected color is displayed in the Start Color or End Color box and blended into the gradient. (Using a Continuous Color display is described in Part 4, Chapter 5. The availability of the gradient Eyedropper is described in a subsequent paragraph.)

To add colors to the gradient between the Start Color and End Color:

1. Click the Bulb Well to select it.

   The Bulb Well is highlighted.

2. Select a color from the Continuous Color space, or pick up a color with the Eyedropper.

   The Color Bulb in the Bulb Well is filled with the color.

3. Drag the Color Bulb from the Bulb Well into position above the gradient bar.

   The selected color is blended into the gradient in both directions from that point.

Repeat Steps 1, 2 and 3 to add additional colors to the gradient. You can place up to 256 Color Bulbs above the gradient bar.

Alternate methods of selecting colors and adding Color Bulbs:

- Outside of the dialog box, the pointer is an Eyedropper that you can use to pick up color for the selected item (Start Color box, End Color box, Bulb Well, existing Color Bulb). Inside the dialog box, press the Command key to switch the pointer to the Eyedropper. The Eyedropper picks up "true" rather than dithered colors (true and dithered colors are described in Part 4, Chapter 5).

- To select a color from the Apple Color Picker, double-click the display bar to the left of the Continuous Color space.

- To position a duplicate of an existing Color Bulb on the gradient bar, Option-drag from the existing bulb.

- To create a Color Bulb over the gradient bar, click a point in the bar. A bulb is added, taking the color of the bar at that point.

To delete a Color Bulb from above the gradient bar:

- Drag the Color Bulb off either end of the bar.

or

- Click the Color Bulb to select it, and press the Delete key.

When you have finished editing gradients:

- Click *OK*, or press Return or Enter, to close the dialog box.

Altered gradients replace existing gradients on the Gradients palette, and new gradients are appended to the palette. The palette will expand or contract to accommodate additions or deletions. (The palette can contain up to 22 gradients, and there must be at least one.)

Note: Gradients created or edited when a document is open are stored with that document. If you want to change SuperPaint's default gradients, edit them with no documents open. If you have done so, the original default gradients can be restored by discarding the SuperPaint Prefs file in the SP Pouch. (Refer to Part 4, Chapter 2 for more information on the SuperPaint Prefs file.)

Transfer Modes

Both the Line Fill and the Area Fill have a Transfer Mode associated with them. This Transfer Mode defines how the fill interacts with existing graphics and the document background when applied with any of SuperPaint's tools in either layer. In addition, the assigned Transfer Mode defines how a selection area interacts with the rest of the Paint layer when it is moved. (Selection areas, and the effect of the current Transfer Mode, are discussed in Part 4, Chapter 7.)

Note: There are two sets of similar modes: Transfer Modes and Fill Modes. Fill Modes are available from the Paint menu and affect the **Fill** command and certain plug-ins. See Part 4, Chapter 8 for a discussion of Fill Modes and the **Fill** command.

Hot Key:
M is the hot key for the Transfer Modes palette.

To change the Transfer Mode of the Line Fill, the Area Fill, or an existing selection area, select the desired mode from the Transfer Modes pop-up on the Line & Fill palette. (The Transfer Modes pop-up can be torn off to create a floating palette.)

Four Transfer Modes are available in black-and-white documents: *Opaque*, *Translucent*, *Paint on Darker*, and *Invert*. Three additional selections are available in color documents: *Transparent, Transparent Bkgnd.*, and *Set Transparent %.*

- **Opaque** – fills and selections cover the underlying image and background completely; this is the default Transfer Mode.

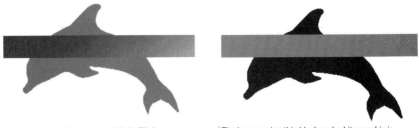

The bar covering this color graphic is filled with an *Opaque* gradient.

The bar covering this black-and-white graphic is filled with an *Opaque* gray pattern.

- **Translucent** – underlying portions of the image are visible through translucent fills and selections. Underlying colors are darkened or replaced by overlaid translucent colors; the effect depends on how light or dark the two colors are, and how far apart they are in the spectrum.

The bar covering this color graphic is filled with a *Translucent* gradient.

The bar covering this black-and-white graphic is filled with a *Translucent* gray pattern.

- **Paint on Darker** – the current fill or selection is visible only against underlying areas that are darker than itself. There is a slight translucent effect.

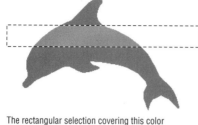 

The rectangular selection covering this color graphic is filled with a gradient assigned the Transfer Mode *Paint on Darker*.

The rectangular selection covering this black-and-white graphic is filled with a gray pattern assigned the Transfer Mode *Paint on Darker*.

- **Invert** – reverses black and white, and produces complementary colors. (In an 8-bit document, the color index is reversed and the result may not be strictly complementary.)

The bar covering this color graphic is filled with a gradient assigned the Transfer Mode *Invert*.

The bar covering this black-and-white graphic is filled with solid black assigned the Transfer Mode *Invert*.

- **Transparent Bkgnd.** – the fill background (whether white or colored) and the white areas of a selection are transparent; all other colors are opaque.

- **Transparent** – the fill or selection area acts as an overlay with the specified percentage of transparency.

Rectangular selection assigned the Transfer Mode Transparent Bkgnd.

This bar is filled with a Transparent (50%) *gradient*

- **Set Transparent %** – opens the Set Transparent % dialog box in which you can define a transparency percentage for the previous Transfer Mode.

Select a pre-set value, or type a percentage in the *Other* text box.

Note: *Transparent Bkgnd.*, *Transparent*, and *Set Transparent %* appear on the Transfer Modes palette only in color documents.

```
┌─────────────────────────────────┐
│  Set Transparent %              │
│  ─────────────────────────────  │
│  ○ 25%                          │
│  ○ 50%     ● Other: [100]       │
│  ○ 75%                          │
│     ( Cancel )    (  OK  )       │
└─────────────────────────────────┘
```

Transfer Modes in the Draw Layer

The Transfer Modes are available in both layers; however, because of a current PostScript limitation, Draw objects with fills that are assigned a Transfer Mode other than *Opaque* will not print correctly on PostScript printers. All Draw objects will print as *Opaque* or *Transparent Bkgnd.* objects; the other modes are evident only on your screen. (This limitation does not exist with QuickDraw printers.) To work around this limitation, you could cut the objects to the Paint layer, or use a film recorder or other screen-capture utility, but the object resolution would be limited to 72 dpi.

Note: Transfer Modes cannot be applied to text in the Draw layer, or to objects in the Draw layer filled with a texture.

Line Widths

Hot Key:
W is the hot key for the Line Widths palette.

Lines, both those produced with the line tools and those outlining shapes, can be up to 99 pixels thick. The Line Widths pop-up palette on the Line & Fill palette lets you select from a number of preset line widths, or you can open the Custom Line Width dialog box and specify separate horizontal and vertical line widths. The current numeric settings are displayed on the drop-shadowed pop-up box; for lines up to eight pixels by eight pixels, a physical representation is displayed also.

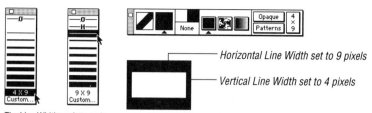

Horizontal Line Width set to 9 pixels

Vertical Line Width set to 4 pixels

The Line Widths palette as it appears in the Paint layer (left) and the Draw layer (right).

To change line widths, open the palette like any other pop-up palette, and drag to make a selection. From the top down, there are bars representing preset options (for which line thickness is the same in both directions); the current setting is highlighted.

The first setting (-0-) is for no lines at all. This Line Widths setting lets you draw shapes without frames (the effect is the same as setting the Line Fill to *None*). The second setting (-H-), available only in the Draw layer, produces hairlines. Lines drawn at this setting appear to be single-pixel lines on the screen, but print at one-quarter of a pixel (approximately 300 dpi) on 300-dpi or higher output devices. The remaining preset options are 1 x 1 to 9 x 9 pixels. To specify line widths larger than 9 x 9 pixels, or different widths for horizontal and vertical lines, select *Custom* from the bottom of the palette.

Custom Line Widths

When you select *Custom* from the Line Widths palette, the Custom Line Width dialog box appears.

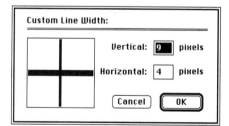

1. Enter a width for vertical lines, press Tab and enter a width for horizontal lines.

   Maximum line width is 99 pixels. A sample of the current settings is displayed in the dialog box.

2. Click *OK*, or press Return or Enter, to close the dialog box with the new line-width settings.

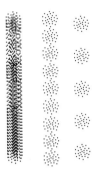

The effect of different Line Widths on the Spray Can.

Line Width Effects

The Line Widths settings affect more than just the lines and frames made by the line and shape tools.

The settings also affect:

- The size of the current arrowhead (see the later section in this chapter on "Arrows").

- The minimum distance between repeat copies when you drag a selection while the Command and Option keys are pressed (see Part 4, Chapter 7).

- The minimum distance between sprays from the Spray Can (see Part 4, Chapter 6).

- Settings for plug-in tools such as the Sprinkler (see Part 4, Chapter 6).

Frequent Fills

Hot Key:
V is the hot key for the Frequent Fills palette.

The Frequent Fills palette holds up to twelve of the most recently used fill combinations (pattern, foreground and background). Each time you use one of the creation tools with a new fill, the fill is added to this palette. Like all floating palettes, this palette can be repositioned and closed.

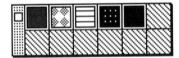

Frequent Fills palette.

The newest fill combination always appears in the upper left cell; the older fills move to the right. When the first row is full, the older fills move onto the second row, from the left. When the palette is full, the oldest fill combination, in the lower right cell, is removed when a new fill is used.

You can reselect any fill combination, making it the current Line Fill or Area Fill, by clicking the appropriate cell.

Arrows

In both layers, lines drawn with the two line tools can automatically have arrowheads at either or both ends. A selection of arrowhead shapes is available, and they can be customized.

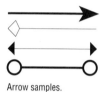

Arrow samples.

To produce arrows, choose **Arrow on Start**, **Arrow on End**, or **Arrows on Both** from the **Arrows** submenu of the Options menu. Now when you use the Line tool or the Perpendicular Line tool, the current arrowhead shape is added automatically to either or both ends. Arrowheads are filled with the current Area Fill, and their size is changed by changing the Line Widths.

To stop producing arrows, choose **No Arrows** from the **Arrows** submenu. The current mode is indicated by a check before the appropriate command in the **Arrows** submenu.

Changing Arrowheads

You can change the currently selected arrowhead in the Custom Arrows dialog box — you can select one of the arrowheads provided, and you can edit it to create a new shape.

Note: Arrowheads customized when a document is open are stored with that document. If you want to change SuperPaint's default arrowheads, edit them with no documents open. If you have done so, the original default arrowheads can be restored by discarding the SuperPaint Prefs file in the SP Pouch. (Refer to Part 4, Chapter 2 for more information on the SuperPaint Prefs file.)

To change the current arrowhead shape:

1. Choose **Custom Arrows** from the **Arrows** submenu of the Options menu, or double-click the Line tool icon on the Tools palette, to display the Custom Arrows dialog box.

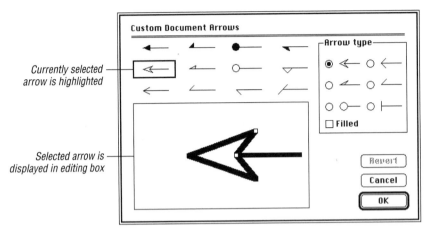

Currently selected arrow is highlighted

Selected arrow is displayed in editing box

2. Click one of the twelve displayed arrows to select it.

    If none of the displayed shapes is suitable, you can customize an arrowhead, as described in the following section.

3. Click *OK*, press Return or Enter, or double-click one of the twelve arrow selections, to make the selected shape the current arrowhead and close the dialog box.

    The arrow highlighted when the dialog box is closed will be produced by the line tools when any command but **No Arrows** is checked in the **Arrows** submenu of the Options menu.

Note: In the Paint layer, the desired arrow shape must be selected before a line is drawn. In the Draw layer, arrowheads can be added to or changed on existing lines at any time.

Customizing an Arrowhead

The shape highlighted in the block of twelve in the upper left portion of the Custom Arrows dialog box is displayed in the editing box at the bottom of the dialog box, and its type indicated by the highlighted button in the *Arrow type* section.

To change the shape displayed in the editing box:

- Select the arrowhead closest to the shape you want from the twelve above the editing box, or from those in the *Arrow type* section.

  Be aware that if you select from the *Arrow type* section, the shape currently highlighted in the block of twelve is replaced by the *Arrow type* selection (so be sure the highlighted shape is one you are willing to discard).

Arrowheads that are shapes (rather than lines) can be hollow or filled:

- Click the *Filled* checkbox in the *Arrow type* section to select or deselect the option. (A "hollow" arrowhead actually is filled with white.)

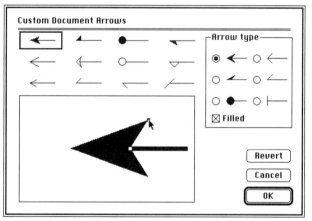

Custom arrow.

To customize the current arrowhead shape:

- Drag the handle(s) on the arrowhead in the editing box to change its size and shape:

Dragging a handle to change the shape of an arrow.

For circular arrowheads, the handle is moved up or down to change the size of the circle.

For all others, the handle above or below the shaft is moved horizontally and vertically to reshape the arrowhead.

If there is a second handle on the shaft, it can be moved back and forth on the shaft to reshape the arrowhead.

Dashes

In both layers, lines drawn with the two line tools can be dashed. A selection of dash schemes is available, or you can create your own.

To produce dashed lines, choose **Dashed** from the **Dashes** submenu of the Options menu. Now when you use the Line or the Perpendicular Line tool, dashed lines are produced automatically. To return to undashed lines, choose **Not Dashed** from the Dashes submenu. The current mode is indicated by a check before the appropriate command.

Note: The shape tools will not produce dashed outlines.

Examples of dashed lines.

Changing Dash Schemes

The current dash scheme is changed in the Custom Dashes dialog box — you can use one of the schemes provided, or you can edit them to create new ones.

Note: Dash schemes edited when a document is open are stored with that document. If you want to change SuperPaint's default dash schemes, edit them with no documents open. If you have done so, the original default dash schemes can be restored by discarding the SuperPaint Prefs file in the SP Pouch. (Refer to Part 4, Chapter 2 for more information on the SuperPaint Prefs file.)

To change the current dash scheme:

1. Choose **Custom Dashes** from the **Dashes** submenu of the Options menu, or double-click the Perpendicular Line tool icon on the Tools palette, to display the Custom Dashes dialog box.

Currently selected dash scheme is highlighted

Custom Document Dashes
Measure in:
Inches
1st Pair:
0.04
0.04
Dash
Gap
Revert
Cancel
OK
Fewer Pairs
More Pairs

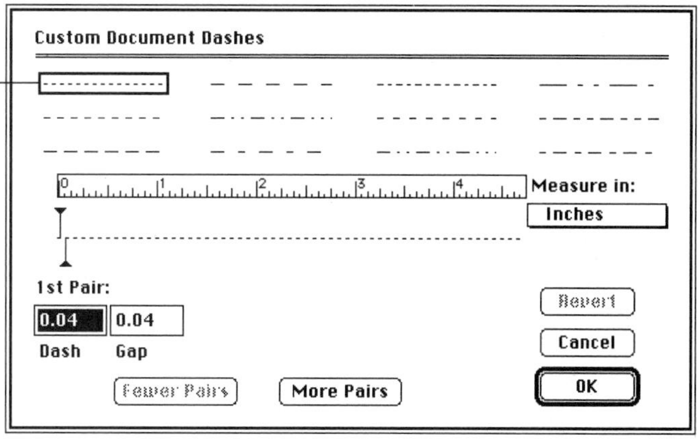

2. Click one of the twelve dash schemes (displayed above the ruler) to select it.

   If none of the displayed schemes is suitable, you can alter one of them, as described in the following section.

3. Click *OK*, press Return or Enter, or double-click one of the twelve dash schemes, to make the highlighted scheme the current dash scheme and close the dialog box.

The dash scheme highlighted when the dialog box is closed will be produced by the line tools when **Dashed** is checked in the **Dashes** submenu of the Options menu.

Note: In the Paint layer, the desired dash scheme must be selected before a line is drawn. In the Draw layer, the dash schemes of existing lines can be changed at any time.

Customizing a Dash Scheme

The dash scheme highlighted in the block of twelve is displayed in the editing area under the ruler in the Custom Dashes dialog box. To change the scheme displayed in the editing area, click another in the block of twelve.

Dash schemes are defined as dash-gap pairs; that is, you define the length of a dash and the length of a gap. Your dash pattern can consist of a single dash-gap pair that is repeated continuously, or you can define up to three dash-gap pairs that repeat sequentially.

To add or delete dash-gap pairs to the selected dash scheme:

- Click the *More Pairs* button or the *Fewer Pairs* button.

   When you add a pair to the scheme, the new pair has the same dash and gap lengths as the previous pair. When you delete a pair, the last pair added is removed.

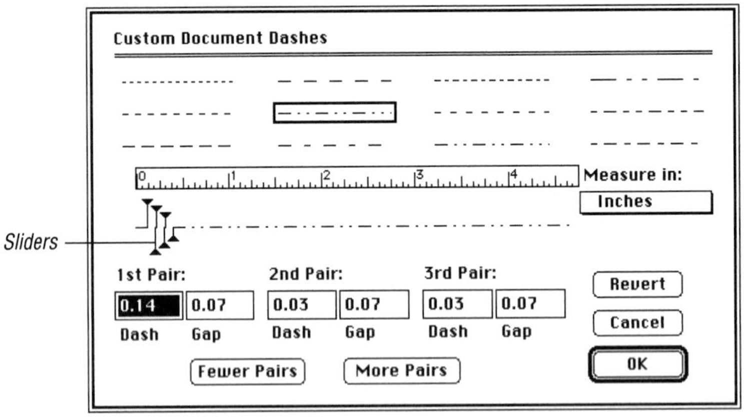

Sliders

Dash scheme edited by adding two pairs and moving sliders.

There are two ways to adjust the lengths of the dashes and gaps in the selected scheme:

- Drag the slider controls below the ruler to lengthen and shorten the dashes and gaps. The sliders for the dashes are above the line; the sliders for the gaps are below the line. As a slider is moved, the length measurement in the associated text box is updated.

or

- Type new lengths into the *Dash* and *Gap* text boxes (the changes are displayed in the sample line).

   In addition, the *Measure in* pop-up menu can be used to change the units of measurement for the document.

Part 4

Chapter 5: Color

This chapter describes SuperPaint's color capabilities. SuperPaint provides a consistent, easy-to-use interface whether you're working in black and white or with 16.8 million colors.

Dots, Bits and Colors

The basic unit of image composition for scanners, monitors and printers is the dot: all computerized images (and this includes text characters) are composed of tiny dots. For instance, the illuminated dots on your monitor screen, known as picture elements or *pixels*, are $1/72$ of an inch in diameter and are capable of displaying between two (black and white) and almost 16.8 million colors, depending on the system and monitor. An image is thus the result of a combination of points of colored light. (The resolution of the image, determined by dot size, is discussed in Part 4, Chapter 9.)

Similarly, the basic unit of information for computers and all digital devices is the binary digit or *bit*. A bit can be either off or on, representing the values zero or one. With strings of bits and a coding system in which, for example, numbers are assigned to colors, a great deal of information can be represented in binary form.

Accordingly, the term *bit depth* refers to the number of bits used to encode color or gray-scale information for each dot in an image. In black-and-white images, each dot is either black or white, and so only one bit is necessary for each dot. If eight bits are stored per dot, then 256 (2^8) separate code combinations, representing 256 colors, are possible for each dot. And with a bit depth of 24, approximately 16.8 million (2^{24}) color codes are available. So basically, an image document is simply a matrix of bit strings representing color codes for each dot.

An image is the result of a combination of gray-shaded pixels. (See detail, right.)

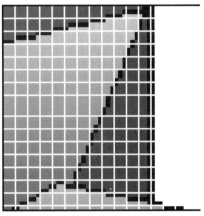

Detail of picture elements.

Note: Bit depth can refer to both the number of colors that can be stored by an image document, and the number of colors a device is capable of recording or displaying. For example, a black-and-white document is a 1-bit document, and an 8-bit scanner is capable of recording 256 colors (or grays).

SuperPaint provides four document bit depths — 1 bit, 8 bit, 16 bit, and 32 bit. The following chart indicates the number of colors available with each bit depth.

Document Bit Depth	Number of Colors
1	2
8	256
16	32,768
32	16,777,216

Note: As you may have noticed, there is a discrepancy with both the 16- and 32-bit figures. The number of colors actually represents 15 bits (2^{15}) and 24 bits (2^{24}) respectively. The extra bit in 16-bit documents and the extra eight bits in 32-bit documents are unused (system programming works most efficiently with strings of 32 bits; thus, one-half and one-quarter units of these strings are handled more easily than other divisions). So, you will find references to 24-bit and 32-bit color that are actually references to the same color capacity; for example, a 24-bit display and a 32-bit document both provide access to nearly 16.8 million colors.

Dithered color,
normal magnification.

Dithered color, 8x
magnification.

With SuperPaint, the bit depth of a document and the display capabilities of your system are not interdependent. This means that 24-bit hardware is not required to work with 16.8 million colors. SuperPaint uses a technique called *dithering* to simulate colors your system cannot display directly. Dithering mixes available colors (or black and white) to create the illusion of a different color (or gray). Thus on an 8-bit machine, the screen may show dithered colors as you work in a 32-bit document; however when you transport the document to a 24-bit system, the monitor will display the "true" colors. (Conversely, the system will only display whatever information is available in the document. A 24-bit system can display only the 256 colors actually saved in an 8-bit document.)

Setting Document Bit Depth

The default bit depth for new documents is specified in the Preferences dialog box. The bit depth of the active document can be changed at any time in the Document Info dialog box (choose **Document Info** from the File menu). Setting the default bit depth and changing the bit depth of the active document are fully explained in Part 4, Chapter 3.

Note: On color machines, you can override the default bit depth for new documents and open a new, 1-bit document by pressing the Shift key while opening the File menu and choosing the **New** command.

Bit Depth and Document Size

As stated, bit depth is the number of bits assigned to each dot or pixel to define its color. It follows, then, that 32-bit documents can be significantly larger than 1-bit and 8-bit documents. This means that color graphics files can become very large, requiring a large amount of disk storage space, and slowing processing times considerably. We recommend that you give some thought to the expected use of your images and set the document bit depth accordingly — if the image is to be printed on a black-and-white printer, 32-bit color is probably unnecessary. The following illustration indicates the document size of the same image when defined at bit depths of 1, 8, 16, and 32 bits.

Note: Predicting the storage requirements for color documents is imprecise. The requirements depend on the dimensions of the document, the document's bit depth, and the area of the document occupied by graphics.

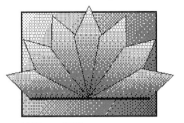

1-bit image (19 K).   32-bit image (206 K).

System Considerations

SuperPaint behaves as consistently as possible on black-and-white and color systems; however, the capability of your system can affect its ability to work with color. For the purposes of this discussion, there are two kinds of Macintosh: those that are color-capable and those that are not. Color-capable means that with the addition of a color display board, a color monitor, and 32-bit QuickDraw you can view colors. With a non-color-capable machine, attaching the same hardware and software does not provide color viewing.

On non-color-capable systems (Macintosh Plus, Classic, SE, and Portable models), you can create and save only 1-bit documents. You can open existing multi-bit documents, but they will be displayed as black and white (use **Save As** to avoid altering the original color document).

On a color-capable machine without a color display board and a color monitor (such as the SE/30), if you put 32-bit QuickDraw in the System folder, you can create and save multi-bit documents. The foreground and background options on the Line & Fill palette will be represented by dithered black and white, yet a color document produced on this system and transported to a color system will display the correct colors.

Viewing colors as you work requires a color system with 32-bit QuickDraw in the System folder, and a color monitor. To see 16.8 million "true" colors, you need a 24-bit color board in your system. If you have an 8-bit color board, most of the 16.8 million colors are displayed by dithering the 256 available colors.

The following functions require a color-capable system and 32-bit QuickDraw:

- Create and save 8-, 16-, and 32-bit documents.

- Use and edit the colors on the Colors palette.

- Use the Transfer Modes and the Fill Modes **Transparent Bkgnd.**, **Transparent**, and **Set Transparent %**.

- Use the Brightness & Contrast and Color Balance controls.

- Create and save custom gradients.

- Multiple colors in the Paint layer (color assignments made in 1-bit documents apply to all black dots in the layer).

Color on Black-and-White Systems

Non-color-capable systems and color-capable systems without 32-bit QuickDraw can only create 1-bit documents. Any color textures and gradients installed in the SP Pouch will be displayed and printed as dithered black and white. (The appearance of the black-and-white and Draw textures will not be affected.) Spot color assignments can be made using the eight ImageWriter II or Scrapbook colors (as described in the section "Color Palettes in Black-and-White Documents" later in this chapter). These color assignments can be viewed by printing to a color printer, or by previewing the document on a color system.

Note: If you are working on a color-capable black-and-white system, you may want to change the default document bit depth to one in the Preferences dialog box.

Black and White on Color Systems

You can work in black and white on a color system by setting the document's bit depth to one. The selections on the Textures and Gradients palettes are displayed, and applied in the Paint layer, as dithered black and white, as they would be on a black-and-white system.

A document created in SuperPaint 2.0 opens as a 1-bit document.

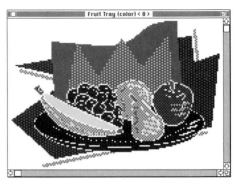

Spot color assignments made in SuperPaint 2.0 are displayed when the bit depth is changed.

Conversely, you can open any SuperPaint 2.0 or other compatible 1-bit document in Version 3.0, change its bit depth and color the graphics. Color assignments made in a 1-bit document are automatically displayed as the appropriate color if the document bit depth is increased.

Colors Palette

Hot Key:
C is the hot key for the Colors palette.

A separate color can be applied to the pattern foreground and background of both the Line Fill and the Area Fill (except in the Paint layer of 1-bit documents — background color assignments cannot be made). To change the current foreground color, position the pointer on the foreground Colors pop-up box, and press the mouse button to open the palette. Drag to the cell displaying the color you wish to select and release the mouse button. The palette closes and the selected color is applied to the foreground of the Area Fill or Line Fill (whichever is the active display). A background color is selected from the same Colors palette by opening the palette from the area surrounding the three foreground element boxes on the Line & Fill palette.

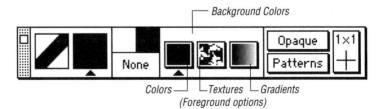

Background Colors

Colors — Textures — Gradients
(Foreground options)

As with all pop-up palettes, the Colors palette can be "torn off" to form a floating palette with a "title" bar and a close box. Drag the title bar to reposition the palette; click the close box in the title bar to close the floating palette. The Colors palette can be torn off when opened to select either a background or foreground color. However, only foreground colors can be selected from the floating palette; to select a background color, open the background Colors palette from the Line & Fill palette normally.

In black-and-white (1-bit) documents, the Colors palette displays the names of eight spot colors. In color documents, the Colors palette provides access to a table of 256 color cells, the Continuous Color palette, and the Apple Color Picker. The color table displayed on the Colors palette is intended to provide rapid access to colors you use frequently; that is, you are not limited to only those colors, and the colors displayed can be modified: a number of different color tables are provided, and all of them can be edited to change the colors displayed in the cells.

Colors Palette in Black-and-White Documents

If you are working in a 1-bit document, the Colors palette displays the names of either the eight ImageWriter II or the eight Scrapbook colors, depending on the setting of the *Color Palette matches* option on the *Miscellaneous Settings* page of the Preferences dialog box. (The Preferences dialog box is discussed in Part 4, Chapter 2.)

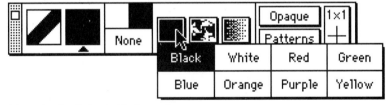

Colors palette in a black-and-white document.

When you select one of these colors in the Paint layer of a 1-bit document, all existing and subsequent foreground pixels in the layer are assigned that color (i.e., instead of a black-and-white document, you have a single-color-and-white document). The color assignment applies to both Area Fill and Line Fill, and you cannot make a background color assignment in the Paint layer because there is no differentiation between the white pixels of the pattern background and the untouched white areas of the document.

In the Draw layer, separate foreground and background assignments can be made to individual objects, and the Eyedropper can be used to pick up those assignments. Also, if you are working in a 1-bit document on a color system, the textures or gradients used to fill Draw objects are represented on the screen as dithered black and white, but they are actually full color, as you will see if the document is color previewed, printed on a color printer, or converted to a multi-bit document.

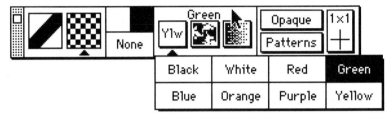

In the Draw layer, separate foreground and background color assignments can be made.

If you are working in a 1-bit document on a color system with a color monitor, you can preview the color assignments by choosing **Color Preview** from the View menu. You cannot edit graphics while in Color Preview mode. Choose **Color Preview** again to return to your work.

Colors Palette in Color Documents

The cells of the color table on the Colors palette provide convenient access to 256 colors; these can be any combination of colors selected from nearly 16.8 million. However, you are not limited to this current selection of colors — the Continuous Color palette and the Apple Color Picker are both available, providing access to other colors.

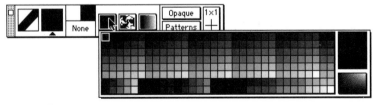

The default Colors palette.

The default color table in the Colors palette contains the 256 Apple System colors. These colors represent an even distribution throughout the spectrum, and more importantly, they are the default colors used by most 8-bit monitors and recognized by most other Macintosh applications. This is particularly important if you transport an 8-bit document to another application that does not dither colors the way SuperPaint does — if the image contains only colors selected from the default Colors palette, it will look the same, for example, in Aldus Personal Press as it does in SuperPaint. (However, other color tables are available, as described later in this chapter.)

The cell of the currently selected color is highlighted — with a solid white outline if the color itself is selected, or with a dotted outline to indicate that the highlighted color is the closest one on the palette to the selected color. To change colors when the palette is torn off, simply click the appropriate cell, or use the Continuous Color palette or the Apple Color Picker.

The Continuous Color Palette

Hot Key:

Q is the hot key for the Continuous Color palette.

The drop-shadowed box in the lower right corner of the Colors palette represents the Continuous Color pop-up palette. The Continuous Color palette provides access to 16.8 million colors (even in 8- and 16-bit documents) and the Apple Color Picker. When the Colors palette is torn off, the Continuous Color palette can be popped up and torn off. (The Continuous Color palette can be open when the Colors palette has been closed.) Like other floating palettes, it has a "title" bar with a close box; unlike the others, it has a zoom box on the right side of the title bar. Click the zoom box to increase the size of the Continuous Color palette, allowing more precise color selection; click the zoom box again to return the palette to its original size.

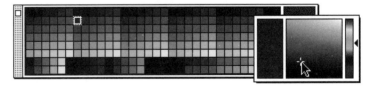

The Continuous Color floating palette.

The Continuous Color pop-up palette.

The Continuous Color palette uses the *HSB* (hue, saturation, brightness) color model to define colors. (Color models are discussed in the "Using Color Models" section later in this chapter.) *Hue* is the shade of color (red, blue, etc.). *Saturation* represents the purity of the hue versus dilution with white; that is, if no white is present, the color is at its highest saturation. *Brightness* represents the purity of the hue versus dilution with black; colors with no added black are at maximum brightness (black represents no brightness at all). Colors with low brightness values do not reflect light well, and therefore appear "dull."

The Continuous Color palette consists of a current-color bar, a color space, and a multi-colored hue bar. The hue bar and pointer on the right side of the palette determine the hue. Drag the pointer, or click anywhere in the bar, to change the hue.

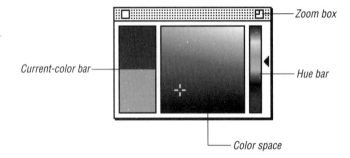

The position of the crosshair in the color space determines the saturation and brightness of the selected hue. Drag the crosshair, or click anywhere in the color space, to change the saturation and brightness. Horizontal crosshair movement changes the saturation, increasing from right to left, and vertical movement changes brightness, increasing from bottom to top. When the crosshair is at the upper left corner of the color space, the selected hue is at its highest saturation and brightness. When the crosshair is at the lower right corner, the hue is at its lowest saturation and brightness.

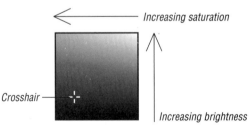

The current-color bar is actually two displays. The lower half is the color most recently used in the document — click the lower swatch to reset the hue bar and color space to that color. The upper half of the current-color bar continuously displays the color defined by the hue-bar pointer and the crosshair in the color space as you move either of them. Double-click either swatch to open the Apple Color Picker (the swatch color is selected on the color wheel).

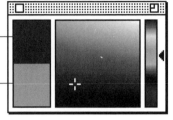

Color currently defined by the hue bar and color space

Color most recently used in the document

The current-color bar is on the left side of the Continuous Color palette.

Using True Colors

"True" colors are pure, undithered colors, and they are displayed and printed as such if the hardware is capable. In 32-bit documents, all 16.8 million colors available from the Continuous Color palette are "true" colors, although the display may be dithered if you are working on an 8-bit monitor.

Dithered color, normal magnification.

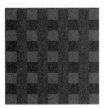

Dithered color, 8x magnification.

In the Paint layer of 8-bit documents, most of the 16.8 million colors available are dithered. (Whether displayed as such or not, colors in the Draw layer are always true.) You can select them with the hue bar and color space, and use them in your documents, and for most purposes the dithered colors are acceptable. However, close inspection will reveal them to be mixtures of other colors, and if you are planning to color separate an image, for example, using only true colors would produce better results since the color-separation program will attempt to separate each component of a dithered color individually.

To be sure that you are using only true colors, either work in a 32-bit document, use only the colors on the default Colors palette, or use the *Change Document Palette* option in the Custom Color Table dialog box to change the selection of true colors available. (The latter is described in a subsequent section.)

The Apple Color Picker

You also can use the Apple Color Picker to select colors. Double-click one of the swatches in the current color bar on the Continuous Color palette to display the Apple Color Picker — the swatch color is the color selected on the wheel. You can drag or click with the circular pointer anywhere in the color wheel to change the color visually, or you can select a color numerically using the Hue, Saturation and Brightness, or Red, Green and Blue text boxes and scroll arrows.

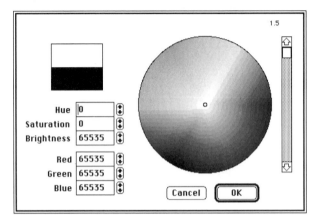

The Apple Color Picker, the Continuous Color palette, and the Colors palette are linked; that is, whenever you select a color from one source, the others also display that color. Thus if you select a particular color, say in the color space, you can open the Apple Color Picker and write down the settings for the color. Then whenever you wish to use that color again, simply open the Apple Color Picker and enter the values for either of the color models.

Note: Because of the variations between different monitors and different printers, any given color image may appear different when viewed or printed on another system. To ensure the most accurate presentation possible, you may want to have your systems color calibrated.

The scope of this manual does not allow an in-depth discussion of the Apple Color Picker, especially the significance of the values in the color-model text boxes (the range of values for each setting is zero to 65535). The purest hues (minimum saturation) are at the outer edge of the color wheel; maximum saturation is at the center. Brightness is controlled with the scroll bar to the right of the wheel. The box in the upper left quadrant of the dialog box consists of two swatches: the upper is the color currently selected on the color wheel, and the bottom is the color currently selected in the active document.

Changing the Color Table

A color table is a matrix of cells, each containing a color; the Colors palette displays a table of 256 cells. The current color table can be changed at any time: a number of color tables are provided with Super-Paint, which you can edit to suit your needs, and save for future use. For example, suppose you are rendering some landscaping ideas for a new building. You might find it useful to change the color table on the Colors palette to one that contains only various shades of greens and browns, so you can quickly select from all the colors you use for foliage.

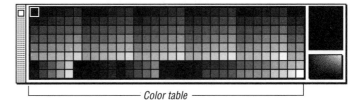

Color table

The currently selected color table is displayed on the Colors palette. You can use any number of color tables in your document, although only one table can be displayed at a time. Color tables are selected and edited in the Custom Color Table dialog box, which is displayed when you choose the **Colors** command from the Options menu. This dialog box is unique because it includes pull-down menus.

Note: The **Colors** command is not available in 1-bit documents.

To change the color table displayed on the Colors palette:

1. Choose **Colors** from the Options menu, or double-click a cell on the floating Colors palette, to display the Custom Color Table dialog box.

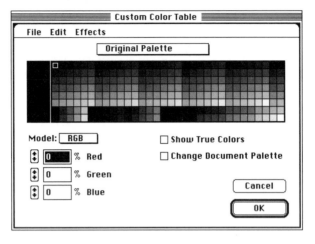

2. Select the name of a table from the pop-up menu above the color table.

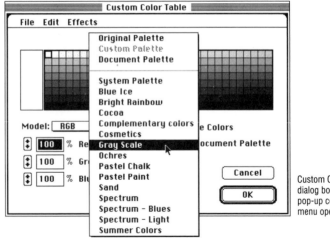

Custom Color Table dialog box with the pop-up color-table menu open.

or

Choose **Open Palette** from the File menu (in the dialog box) and select a color-table document from another drive or folder.

The selected color table is displayed in the matrix of color cells in the dialog box.

To be listed in the pop-up color-table menu each time you begin SuperPaint, a color-table document must be saved in the SP Pouch, or in a folder in the SP Pouch. Those opened with the **Open Palette** command are appended to the menu only until you quit SuperPaint.

3. Click *OK*, or press Return or Enter, to close the dialog box.

The selected color table is displayed on the Colors palette of the active document.

The *Show True Colors* option is available only in 8-bit documents when you are working on an 8-bit or a 24-bit system. If you choose a color table that contains some dithered colors, selecting this option shifts the display capabilities of your monitor to show the colors in the table in their undithered form. This shift is for viewing purposes only while the dialog box is open; the monitor is returned to its normal state (and the dithered representations re-appear in the color table) when you close the dialog box. To convert the dithered colors in the selected color table to true colors, you must alter the document color table, as described in the next section.

Changing the 8-Bit Document Color Table

In 8-bit documents, because they are capable of storing only 256 colors, the *document* color table serves as the basis of all color in the document. All gradients, textures, and existing graphics are composed of these colors (pure and dithered). This means that the eight bits stored for each pixel do not represent actual color codes, as is the case in 16-bit and 32-bit documents. Each 8-bit code is an index to a cell in the current *document* color table; the colors are mapped from the color table to the document. Therefore, if you select the *Change Document Palette* option in the Custom Color Table dialog box and change the set of colors available in the document, every color item in the document will change, since each indexed cell now contains a different color (only the active document is affected).

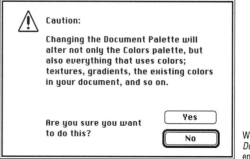

When you select the *Change Document Palette* option, you will encounter this dialog box.

For example, if you choose the Blue Ice color table, and select *Change Document Palette*, the textures on the Textures palette, the gradients on the Gradients palette, and any graphics already in the document will be displayed in shades of blue (and perhaps some dithered black and white). Because the **Undo** command has no effect on these changes, you may want to save your document before experimenting with the *Change Document Palette* option.

You can restore the default color table by selecting the *System Palette* table from the pop-up menu in the Custom Color Table dialog box and then selecting *Change Document Palette*. The contents of the Textures and Gradients palettes will appear as they did, and fills in the Draw layer will be updated. However, each remapping of colors affects Paint-layer graphics unpredictably. (If you saved the document prior to changing the document color table, the **Revert to Saved** command will restore your document to its previous appearance.)

Customizing Color Tables

You can edit color tables in the Custom Color Table dialog box and save them for later use. For example, you might create a table of shades of green for use when depicting foliage, and another of bright colors with corresponding darker hues for use when producing shaded shapes.

To customize a color table:

1. Choose **Colors** from the Options menu to display the Custom Color Table dialog box.

2. Select the color table to be altered.

    The pop-up menu in the dialog box lists the color tables in the SP Pouch. To open a table stored elsewhere, choose **Open Palette** from the File menu (in the dialog box) to display a standard Open dialog box. (The names of tables opened with the **Open Palette** command are added to the list in the pop-up menu until you quit SuperPaint.)

3. Define colors for any or all of the 256 cells in the table. (See the instructions in the next section.)

   When you begin to edit the color table, the name displayed on the pop-up menu changes to "Custom Palette."

4. When finished editing, choose **Save Palette As** from the File menu (in the Custom Color Table dialog box).

   A standard Save As dialog box is displayed.

5. Enter a name for the color table, specify where it is to be saved, and click *Save*.

   Color-table documents saved in the SP Pouch, or in a folder within the SP Pouch, are listed in the pop-up menu in the Custom Color Table dialog box the next time you start SuperPaint.

6. Click *OK*, or press Return or Enter, to close the Custom Color Table dialog box.

   The color table displayed in the dialog box appears on the Colors palette for the active document.

Changing the Colors in a Color Table

The colors displayed in the color-table cells can be any mixture of colors you desire. To change its color, a color-table cell must be selected. To select an individual cell, click it. To select a range of cells, click the first and Shift-click the last. Press the Command key while clicking to select non-contiguous cells; for example, you can select the first color in the first row, the second color in the second row, and so on. Choose **Select All** from the Edit menu (in the Custom Color Table dialog box), or use the Command-A shortcut, to select all the cells at once.

Color table with one cell selected.

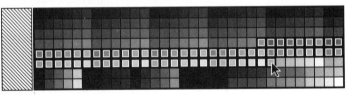

Color table with a range of cells selected.

When a cell or range of cells has been selected, you can use any of the commands available in the Effects menu (in the Custom Color Table dialog box) to alter the cell colors:

- **Lighter** dilutes the color(s) slightly with white.

- **Darker** adds a little black to the color(s).

- **Warmer** adds a little red.

- **Cooler** adds a little blue.

Note: Lighter and **Darker**, and **Warmer** and **Cooler** are not opposite effects. In other words, choosing **Lighter** twice and then choosing **Darker** twice does not result in the original color.

- **Blend** produces a graduated blending from the color in the start cell to the color in the end cell (applicable only to a range of color cells).

- **Reverse** flips the sequence of colors in the selected range of cells (end becomes start and vice versa); applicable only to a range of color cells.

- **Repeat Effect** (Command-E) can be used to repeat the last effect chosen rather than repeatedly choosing the same command from the menu.

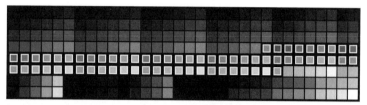

A range of cells is selected.

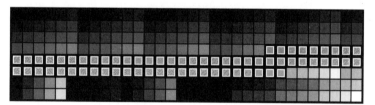

The range of cells after **Blend** was chosen.

You can also copy the colors of a selected cell or range of cells to the Clipboard by choosing **Copy Color** from the Edit menu (in the Custom Color Table dialog box), or use the Command-C shortcut. To paste the color copied to the Clipboard into an individually selected cell or the last cell in a range, choose **Paste Color** from the Edit menu in the dialog box (or use the Command-V shortcut). If a range of color cells was copied to the Clipboard, they can be pasted into the table starting at an individually selected cell or the last cell in a range.

To use the Apple Color Picker to change a cell color, select the cell and then choose **Edit Color** from the Edit menu in the dialog box, or click the current color bar to the left of the color-table matrix to open the Color Picker (or simply double-click the cell to simultaneously select it and open the Apple Color Picker).

You can also change the color of the selected cell by specifying a color numerically according to one of three color models, as described in the next section.

Using the Color Models

White light is a combination of the three primary colors red, green and blue. We see objects as colored because they reflect or absorb each component to some degree. This means there are two basic approaches to utilizing light to produce color: the blending of two or all three primary colors to produce another (this is what happens in your color monitor), or by subtracting two or all three of the colors from white light, leaving another color. (This is what happens in printed images, because while colored lights can be combined to produce another bright colored light, the combination of bright colored inks produces a duller, darker color.)

A color model is a means of defining colors according to one or the other of these two approaches. SuperPaint provides three color models: RGB (red, green, blue), HSB (hue, saturation, brightness), and CMYK (cyan, magenta, yellow, black). The advantage of using a color model is that colors are defined numerically, meaning you can select a very specific color quickly, easily and repeatedly. While the color may appear to be different when displayed on another monitor, its numeric definition will always produce the same color, which is particularly useful in other programs, and for color separations.

To define a color numerically for the highlighted cell in the color table, select the model to be used from the *Model* pop-up menu in the Custom Color Table dialog box. Then highlight the text boxes below the pop-up menu and type new color-component values, or use the scroll arrows to change the values.

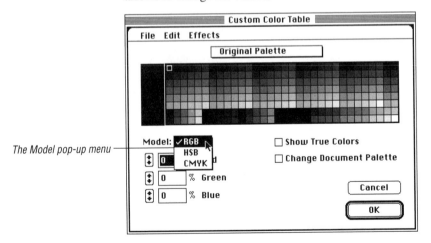

The Model pop-up menu

RGB

Model: **RGB**

‡ |100| % **Red**

‡ |60| % **Green**

‡ |40| % **Blue**

Red, green and blue are known as the "primary additive" colors be-cause all other colors are mixtures of two or all of them. (The RGB model is used for video displays because the three colors can be pro-jected together to form others.) Specify the contribution of red, green and blue as a percentage for each. The absence of all three produces black; the presence of all three equally produces white.

HSB

The HSB (hue, saturation, brightness) model is based on the behavior of light. Hue is the color perceived by the eye (e.g., red or blue). Hue is specified numerically as an angular location on a color wheel, where pure red is zero and the angle is measured counterclockwise. For ex-ample, looking at the color wheel in the Apple Color Picker, the angle for pure blue is 240 degrees.

The color wheel.

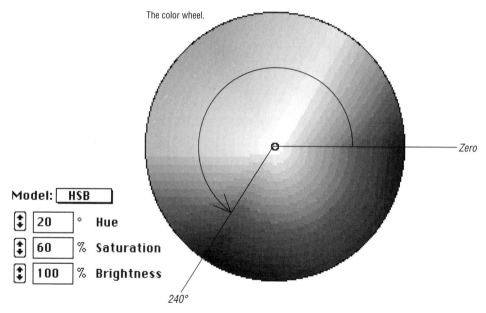

— Zero

240°

Model: **HSB**

‡ |20| ° **Hue**

‡ |60| % **Saturation**

‡ |100| % **Brightness**

Saturation is the purity of the hue with respect to white (fully saturated hues contain no white), and is defined as a percentage, where zero percent saturation produces white, and 100 percent saturation includes no white. Brightness (sometimes referred to as intensity) is the lumi-nance of the color, and it is defined as the absence of black. Brightness is defined as a percentage, where zero percent brightness produces black, and 100 percent brightness includes no black.

CMYK

Cyan, magenta and yellow are known as the "primary subtractive" colors because these colors absorb the primary additive colors, and two or more subtractive colors can be combined to produce nearly all other colors ("neon" colors, for example, have no CMYK equivalents). Black is added to increase contrast and the shadow density. These colors are sometimes referred to as the "process" colors because they are used for color separations.

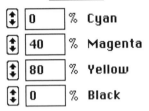

The presence of each of the four colors is specified as a percentage. When all four are present at 100 percent, the result is solid black. When all four are absent (zero percent), the result is white. Pure red is produced with both magenta and yellow present at 100 percent (completely absorbing green and blue respectively), and both cyan and black absent (zero percent).

So, the same color can be defined using any of the three color models:

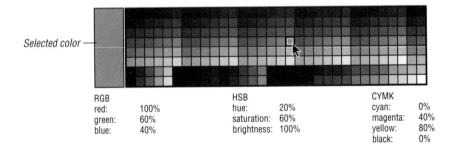

Selected color

RGB		HSB		CYMK	
red:	100%	hue:	20%	cyan:	0%
green:	60%	saturation:	60%	magenta:	40%
blue:	40%	brightness:	100%	yellow:	80%
				black:	0%

Making Color Separations

Color separation refers to separating an image into its CMYK components for printing or other reproduction. Color separations are produced from color documents using color-separation software, such as Aldus® Preprint.™ If you intend to color separate an image, whether you produce the separations yourself or send the document to a service bureau, for best results work in a 32-bit document — this allows you access to 16.8 million colors.

Since color separations can be produced only from TIFF or EPS documents, create the image in SuperPaint, and then export it as a TIFF or EPS document, whichever is appropriate for the image. (The **Export** command is described in Part 4, Chapter 3.)

Chapter 6: Drawing and Painting Tools

All of SuperPaint's tools are found on the Tools palette. These tools provide a powerful set of features for drawing and painting.

The majority of tools are described in this chapter; however, the Selection Tools are described in Part 4, Chapter 7.

The Tools Palette

Draw Layer.   Paint Layer.

The Tools palette consists of a series of icons, each representing a specific tool. Three of these icons are displayed on drop-shadowed boxes; the boxes indicate pop-up palettes (as described in Part 4, Chapter 2) that contain related tools. The most recently selected tool is displayed on the pop-up box.

A few of the tools change when you switch from the Paint layer to the Draw layer, or vice versa. The Airbrush, Pencil, Paint Bucket, and Eraser are dimmed in the Draw layer, indicating that they are unavailable. In the Draw layer, the Selection Arrow replaces the Paint layer's Selection Tools pop-up, and the Two-Layer Selection tool replaces the Paint layer's Brush Tools pop-up.

To select a tool, click its icon; the icon is highlighted. When a tool is selected in either layer and you switch to the other layer, the corresponding tool is highlighted. For example, if you were using the Text tool in the Draw layer and you switch to the Paint layer, the Text tool is still selected. If there is no corresponding tool in the Draw layer, the Selection Arrow is highlighted.

As a floating palette, the Tools palette can be positioned anywhere on the screen by dragging the gray "title" bar, and closed by clicking its close box. To re-open the Tools palette, choose **Show Tools** from the **Floating Palettes** submenu in the View menu.

Hot Key:
T is the hot key for the Tools palette.

Pressing the hot key T will display a copy of the Tools palette centered under the pointer; you can select another tool, tear off a pop-up palette, or use the double-click shortcuts.

Tool Categories

The SuperPaint tools, grouped by category, are:

- Selection Tools: except the Selection Arrow and the Two-Layer Selection tool, these are Paint-layer tools, which are grouped on a pop-up palette. The Selection Tools are described in Part 4, Chapter 7.

- Tools common to both layers: the Grabber, Text tool, Magnifier, Eyedropper, the line and shape tools, and the Draw & Paint Plug-in tools. The Draw & Paint Plug-ins are grouped on a pop-up palette.

- Paint-only tools: the Pencil, Eraser, Paint Bucket, Airbrush, and the Brush Tools.

Interaction with the Line & Fill Palette

All of SuperPaint's creation tools are integrated with the options available on the Line & Fill palette. For example, you can paint with transparent paint, draw a box filled with a gradient, produce textured text, and draw lines that include both patterns and colors. The Line & Fill palette is described in Part 4, Chapter 4.

Note: Area Fill and Line Fill refer to the combination of a pattern with a background color and a foreground color, texture, or gradient. Both fills are assigned independent Transfer Modes.

Interactions with Other Features

In addition to the options on the Line & Fill palette, other features or settings affect the way some of the tools work. These settings (and where you can find complete details on them) are:

- Grid snap (Part 4, Chapter 2).

- Paint/Draw-from-Center or Paint/Draw-from-Corner mode (Part 4, Chapter 8).

- Paint Multiple (Part 4, Chapter 8).

- Brush Symmetry (Part 4, Chapter 8).

Pointers

The on-screen indicator that moves when you move the mouse, often called the "pointer" or "cursor," may change depending on the tool selected. Many tools have pointers that resemble their icons, such as the Pencil. Other pointers match their function, such as a spray pattern for the Spray Can, or a square for the Eraser. Some tools, like the Paint Brush, have pointers that change according to their configuration. In addition, the crosshair pointer used with the line tools changes based on the Line Widths selected.

Cursors: Pencil, Lasso, crosshair.

Each pointer has a *hot point:* the spot that "counts." The tip of the Pencil, for instance, is the part that draws the lines; the center of the crosshair, and the trailing tip of the Lasso are other hot points.

Click Shortcuts

A double-click, an Option-click, or a Command-click is often a short-cut for some operation or command. Double-clicking the Paint Brush, for instance, displays the Custom Brushes dialog box. Shortcuts are detailed with the discussion of each tool.

Keyboard Tool Modifiers

Many tools have keyboard modifiers: pressing the Shift, Option, or Command keys singly or together constrains or modifies the action of the tool. For instance, pressing the Shift key constrains many of the tools to horizontal-only or vertical-only operation. Modifiers are included with the discussion of each tool.

Tool Configurations

The operation of many of the tools can be altered to some extent to suit your purposes. These tools are configured through dialog boxes displayed by menu commands, or by double-clicking the tool icon on its palette. The specifics of tool configuration are covered with each tool description.

Tools Available in Both Layers

The following tools are available in both layers: the Text tool, the Draw & Paint Plug-ins, the Two-Layer Selection tool, the line and shape tools, the Eyedropper, the Grabber, and the Magnifier.

Text Tool

Text in the Paint layer is bitmapped, printing at 72 dpi, while Draw-layer text prints at the resolution of the output device.

This discussion of the Text tool covers the basics of entering text into your document. Part 4, Chapter 10 discusses text formatting in detail, including how to change the font, size, and justification.

To enter text into your document:

I-beam.

1. Select the Text tool from the Tools palette.

   In the document window, the Text tool is represented by an I-beam.

2. Click to specify where the text is to start, and then type your text. The spacing and justification are set in the Text menu.

In the Paint layer, text continues on one line until you press Return to begin a new line. While in text-entry mode, you can backspace and change characters; when you select another tool or click elsewhere in the document, Paint-layer text is pasted down and cannot be changed.

SuperPaint|

Text frame in Draw layer.

In the Draw layer, a gray text frame is created when you click in the document; new lines are added whenever the text reaches the right side of the frame. Instead of clicking to begin, you can also drag out a text frame that is approximately the width you want before entering the text. Existing text in the Draw layer is editable; with the Text tool, click or drag to select the text to be edited.

Text object in Draw layer.

The text box can be moved or resized with the Selection Arrow like any other object in the Draw layer. When you select an existing text object with the Selection Arrow, in addition to the handles, you will see a symbol (either an arrow or a small hollow rectangle) centered on the top of the text object. The arrow means that the text box will expand vertically so all text is displayed. The hollow rectangle means the size of the text box is fixed; text that does not fit into the box is not visible (not gone, just not displayed). Clicking the symbol switches the text box (and the symbol) from expanding to fixed and vice versa.

Configuration & Interaction

- Text appearance is controlled by means of the commands in the Font and Text menus.

- Text characters can be filled with the current Area Fill and a Transfer Mode assigned. However, patterns cannot be applied to text in the Draw layer of 8-, 16- or 32-bit documents.

- If grid snap is on, the initial character is aligned with the nearest grid point.

Grabber

The Grabber is available in both layers, at all levels of magnification. It moves the document in the window, and the frame in the left pane of the reduced and enlarged views. Using the Grabber to drag the document has the same effect as moving the scroll bars.

Hot Key:
The space bar is the hot key for the Grabber.

The Grabber lets you continue moving your document in the window when you've reached the boundary of the working area and auto-scrolling stops (refer to the explanation of virtual documents in Part 4, Chapter 3 for more information).

Magnifier

Magnifier cursors with plus and minus signs.

The Magnifier is available in both layers to change the current level of magnification. The new view is centered on the point clicked with the tool.

Hot Key:
E and R are hot keys for the Magnifier; E enlarges, and R reduces.

Select the tool — the magnifying-glass cursor displays a plus sign — and click anywhere in the document window to zoom in one level of magnification. Press the Option key — the magnifying-glass cursor displays a minus sign — and click anywhere in the document window to zoom out one level of magnification. More information on zooming and levels of magnification is available in Part 4, Chapter 2.

Eyedropper

The Eyedropper is available in both the Paint and Draw layers. In the Paint layer of a color document, it picks up the color beneath the tip of the tool; the color is applied to the foreground of the Line Fill or Area Fill, depending which display is active on the Line & Fill palette. If the point under the tip of the tool is a boundary between divergent colors, SuperPaint will blend them. (In the Paint layer of a black-and-white document, the Eyedropper picks up black or white.)

Hot Key:
D is the hot key for the Eyedropper.

In the Draw layer, the Eyedropper picks up the Area Fill or Line Fill of an object, depending on the active display, and replaces the current fill combination with the picked-up combination.

The Line and Shape Tools

Two line tools and seven shape tools — the Rounded Rectangle, Rectangle, Multigon, Oval, Polygon, Arc, and Freehand tool — are available in both layers.

Note: In the Draw layer, when a line or shape is completed, it is automatically selected. The tool in use remains selected, or the Selection Arrow is automatically selected, depending on the setting of the *After using a Shape tool* option in the Preferences dialog box (refer to Part 4, Chapter 2 for more information).

The Line Tools

The two line tools produce straight lines; the Perpendicular Line tool makes a line at a specific angle (horizontal, vertical, 30, 45, or 60 degrees), while the Line tool draws a line at any angle.

Lines with arrows, and dashed lines.

Lines are filled with the current Line Fill, they can be solid or dashed, any thickness up to 99 pixels, and can have arrowheads at either or both ends. Refer to Part 4, Chapter 4 for descriptions of the **Arrows** and **Dashes** submenus of the Options menu, and the Line Fill and the Line Widths options available on the Line & Fill palette.

To draw a line:

1. Select the Perpendicular Line tool or the Line tool from the Tools palette.

   The pointer is a crosshair in the document window; at higher Line Widths, the pointer is represented by thicker crossed bars.

2. Position the pointer where you want the line to begin, press the mouse button, and drag to the spot where you want the line to end.

   As you drag, a line is drawn from the starting point; the line moves like an elastic band with the starting point tacked down. If you're using the Perpendicular Line tool, the line jumps to the nearest constraint angle — horizontal, vertical, 45 degrees — as you move the pointer.

3. Release the mouse button to end the line.

Modifiers

- Pressing the Option key constrains the Perpendicular Line tool to horizontal, vertical, 30-degree, and 60-degree lines.

- Pressing the Shift key constrains the Line tool to horizontal, vertical, and 45-degree lines (in effect turning it into the Perpendicular Line tool). Similarly, pressing Shift-Option constrains the Line tool to horizontal, vertical, 30-degree, and 60-degree lines.

Interactions & Click Shortcuts

- If grid snap is on, the ends of the line will snap to the nearest grid point.

- Double-click the Line tool icon on the Tools palette to display the Custom Arrows dialog box.

- Double-click the Perpendicular Line tool icon on the Tools palette to display the Custom Dashes dialog box. (Information on arrows and dashes appears in Part 4, Chapter 4.)

The Shape Tools

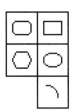

Shape-tool icons.

The shape tools — Rounded Rectangle, Rectangle, Multigon, Oval, and Arc (one quarter of an oval) — produce symmetric shapes that are filled with the current Area Fill, and bounded by lines of current Line Fill and Line Widths. Both fills can have separate Transfer Modes.

In the Draw layer, these shapes can be converted to Bezier objects and reshaped (see Part 4, Chapter 8 for more information).

The shape tools all work in a similar manner:

1. Select a shape tool from the Tools palette.

   The pointer is a crosshair in the document window.

Shape tool-icons in Paint/Draw-from-Center mode.

2. Position the pointer where you want one corner of the shape (or its bounding box), and drag to the diagonally opposite corner.

   If earlier you chose **Paint** (or **Draw**) **from Center** from the Options menu, begin at the center of the shape.

The orientation of a shape depends on the direction in which the pointer is moved. Also, the *Objects are dragged as* option on the Draw Layer Settings page of the Preferences dialog box controls how shapes are displayed while being drawn in the Draw layer. If *Objects* is selected, the shape is filled with the current Area Fill, and bounded by lines of the current Line Fill and Line Widths, as you drag it out. If *Outlines* is selected, only a gray outline of the shape is displayed until the mouse button is released; the object is then filled.

Rounded Rectangle

The Rounded Rectangle tool is configurable — you can produce shapes with rounded ends or rounded corners, and you can specify the radius of the rounded corners.

To change the rounding of the shape produced by the Rounded Rectangle:

1. Display the Round Corners dialog box by choosing **Round Corners** from the Options menu, or by double-clicking the Rounded Rectangle icon on the Tools palette.

Round Corners

Measure in:
| Inches |

○ Round ends
● Round corners

┌─ Corner Radius ─
○ 0   ● 1/8   ○ 3/16
○ 1/4 ○ 5/16 ○ 3/8

○ Other: | 1/8 |

[Cancel]   [OK]

2. Click the *Round ends* or the *Round corners* button.

3. For *Round corners*, select a preset corner radius, or click *Other* and type a radius value.

   This is the radius of the 90-degree arc of the rounded corners, in current units of measurement. (If you select a radius, *Round corners* is selected automatically.)

4. If you want to change the units of measurement for this document, use the *Measure in* pop-up menu.

5. Click *OK*, or press Return or Enter, to close the dialog box.

Rounded rectangles created by dragging vertically.

If you select the *Round ends* option, the narrower ends of the "rectangle" are rounded; this is a function of how you move the cursor while drawing the shape. If you drag more horizontally than vertically, the left and right sides are rounded; if you drag more vertically, the top and bottom are rounded. (Dragging equally in both directions produces a circle.)

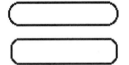

Rounded rectangles created by dragging horizontally.

Rectangle

The Rectangle produces rectangles filled with the current Area Fill, and bounded by lines of current Line Fill and Line Widths. Both fills can have separate Transfer Modes.

Press the Shift key to restrict the tool to producing squares.

Double-click the Rectangle icon on the Tools palette to switch back and forth between Paint/Draw-from-Corner and Paint/Draw-from-Center modes.

Multigon

The Multigon makes equilateral polygons with a definable number of sides. The default Multigon shape is a hexagon, but you can configure the tool to produce from 3 to 36 sides.

To specify the number of sides for the Multigon:

1. Choose **Multigon Sides** from the Options menu, or double-click the Multigon icon on the Tools palette to display the Multigon Sides dialog box.

2. Double-click one of the five shapes to simultaneously select the shape and close the dialog box.

or

Type the number of sides you want for the Multigon, and click *OK*, or press Return or Enter, to close the dialog box.

Note: In the Draw layer, a Multigon is treated as a polygon — you can reshape it with the **Reshape Polygon** command in the Draw menu.

Interactions

*   The Multigon is affected by grid snap, and by the Paint/Draw-from-Center/Corner mode.

*   When you produce a Multigon in Paint/Draw-from-Corner mode, the bottom of the figure is always horizontal.

*   When you're working in Paint/Draw-from-Center mode, the shape will spin about its center if you move the pointer in a circle. Pressing the Shift key prior to beginning a Multigon in Paint/Draw-from-Center mode, restricts one of the Multigon sides to being either horizontal or vertical, as well as keeping the Multigon from spinning as you create it. The horizontal or vertical restriction depends on the number of sides in the shape, and the initial pointer direction.

Oval

The Oval produces ovals filled with the current Area Fill, and bounded by lines of current Line Fill and Line Widths. Both fills can have separate Transfer Modes.

Press the Shift key to restrict the tool to producing circles.

Double-click the Oval icon on the Tools palette to switch back and forth between Paint/Draw-from-Corner and Paint/Draw-from-Center modes.

Polygon

The Polygon creates an irregular shape of current Area Fill bounded by straight lines of the current Line Fill and Line Widths.

To use the Polygon:

1. Select the Polygon from the Tools palette.

   The pointer is a crosshair in the document window.

2. Click to specify each corner of the polygonal shape.

3. Double-click or click outside the window to end the shape. SuperPaint closes the polygon for you by joining the last point and the first.

Creating a polygon (polygons are not filled until shape is complete).

Polygon with an Area Fill of None.

If you selected *None* as the Area Fill before beginning the polygon, SuperPaint does not close the polygon; i.e., you are left with a series of straight lines that end where you double-click.

In the Draw layer, you can reshape the polygon by choosing the **Reshape Polygon** command from the Draw menu (see Part 4, Chapter 8 for more information).

Modifiers

- Pressing the Shift key restricts the current polygon side to be vertical, horizontal, or at a 45-degree angle.

- Pressing Shift-Option restricts the current line to vertical, horizontal, 30-degree, or 60-degree angles.

Note: Unlike the Shift constraint for other tools, you don't have to press Shift before you press the mouse button. Pressing Shift or Shift-Option at any time shifts the current side to one of the constraint angles.

Arc

The Arc tool creates a one-quarter oval of current Area Fill that is bounded by an arc of current Line Fill and Line Widths.

In the Draw layer, you can choose the **Reshape Arc** command from the Draw menu to reshape the arc (see Part 4, Chapter 8 for more information).

Left: Arc with an Area Fill of *None*.
Right: Arc with a gray Area Fill.

Modifiers

- Pressing the Shift key restricts the shape to one quarter of a circle (versus one quarter of an oval).

Freehand Tool

The Freehand tool lets you draw free-form shapes of the current Area Fill, bounded by lines of the current Line Fill and Line Widths.

To use the Freehand tool:

1. Select the tool from the Tools palette.

   The cursor is a crosshair in the document window.

2. Drag the crosshair to outline your shape.

3. When you release the mouse button, if the shape is not closed, SuperPaint closes it by joining the end of the outline and the starting point.

If you selected *None* as the Area Fill before using the Freehand tool, SuperPaint does not close the shape; i.e., you are left with a freehand line.

In the Draw layer, the shapes are objects outlined by editable Bezier paths or curves. A Bezier path consists of anchor points joined by line and curve segments that can be individually reshaped (choose the **Reshape Bezier** command from the Draw menu). See Part 4, Chapter 8 for more information on using and editing Bezier curves.

Freehand shape drawn with an Area Fill of *None*.

Freehand shape drawn with a patterned Area Fill.

Configuring the Freehand Tool in the Draw Layer

Prior to using the Freehand tool in the Draw layer, you can set the controls in the Bezier Settings dialog box to influence the definition and smoothing of the Bezier-path outline.

To configure the Freehand tool in the Draw layer:

1. Choose **Bezier Settings** from the Draw menu, or double-click the Freehand tool icon on the Tools palette, to display the Bezier Settings dialog box.

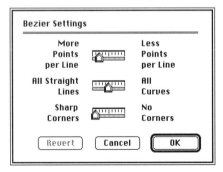

2. Drag the slider controls to the desired settings.

The controls are fairly straightforward, but there may be some trial-and-error involved in achieving the influence you desire. (Bezier curves are described in detail in Part 4, Chapter 8.) Click *Revert* to restore the original settings.

3. Click *Cancel* to close the dialog box and discard any changes to the sliders; click *OK*, or press Return or Enter, to close the dialog box and establish the new settings.

Generally, a Bezier path with more points, straighter lines, and sharper corners is smoothed less; that is, the path more closely resembles the line you drew on the screen. However, paths with fewer points, more curves, and fewer corners print more smoothly.

Draw & Paint Plug-in Tools

Hot Key:
Z is the hot key for the Draw & Paint Plug-ins palette.

The Draw & Paint Plug-ins palette is available in both layers. The tools found on this palette are those plug-in tool modules in the SP Pouch that work in both the Paint and Draw layers.

Draw & Paint Plug-ins palette.

SuperPaint is shipped with the following Draw & Paint Plug-in tools: 3-D Box, AllGon, Bubbles, Cycloid, QuickShadow, and Spiral.

Information about plug-in tools is usually provided by their developers. To see this information, choose **About SuperPaint** from the Apple menu and click the *Plug-ins* button. A scrolling list of the plug-ins in the SP Pouch is displayed. Select a tool from the list and click *About*.

3-D Box

This tool creates a three-dimensional wireframe box. The box outlines use the current Line Fill and Line Widths; the box can be filled or shaded with the current Area Fill.

To use the tool:

1. Select the 3-D Box from the Draw & Paint Plug-ins palette.

2. Drag a rectangle for the "back" of the box.

The back of the box.

3. Release the mouse button and move the mouse to give the box its depth and orientation.

   Press the Option key, the Command key, or the Option and Command keys together as you move the mouse to fill and shade the box. Press Shift to restrict the angle of perspective to 45 degrees.

4. Click to complete the box.

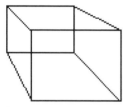

Completed 3-D Box.

AllGon

The AllGon lets you create shapes, each of which is composed of a specific grouping of a symmetric polygon. You can define the number of sides, create repeating effects of one or two levels deep, and render the polygons in four styles. You can create one AllGon at a time, "smear" them continuously, or sprinkle AllGons of random sizes. Current Area Fill, Line Fill, and Line Widths are used.

Four-sided AllGon at one and two levels deep.

To use the tool, select it from the Draw & Paint Plug-ins palette, and drag in the document window. The results depend on the settings in the AllGon Settings dialog box and the speed of the mouse. To display the AllGon Settings dialog box, double-click the AllGon icon on the Draw & Paint Plug-ins palette.

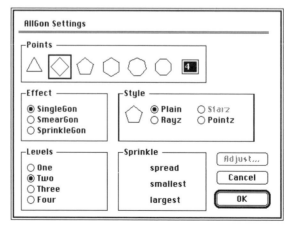

Starbursts created with the AllGon tool. (Drop shadows are filled duplicates.)

Modifier

- Press Shift to orient the figure(s) horizontally and vertically, and prevent its rotation.

Note: The SmearGon and SprinkleGon effects in the AllGon Settings dialog box are available in the *Paint layer only*.

Bubbles

The Bubbles tool produces a stream of bubbles that vary in size and shape according to the speed and direction of the pointer movement. The bubbles are outlined by lines of the current Line Fill and Line Widths, and filled with the current Area Fill.

To use the tool, select it from the Draw & Paint Plug-ins palette, and drag in the document window.

In the Draw layer, all of the bubbles are selected — the bubbles can be dragged or otherwise manipulated as a group with the Selection Arrow. The group can be deselected and individual bubbles selected.

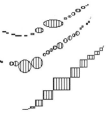

Top: Bubbles.
Center: Shift-Bubbles.
Bottom: Option-Bubbles.

Modifiers

- Press the Shift key to produce round bubbles.

- Press the Option key to produce rectangles.

- Press Option-Shift to produce squares.

Cycloid

The Cycloid creates a geometric shape based on rolling circles, using a line of current Line Fill and Line Widths.

To create a Cycloid:

1. Select the Cycloid from the Draw & Paint Plug-ins palette.

2. Drag a circle that defines a size for the cycloid.

When you release the mouse button, the cycloid is created according to the settings in the Cycloid Settings dialog box. (Double-click the Cycloid icon on the Draw & Paint Plug-ins palette to display the dialog box.)

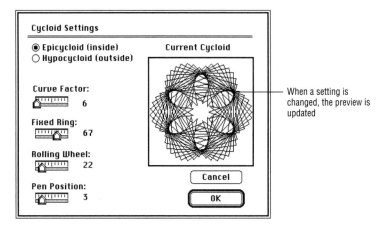

When a setting is changed, the preview is updated

QuickShadow

The QuickShadow tool produces a symmetric shape with a drop shadow. You can specify the number of sides for the shape (3 to 36), and define the size of the shadow and its placement relative to the shape.

Select the tool and drag the shape; the drop shadow appears when you release the mouse button. The shape is filled with the current Area Fill. The shape outline uses the current Line Widths and Line Fill; the drop shadow also uses the current Line Fill (for some fill combinations, you may want to set the Line Widths to zero).

Double-click the QuickShadow icon on the Draw & Paint Plug-ins palette to display the QuickShadow Settings dialog box.

In the Draw layer, the QuickShadow object is a grouped object; you can ungroup it and change the Area Fill for the shape and the shadow separately.

Examples of the QuickShadow at various settings.

Spiral

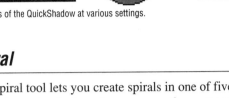

The Spiral tool lets you create spirals in one of five shapes. The point at which you begin dragging serves as the center of the spiral. The current Line Fill and Line Widths are used.

To select one of the five spiral shapes, display the Spiral Shapes dialog box by double-clicking the Spiral tool icon on the Draw & Paint Plug-ins palette.

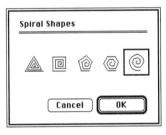

Modifiers

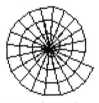

Pressing Command while making a Spiral creates spokes.

- Press the Command key to produce a spiral with spokes.

- The number keys 1 through 9 (either across the top of the keyboard, or on the keypad) control the spacing of the spiral's lines, with 1 being the tightest and 9 the loosest.

Note: The **Paint Multiple** command does not work with the Spiral tool.

The Paint-only Tools

Some of the tools available only in the Paint layer are located on the Tools palette; the others are on the Brush Tools pop-up palette. In addition, any plug-in tools in the SP Pouch that work only in the Paint layer are added to the Brush Tools palette.

Airbrush

 The Airbrush lets you paint as if you were using a real airbrush, spraying the current Area Fill. You can adjust the spray area, rate of flow, dot size, nozzle shape, and spray distribution in the Airbrush Settings dialog box, or from the keyboard while you're spraying.

To use the Airbrush:

1. Select the Airbrush from the Tools palette.

   The cursor appearance depends on the nozzle shape and spray area set in the Airbrush Settings dialog box. If you're using a round nozzle and the spray area is 16 pixels or less across, the cursor is a black circle the size of the spray area; if the spray area is larger than 16 pixels, the cursor is a hollow circle with a small cross in the middle. The Airbrush nozzle can also be the current brush shape; the appropriate cursor is used.

2. Press the mouse button to spray. Release the button when finished.

Airbrush Configuration

Five items can be set in the Airbrush Settings dialog box. The effect of current settings is previewed in the box in the upper right corner of the dialog box.

To configure the Airbrush:

1. Choose **Airbrush Settings** from the Paint menu, or double-click the Airbrush icon on the Tools palette, to display the Airbrush Settings dialog box.

2. Select *Spray Distribution* and *Nozzle Shape* options by clicking the appropriate buttons.

3. Set the *Flow*, *Spray Area,* and *Dot Size* with the slider controls.

   You can move a slider anywhere along its ruled control bar; the left side is the minimum setting and the right is the maximum. As an alternative, you can also type a value in the associated text box.

4. To establish the settings and close the dialog box, click *OK*, or press Return or Enter.

   Cancel closes the dialog box without changing the Airbrush Settings. *Revert* restores the previous settings without closing the dialog box.

Airbrush Settings

Spray Distribution: With *Even* selected, the Airbrush sprays uniformly throughout the spray area. *Faded* is less dense at the edges of the spray area, producing a shaded effect.

Nozzle Shape: The Airbrush can use a standard round nozzle or the current brush shape. With the *Current Brush Shape* option, only the shape itself is used: the *Spray Area* option controls the size of the area sprayed.

Flow: The *Flow* rate controls how quickly the spray area fills when you press the mouse button. The rate can be set from 1% to 100%. The time required to completely fill the spray area depends on its size.

Spray Area: The diameter of the area affected by the Airbrush can range from one pixel to a maximum of 256 pixels.

Dot Size: This setting ranges from zero to eleven pixels. With settings above one pixel, the dots sprayed are a random mix of sizes between one and the size specified. For example, if the slider was set at four pixels, the spray would consist of dots one, two, three, and four pixels in diameter. Mixing dot sizes gives the spray a splotchy effect. The zero setting, available only in color documents, provides a smooth airbrushed effect.

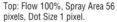

Top: Flow 100%, Spray Area 56 pixels, Dot Size 1 pixel.

Bottom: Flow 50%, Spray Area 56 pixels, Dot Size 1 pixel.

Top: Flow 100%, Spray Area 26 pixels, Dot Size 1 pixel.

Bottom: Flow 100%, Spray Area 26 pixels, Dot Size 6 pixels.

Keyboard Controls for the Airbrush

You can change the Airbrush Settings without opening the Airbrush Settings dialog box by pressing certain keyboard keys. The keyboard controls can be divided into groups: number keys, alphabet keys, and symbol keys. The number and symbol keys work whenever the Airbrush is selected. The alphabet keys work only while the Airbrush is spraying (i.e., while the mouse button is pressed), or while the Caps Lock key is engaged; otherwise, they serve as hot keys for various palettes and tools.

Number Keys

The number keys, both those across the top of the keyboard, and those on the keypad on the right side, control the size of the *Spray Area*:

Key	Spray Area
1	2 pixels
2	4 pixels
3	8 pixels
4	16 pixels
5	32 pixels
6	64 pixels
7	96 pixels
8	128 pixels
9	192 pixels
0	256 pixels

The minus key gradually reduces the spray area as you paint; the equals key (and the plus key) gradually increases it.

Alphabet Keys

With the mouse button down, or the Caps Lock key engaged, the bottom row of keys, with the exception of B, control the rate of *Flow*:

Key	Flow
Z	1%
X	6%
C	15%
V	50%
N	60%
M	100%

The comma key gradually increases, and the period key gradually decreases, the *Flow* as you paint.

The letters B and R, respectively, set the *Nozzle Shape* to the current brush shape or the Round Brush nozzle.

The letters F and E, respectively, set the *Spray Distribution* to *Faded* or *Even* distribution.

Symbol Keys

The symbol keys (Shifted number keys) control *Dot Size*:

Key	Dot Size	
!	(Shift-1)	1 pixel
@	(Shift-2)	1 and 2 pixels
#	(Shift-3)	1 to 3 pixels
$	(Shift-4)	1 to 4 pixels
%	(Shift-5)	1 to 5 pixels
^	(Shift-6)	1 to 6 pixels
&	(Shift-7)	1 to 3 pixels
*	(Shift-8)	1 to 4 pixels
(	(Shift-9)	1 to 5 pixels
)	(Shift-0)	1 to 6 pixels

Note: There is no symbol-key shortcut for setting the Dot Size to zero.

Modifiers

- Press the Shift key before spraying to restrict the motion of the Airbrush to horizontal or vertical, depending on its initial movement. This does not interfere with the operation of the keyboard controls.

- Press the Command key to hide the nozzle cursor while spraying.

- While the Option key is pressed, the nozzle is the current brush shape.

Pencil

 The Pencil writes a one-pixel line. In black-and-white documents, it writes a black line, unless you begin dragging on a black pixel, in which case it erases a one-pixel line. In color documents, the Pencil writes a line of the current Area Fill, unless you begin dragging in an area of current Area Fill, in which case it erases a one-pixel line.

Modifiers & Click Shortcuts

- Press the Shift key to restrict motion to vertical or horizontal, depending on the initial movement of the tool.

- Command-click to zoom into and out of 8x magnification; the magnification is centered on the Pencil cursor.

- Double-click the Pencil icon on the Tools palette to zoom into and out of 8x magnification; the magnification is centered in the document window.

Paint Bucket

The Paint Bucket "pours" the current Area Fill over all contiguous pixels that are the color of the pixel under the cursor hot point (the tip of the pouring paint) when you press the mouse button. Thus, you can use the Paint Bucket to quickly fill the document, or change specific areas of an image.

Note: If you are working in a virtual document, the portion of the document outside the working area is not filled.

Top: Dolphin filled with solid black.

Bottom: Dolphin filled with a grayscale gradient (Peaked type).

Modifiers

- Press the Option key to fill only the area in the document window.

Eraser

The Eraser erases the area under the pointer as it is dragged. The pointer is a square 16 by 16 pixels.

Modifiers & Click Shortcuts

- Press the Shift key to restrict the Eraser to vertical or horizontal motion, depending on its initial movement.

- Press the Option key to halve the size of the Eraser (to 8 x 8 pixels).

- Double-click the Eraser icon on the Tools palette to erase everything in the document window. If you're working in magnified or reduced view, double-clicking the icon erases everything in the right pane of the window.

Note: Double-clicking the Eraser doesn't select the Eraser; the tool you were using remains selected. The **Undo** command restores graphics in the Paint layer if necessary.

- Command-Option-double-click to erase everything in the working area of a virtual document.

Erasing in a solid black rectangle.

Brushes and Paint Plug-in Tools

Hot Key:
B is the hot key for the Brush Tools pop-up palette.

The Paint Brush, Spray Can, and any plug-in tools that work only in the Paint layer are contained on the Brush Tools pop-up palette.

Brush Tools pop-up palette.

Paint-only plug-in tools provided with SuperPaint are the Calligraphy Brush, Charcoal, Dry Brush, Smudge tool, Spin tool, Sprinkler, Texture Brush, and Twister. Other pixel-manipulation tools may appear on the palette, depending on the contents of the SP Pouch.

As with the Draw & Paint Plug-in tools, to view information provided by the developers about their plug-in tools, choose **About SuperPaint** from the Apple menu and click the *Plug-ins* button. A scrolling list of the plug-in modules in the SP Pouch is displayed. Select the name of a tool from the list and click *About*.

Note: If you seldom use certain of the Paint-only (or any other) plug-ins, you can remove those files from the SP Pouch. The tools then will not appear on the palette, and SuperPaint will use less memory.

Paint Brush

The Paint Brush uses the current brush shape to "paint" with the current Area Fill; the paint has the property of the selected Transfer Mode.

You can choose from 40 pre-defined brush shapes, or create your own. Brush shapes are selected and edited in the Custom Brushes dialog box.

To change the current brush shape:

1. Choose **Brush Shapes** from the Options menu, or double-click the Paint Brush icon on the Brush Tools palette, to display the Custom Brushes dialog box.

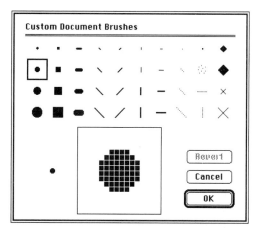

2. Click one of the 40 brush shapes to select it, and then click *OK*, or press Return or Enter.

or

Double-click the new brush shape to simultaneously select the shape and close the dialog box.

Designing Custom Brushes

You can design your own brush by editing one of the default brush shapes, or by picking up any 16-square-pixel area on the screen.

Note: The brush shapes you design while a document window is active are stored with that document (the dialog box is labeled Custom Document Brushes). To change SuperPaint's default brush collection, edit the brush shapes when no document windows are open (the dialog box is labeled Custom Preferences Brushes). The new brush shapes are saved in the SuperPaint Prefs file in the SP Pouch (see Part 4, Chapter 2 for more on the SuperPaint Prefs file). To restore the original default brush shapes, discard the SuperPaint Prefs file, restart the program, and create a new SuperPaint Prefs file.

To design a new brush shape in the Custom Brushes dialog box:

1. Select one of the pre-defined brush shapes.

or

Click or drag anywhere outside the dialog box to pick up a 16-by-16-pixel area as the brush shape; the area is centered on the cursor.

The currently selected brush shape or picked-up area is displayed in the lower half of the dialog box, both at normal magnification, and at 8x magnification in the editing box.

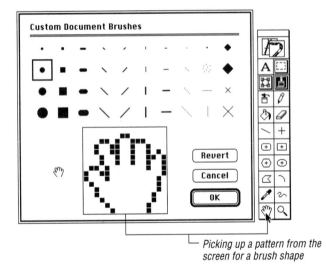

Picking up a pattern from the screen for a brush shape

2. The pointer becomes a Pencil inside the editing box: edit the brush shape by clicking or dragging to turn pixels on or off.

    Command-click in the editing box to reverse the black and white pixels of the shape.

    Click *Revert* to discard changes made in the editing box.

Painting with a hand-shaped brush.

3. Click *OK*, or press Return or Enter, to close the dialog box and use the brush.

Click the *Cancel* button to close the dialog box with no change to the brush shapes.

Paint is applied by the black pixels of the brush shape; like a rubber stamp, if you drag the brush, the outline is smeared.

Note: The current brush shape also can be used by the Spray Can, the Airbrush, the Smudge tool, and any other Paint plug-in tool designed to do so.

Modifiers

• Press the Shift key to restrict the brush to vertical or horizontal motion, depending on its initial movement.

Spray Can

The Spray Can "sprays" a repeating pattern of the current Area Fill. The tool is useful for various special effects, such as shading and softening edges.

The Spray Can cursor is the spray pattern used. If you move it slowly, or move over the same area repeatedly, a "thicker coat" of paint is applied.

Spray Can cursor

Moving the Spray Can at two different speeds (bottom more slowly than top).

Left: Spray Can used with a horizontal Line Width setting of 1 pixel.

Right: Spray Can used with a horizontal Line Width setting of 12 pixels.

Note: Generally, the Spray Can produces a heavier, more coherent spray pattern than the Airbrush.

The distance between succeeding sprays of the pattern is controlled by the horizontal and vertical Line Widths: the larger the Line Width in either direction, the farther apart each spray when the Spray Can is moved in that direction.

Modifiers

• Press the Shift key to restrict the tool to vertical or horizontal motion, depending on its initial movement.

- Press the Option key to toggle the spray pattern to the current brush shape, which is stamped into the document at increments of the current Line Widths.

- When you use the Spray Can with grid snap on, the spray patterns appear only at grid points.

Calligraphy Brush

With the Calligraphy Brush, you apply the current Area Fill with a brushstroke that varies with the speed of the mouse. The result is a liquid appearance, more like ink than paint.

A set of eight brush shapes and two types of stroke are available. If you are using a pressure-sensitive tablet, the width of the brush stroke can be controlled by pressure on the stylus.

From left to right, the results of moving the Calligraphy Brush with increasing speed.

Configuration

To change the Calligraphy Brush settings:

1. Double-click the Calligraphy Brush icon on the Brush Tools palette to display the Calligraphy Brush Settings dialog box.

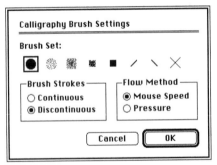

2. Select the brush shape and type of brush stroke you want to use.

   Click the *Pressure* button only if you are using a pressure-sensitive tablet.

3. Click *OK*, or press Return or Enter, to close the dialog box.

Modifiers

- Press the Shift key to restrict the brush to vertical or horizontal motion, depending on its initial movement.

Charcoal

This tool lets you produce a textured, charcoal-on-paper effect with the current Area Fill. To use the Charcoal tool, select it from the Brush Tools palette and drag as with any tool. The tool has no special settings.

Modifiers

- Press the Shift key to restrict the tool to either vertical or horizontal motion, depending on its initial movement.

Dry Brush

The Dry Brush works like a watercolor brush — it runs out of paint. The faster you paint, the faster it dries out. To use the Dry Brush, select it from the Brush Tools palette and drag as with any brush. It has no special settings.

Modifiers

- The length of the brushstroke (the "amount of paint" on the brush) is controlled by the larger of the Line Widths settings. A smaller width results in shorter brush strokes, while a larger width results in longer brushstrokes. The Line Widths do not change the width or shape of the brush.

- Press the keys 1 or 2 to switch between uneven and even modes (the brush runs out of paint unevenly or evenly). The pointer changes to indicate the selected mode.

- Press the Shift key to restrict the brush to vertical or horizontal motion, depending on its initial movement.

Smudge Tool

The Smudge tool uses the current brush shape to lighten and blend the pixels over which it passes. The effect is most apparent in areas of high contrast.

Modifiers

- Double-click the Smudge tool icon on the Brush Tools palette to display the Custom Brushes dialog box.

- Press the Shift key to restrict the tool to either vertical or horizontal motion, depending on its initial movement.

Before and after Smudging.

Spin Tool

The Spin tool is two lines joined end to end, swinging about that point, being stamped into the document as they spin, in a rapid "freeze frame." The lines can spin in the same direction, through a full circle, or in opposing directions, through a 90-degree arc before reversing directions. (For example, one of the options resembles the movement of the wings of a butterfly.)

The lines are filled with the current Area Fill, and the Line Widths can be varied to produce blocks and bars in place of the lines.

To change the line length and rate of spin:

1. Double-click the Spin tool icon on the Brush Tools palette to display the Spin Tool Settings dialog box.

2. Change any or all three options:

> **Spin Tool Settings**
>
> Line Length: [16] pixels
>
> Delay spin by [◁|▭▦▦▦▦|▷] 0 %
>
> ☐ Filled Gradient
>
> [Cancel] [OK]

Enter a line length into the *Line Length* text box. Each line is this length; the value can be from 1 through 99 pixels.

Set a rate of spin with the *Delay spin by* slider. Zero percent delay is the fastest rate of spin, while 90 percent delay is the slowest.

Click the *Filled Gradient* checkbox to delay application of a gradient fill until you finish using the tool; otherwise the gradient is applied to the lines as the tool is spinning.

3. Click *OK*, or press Return or Enter, to close the dialog box.

You can use the keys 1 and 3 on the keyboard or keypad to respectively lengthen and shorten the line length while using the tool.

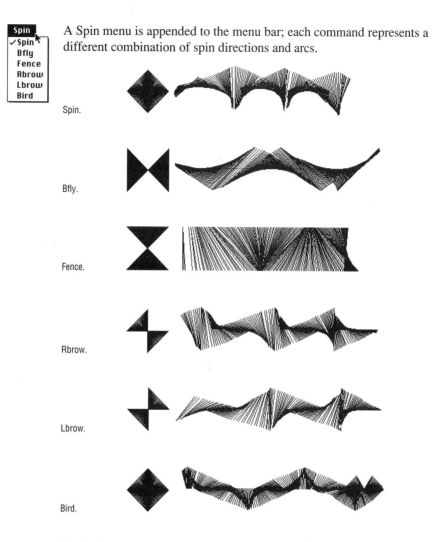

A Spin menu is appended to the menu bar; each command represents a different combination of spin directions and arcs.

Spin.

Bfly.

Fence.

Rbrow.

Lbrow.

Bird.

Sprinkler

The Sprinkler lets you randomly "sprinkle" a set of related shapes into your document (for example, stars, musical notes, or snowflakes), using the current Area Fill. A Sprinkler menu is added to the menu bar; you can select, create, edit, delete, and rename sets of shapes.

The cursor changes to indicate each shape. The **Brush Mode** command in the Sprinkler menu freezes the Sprinkler at the current shape for use as a brush, similar to the Paint Brush.

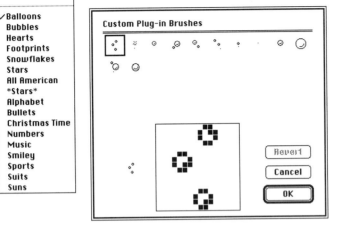

To edit the set of shapes currently chosen in the Sprinkler menu:

1. Choose **Edit** from the Sprinkler menu, or double-click the Sprinkler icon on the Brush Tools palette, to display the Custom Plug-in Brushes dialog box.

The currently chosen set of shapes is displayed across the upper portion of the dialog box.

The Sprinkler can be used to create a custom border.

2. Click the shape you wish to edit.

or

To add a new shape to the set, click a blank slot following the last shape displayed.

The highlighted shape is displayed in the lower half of the dialog box, both at normal magnification, and at 8x magnification in the editing box. You can also click or drag anywhere outside the dialog box to pick up an area 16-by-16 pixels as a new shape; the area is centered on the cursor.

3. The pointer becomes a Pencil inside the editing box: edit the Sprinkler shape by clicking or dragging to turn pixels on or off.

   Command-click in the editing box to reverse the black and white pixels of the shape.

   Click *Revert* to discard changes made in the editing box.

4. Click *OK*, or press Return or Enter, to close the dialog box, assigning the new shape to the selected set.

   Click the *Cancel* button to close the dialog box with no change to the shapes.

Modifiers

- The distance between succeeding shapes is controlled by the horizontal and vertical Line Widths: the larger the width in either direction, the farther apart each shape in that direction.

- Press the Shift key to restrict the Sprinkler to either vertical or horizontal motion, depending on its initial direction.

- Press the Option key to halt the random cycling through the shapes; the current shape is repeated.

- Press the Command key to cycle through the set of shapes, one at a time, without stamping the shapes into the document.

- Press the Command and Option keys together to cycle through the set of shapes, stamping them into the document one at a time, in the order they appear in the dialog box (rather than randomly).

Texture Brush

The Texture Brush combines a Line-Fill effect with an Area-Fill effect around the center of the cursor. The result can range from a multi-colored-airbrush to a tinsel-garland effect. The two Effects are selected from separate pop-up menus. In addition, the Flow rate and Spray Area can be set independently for each.

To configure the Texture Brush:

1. Double-click the Texture Brush icon on the Brush Tools palette to display the Texture Brush Settings dialog box.

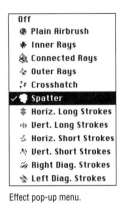

Off
* Plain Airbrush
* Inner Rays
* Connected Rays
* Outer Rays
* Crosshatch
✓* Spatter
* Horiz. Long Strokes
* Vert. Long Strokes
* Horiz. Short Strokes
* Vert. Short Strokes
* Right Diag. Strokes
* Left Diag. Strokes

Effect pop-up menu.

Texture Brush Settings

┌─Area Fill Brush──────────
Effect: Flow:
  [* Spatter]   ●▭▭▭ ● [100] %
            Spray Area:
            ● ▭▭▭ * [16] pixels
────────────────────────────

┌─Line Fill Brush──────────
Effect: Flow:
  [* Outer...]   ●▭▭▭ ● [100] %
            Spray Area:
            ● ▭▭▭ * [20] pixels
────────────────────────────

[Clear Test Area]

[Revert]

[Cancel]

[OK]

2. Select an effect for the Area Fill Brush and the Line Fill Brush from their respective *Effect* pop-up menus.

3. Set the *Flow* and *Spray Area* for both components of the Texture Brush.

   As you move the sliders, the numbers in the text boxes to their right change to reflect the new settings. As an alternative, you can also enter numbers into the text boxes.

4. You can preview the effects by painting in the test area.

   Click the *Clear Test Area* button to clear the test area and experiment with other settings.

   Click *Revert* to discard changes made to the Texture Brush settings.

5. Click *OK*, or press Return or Enter, to close the dialog box with a new Texture Brush.

   Click the *Cancel* button to close the dialog box with no change to the Texture Brush.

Modifiers

- The vertical Line Widths setting applies to the Line Fill texture, and the horizontal Line Widths setting applies to the Area Fill texture.

- Press the Shift key to restrict the Texture Brush to either vertical or horizontal motion, depending on its initial movement.

Twister

The Twister randomly scatters the pixels under the tip of the tool. The effect diffuses and softens sharp edges and other areas of contrast.

Effect of the Twister on a grid pattern.

Press 1, 2, 3, or 4 to change the size of the area affected:

1	2 x 2 pixels
2	4 x 4 pixels
3	8 x 8 pixels
4	16 x 16 pixels

Part 4

Chapter 7: Selecting, Editing, and Transforming Graphics

This chapter describes selections, some of the editing commands, and the Transform menu commands.

What are Selections?

To edit or transform existing graphics, you must first specify the objects in the Draw layer or the area of the Paint layer that you wish to change. In other words, you must *select* them.

In the Draw layer, you select or activate existing objects with the Selection Arrow. A selected object has "handles" at the four corners of its bounding box; lines have handles at each end. (When you create an object or move an object into the Draw layer, it is automatically selected.)

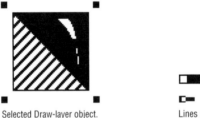

Selected Draw-layer object.   Lines selected in the Draw layer.

In the Paint layer, there are five area Selection Tools that you can use to define an area you want to manipulate. Selection areas are indicated by moving-dash lines.

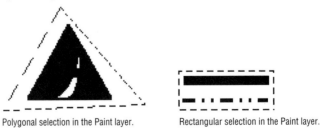

Polygonal selection in the Paint layer.   Rectangular selection in the Paint layer.

In addition, the Two-Layer Selection tool and the **Select All** command can be used in both layers, as described in subsequent sections.

Selecting Objects

In the Draw layer, when an object is selected, you can drag one of its handles with the Selection Arrow to resize the object. To move a selected object or group of objects, drag the object with the Selection Arrow.

To select an object in the Draw layer:

- Click the object with the Selection Arrow; the object's handles appear.

  To select additional objects, press the Shift key prior to clicking the objects. If you Shift-click a selected object, it is deselected.

or

- With the Selection Arrow, drag a frame that encloses the objects you wish to select.

  When you release the mouse button, all objects completely within the frame are selected.

  Press the Tab key to start the frame on an object without selecting and dragging that object.

  Press Shift to drag another selection frame without deselecting the currently selected objects.

Selecting Areas

Hot Key:
S is the hot key for the Selection Tools palette.

In the Paint layer, five area Selection Tools are available on the Selection Tools pop-up palette. The Selection Tools are the Rectangle, Lasso, Oval, Polygon, Freehand Selection tool, and the Two-Layer Selection tool. The Selection Tools pop-up can be torn from the Tools palette to create a floating palette.

Note: The Two-Layer Selection tool is unique in that it is available in both layers; it is discussed later in this chapter.

The Rectangle, Oval, Polygon, and the Freehand Selection tool are similar to their shape-tool counterparts, but instead of producing a filled shape, each selects an enclosed area of the Paint layer, including white space. If you move a selection, the enclosed white space moves with it and overlays anything on which it is placed, unless you select *Transparent Bkgnd.* from the Transfer Modes palette on the Line & Fill palette.

Rectangular selection area, *Opaque* Transfer Mode.

Same selection, Transfer Mode is *Transparent Bkgnd*.

To use an area Selection Tool:

1. Select the tool from the Selection Tools palette.

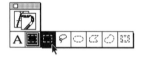

2. Select an area of the active document, as described in the following sections.

   For precise area selection, the tools can be used at any level of magnification.

Inside a selection area, the pointer is a "selection arrow."

Selected areas are indicated by moving-dash lines, sometimes known as "marching ants." (The boundary of a rectangular selection area is also referred to as a *marquee*).

When you move the pointer into a selection area, it becomes a "selection arrow" that you can use to move and transform the selection.

The **Fill** command can be used to fill a Paint-layer selection area with the current Area Fill (according to the selected Fill Mode); refer to Part 4, Chapter 8 for details.

Grid snap affects the Rectangle, Oval, Polygon, and Two-Layer Selection tools, but not the Freehand Selection tool or the Lasso.

The Transfer Modes can be assigned to selection areas to control their interaction with other graphics in the document; see "Transfer Modes and Selection Areas" later in this chapter.

Rectangle

To define a rectangular selection area, select the Rectangle selection tool and, beginning at any corner of the area you want to select, drag to the diagonally opposite corner.

Modifiers

- Press the Shift key while defining the selection to restrict the selection area to a square.

- If you press the Command key while defining the selection, when you release the mouse button the rectangle will contract to exclude as much white space or surrounding color as possible.

Left: Defining a rectangular selection area with the Command key pressed. Right: The resulting selection.

If the initial selection boundary is wholly on an area of one color, the rectangle will contract to exclude as much of that color as possible. With a selection boundary that crosses complex color changes, the result may not be exactly as you intended. You may wish to edit the selection as a mask (refer to Part 4, Chapter 8).

- Press the Option key while defining the selection to cause the contraction to exclude all areas of white or initial color; the effect is the same as using the Lasso and defining a rectangular outline.

- Double-click the selection Rectangle icon to select the area in the document window, or the right pane of any of the zoom windows.

- Press Command and double-click the Rectangle icon: the selection rectangle starts at the size of the document window and contracts to exclude as much white space (or initial color) as possible.

Lasso

Use the Lasso to select irregular shapes that contrast with their surroundings. Select the tool and drag a free-form line around the area you want to select. When you release the mouse button, if the area is not closed, SuperPaint closes it with a straight line and the selection area contracts to exclude any surrounding white space or color. For example, if the initial lassoed outline is wholly on an area of solid blue, the outline will contract to select all non-blue pixels.

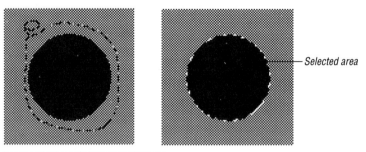

Lassoed selection excludes surrounding color.

Note: When you use the Lasso in areas of complex color variations (for example, the subtle shadings of a scanned image), the result may not be exactly as you intended. You may wish to edit the selection as a mask (refer to Part 4, Chapter 8).

Areas of white space or initial color completely enclosed by other colors are included as part of the selection (unless you press the Command key while using the Lasso). If the selected item has a break in an otherwise enclosed space, the Lasso slips inside as it tightens.

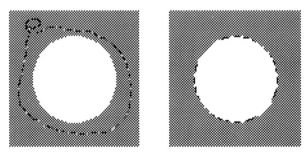

Lassoing white space surrounded by another color.

Lassoing will select more than one item at a time if they are separated within the color being excluded. If you copy or move the items, they behave as a unit, and the intervening space is ignored.

Modifiers

- In the Paint layer, double-click in the document window to select all contiguous pixels of the color under the tip of the Lasso (be wary of dithered colors). Command-double-click a non-white pixel to select all contiguous non-white pixels.

- Double-click the Lasso icon to begin the selection contraction from the edges of the document window; the effect is the same as pressing the Option key and using the selection Rectangle to drag a rectangular selection the size of the document window.

- Press the Option key while defining the selection to keep the selection outline from contracting; the effect is the same as using the Freehand Selection tool.

- Press the Command key while defining the selection to also exclude areas of white space or initial color completely enclosed by the selected area (this is sometimes known as the "x-ray" lasso).

Oval

To define an oval selection area, select the Oval selection tool, and, beginning at any corner of the bounding box of the area you want to select, drag to the diagonally opposite corner.

Selection defined using the Oval tool with the Shift key pressed.

Modifiers

- Press the Shift key while defining the selection to restrict the selection to a circular area.

- Double-click the selection Oval icon to select the largest oval possible in the document window, or in the right pane of any of the zoom windows.

Polygon

A polygon is a shape defined by points connected with straight lines. To define a polygonal selection, select the Polygon selection tool, and click at each corner of the area you want to select. Double-click to signal the last corner; SuperPaint will close the polygon. (You may find this to be the best tool for selecting complex shapes, particularly in scanned images.)

Polygonal selection.

Modifiers

- Press the Shift key at any time to restrict the current polygon side to be vertical, horizontal, or 45 degrees.

- Press Shift-Option to restrict the current polygon side to be vertical, horizontal, 30 degrees, or 60 degrees.

- Press the Option key while defining the selection to cause the selection to contract to exclude all areas of white or initial color; the effect is the same as using the Lasso to define a polygonal selection.

Freehand Selection tool

To define an irregularly shaped area, select the tool, and drag a free-form line around the area you want to select. If the area is not closed when you release the mouse button, SuperPaint closes it with a straight line.

Freehand selection.

Modifiers

- Press the Option key while defining the selection to cause the selection to contract to exclude all areas of white or initial color; the effect is the same as using the Lasso.

Transfer Modes and Selection Areas

When you define a selection area in the Paint layer, its Transfer Mode is *Opaque*, regardless of the mode(s) of the enclosed graphics. However, you can select another Transfer Mode for the selection from the Transfer Modes pop-up palette on the Line & Fill palette, just as you would change the assigned mode of an object in the Draw layer. (The Transfer Modes are described in detail in Part 4, Chapter 6.)

Transfer Mode pop-up palette

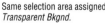

The Line and Fill palette contains the Transfer Mode pop-up palette.

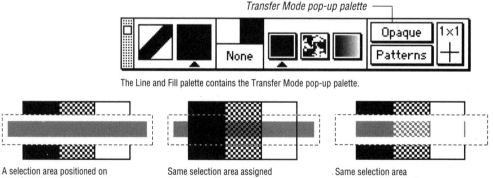

A selection area positioned on top of another graphic. Transfer Mode is *Opaque*.

Same selection area assigned *Transparent Bkgnd*.

Same selection area assigned *Paint on Darker*.

Select All

The **Select All** command, available in the Edit menu, works in both layers. In the Paint layer, **Select All** selects the document's working area. In the Draw layer, **Select All** selects every object in the layer.

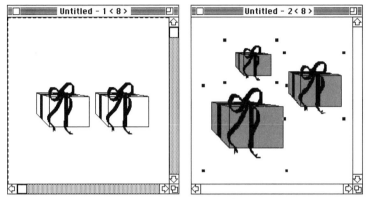

Select All in the Paint layer; notice the marquee at the edges of document window.

Select All in the Draw layer.

In the Paint layer, you can modify the **Select All** command by pressing the Option or Command keys before opening the Edit menu (these modifiers are not available in the Draw layer):

- Option-**Select All** lassos each individual graphic (this is the same as double-clicking the Lasso).

- Command-**Select All** selects all graphics in the Paint layer with the smallest rectangle possible (this is the same as Command-double-clicking the selection Rectangle icon).

Resizing a Selection

To resize a Paint-layer selection area, press the Command key, position the tip of the arrow anywhere on the moving-dash outline, and drag. Some distortion of the shape and fill may be caused by resizing a bitmapped graphic. If you attempt to resize without pressing the Command key, you will move the selection.

To resize a selected object in the Draw layer, simply drag one of the object's handles with the Selection Arrow.

Press the Shift key before beginning to drag a handle to resize the selection area or selected object only vertically or horizontally.

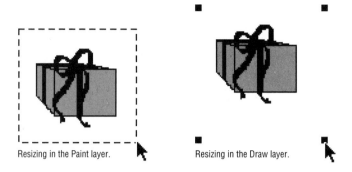

Resizing in the Paint layer.   Resizing in the Draw layer.

Moving a Selection

There are three ways to move a selection area or a selected object:

- Use the commands in the **Nudge** submenu of the Edit menu to move the selection one pixel **Up**, **Down**, **Left**, or **Right**.

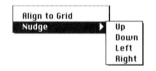

- Use the keyboard arrow keys to move the selection one pixel up, down, left, or right.

- Drag the selection.

Moving a Selection Area

The pointer becomes a "selection arrow" when it is within a selection area in the Paint layer. You can use this arrow to drag the selection to a new location.

When you use any of the three methods listed previously to move a selection area, it is "cut" from the Paint layer, becoming a floating selection, and a "hole" is left behind in the image. To create a floating copy of the area so there is no "hole" when it is moved, press the Option key and click inside the selection (or simply Option-drag it).

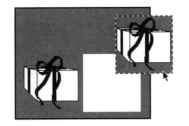

Moving a selected area.

Moving a selected area while pressing the Option key.

Press the Shift key while dragging to restrict the selection area to horizontal or vertical motion, depending on the direction of first movement.

Painting with a Selection Area

Pressing the Command and Option keys while dragging a selection in the Paint layer causes a trail of copies to be made, creating the effect of painting with the selection.

Circular area of Paint-layer graphic selected.

Dragging the selection area with the Command and Option keys pressed to create a brush effect.

The amount of space between each copy varies with the speed of the mouse, although the current Line Widths determine the *minimum* spacing between copies. If grid snap is on, the distance between copies is determined by the grid spacing.

To constrain the copies to a straight line horizontally or vertically, press Shift in addition to the Command and Option keys.

Moving Selected Objects

To move a selected object in the Draw layer, drag it with the Selection Arrow. If the object is a shape with no fill (Area Fill of *None*), the tip of the Selection Arrow must be positioned on the shape's outline.

Press the Shift key while dragging to restrict the object or outline to horizontal or vertical motion, depending on the direction of first movement.

If the *Objects are dragged as* option in the Preferences dialog box is set to *Outlines*, the object remains in position while its outline is dragged to a new location. When you release the mouse button, the object "snaps" into the outline. (This is also true of the interactive transformations described later in this chapter.)

Dragging or transforming objects in *Outlines* mode saves time and uses less memory, although you would notice only with large complex objects.

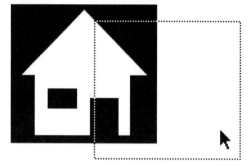

Object dragged in the Draw layer as an outline.

To change the *Objects are dragged as* option:

1. Choose **Preferences** from the Options menu.

    The Draw Layer Settings page of the Preferences dialog box appears.

Preferences: Draw Layer Settings

After using a Shape Tool:

- ● Tool remains selected
- ○ Arrow becomes selected

☐ Go into Reshape mode after drawing a Bezier

Objects are dragged as:

- ● Objects
- ○ Outlines

[Prev]   [Next]   [Cancel]   [OK]

---

2. Select either of the *Objects are dragged as* options.

3. Click *OK*, or press Return or Enter, to close the dialog box.

Deselecting a Selection

When you're finished with a selected area or object(s), deselect it (or paste it down) using any of these methods:

- Click anywhere in the document window outside the selection.

- Select a new area or object.

- Select another tool from the Tools palette or its pop-up palettes.

  When you deselect or paste down a selection area in the Paint layer, it replaces anything under it.

Deleting Selections

To remove a selection from either layer of the document:

- Choose the **Clear** command from the Edit menu.

  This does not place the selection on the Clipboard. **Clear** doesn't work with two-layer selections.

- Choose **Cut** from the Edit menu.

  This removes the selection from the document and places it on the Clipboard. Selections made with the Two-Layer Selection tool can't be cut.

- Press the Backspace, Delete, or Clear keys (depending on your keyboard). This is the same as choosing the **Clear** command.

Two-Layer Selection
tool in the Draw layer.

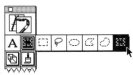

Two-Layer Selection tool in
the Paint layer.

The Two-Layer Selection Tool

The Two-Layer Selection tool is available in both layers. In the Paint layer, this tool is on the Selection Tools pop-up palette. In the Draw layer, it replaces the Brush Tools pop-up palette on the Tools palette.

This tool lets you select simultaneously in both layers of the active document. You can then copy the selection to the Clipboard and paste it into a SuperPaint document, or another program document.

To use the Two-Layer Selection tool:

1. Select the tool and drag a rectangle that encompasses the area you wish to select.

2. Choose **Copy** from the Edit menu (or use the Command-C shortcut) to copy the selected area to the Clipboard.

Note: You can *copy* graphics selected with the Two-Layer Selection tool to the Clipboard. You cannot *cut* two-layer selections to the Clipboard.

The contents of the Clipboard can be pasted normally. Refer to "Cut, Copy, Paste, and Undo" later in this chapter for more information.

How this two-layer selection is copied depends on which layer is active when you define the selection area:

- If the selection is made in the Paint layer, everything enclosed within the rectangle is placed on the Clipboard as a bitmapped graphic. (Only those portions of Draw objects inside the selection rectangle are copied.)

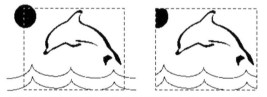

Left: A two-layer selection made in the Paint layer; the waves and the circle are in the Draw layer.
Right: The bitmapped graphic that is placed on the Clipboard; notice that only portions of the Draw objects were copied.

- If the selection is made in the Draw layer, objects partially or wholly within the selection area are placed on the Clipboard as complete objects, and the selected portion of the Paint layer is placed on the Clipboard as a SuperBits object. (Refer to Part 4, Chapter 9 for an explanation of SuperBits objects.)

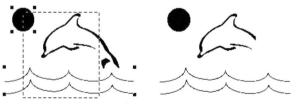

Left: A two-layer selection made in the Draw layer; the dolphin is in the Paint layer.
Right: The objects that are placed on the Clipboard; notice that complete Draw objects are copied, while only the enclosed portion of the Paint graphic is copied (as a SuperBits object).

Note: Using the Two-Layer Selection tool has the same effect as selecting objects or an area in one layer, cutting the selection(s) to the other layer, selecting an area or the objects, and then copying the selection(s) to the Clipboard.

Modifiers & Click Shortcuts

- Press the Shift key while defining the selection to restrict the two-layer selection area to a square.

- Press the Command key before beginning the selection to cause the rectangle to contract to the smallest possible rectangle that encloses the black or colored dots of the selected area *in the Paint layer*. Objects in the Draw layer within the reduced rectangle are then part of the two-layer selection. Using Command with the Two-Layer Selection tool in the Draw layer has no effect.

- Double-click the Two-Layer Selection tool icon to select the area in the document window.

- In the Paint layer, Command-double-click the Two-Layer Selection tool icon to make a rectangular selection just large enough to contain all the black or colored pixels in the document window.

Cut, Copy, Paste, and Undo

The **Cut**, **Copy**, and **Paste** commands in the Edit menu are standard Macintosh application commands. They let you transfer images to and from the Clipboard, and thus between the two layers, between Super-Paint documents, and between SuperPaint and other applications.

The **Cut** command removes the selected graphics from the document, placing them on the Clipboard. The **Copy** command places a copy of the selected graphics on the Clipboard. The **Paste** command places a copy of the graphics on the Clipboard into the active layer.

Note: Special commands in the Edit menu let you cut and copy directly between layers. Those commands are described in Part 4, Chapter 1.

Pasting into the Paint Layer

In the Paint layer, when you chose **Paste** from the Edit menu, or use the Command-P shortcut, a copy of the contents of the Clipboard is pasted into the center of the document window as a rectangular selection.

Anything pasted into the Paint layer becomes a bitmapped graphic, even if it was originally placed on the Clipboard as an object or as text.

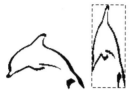

The graphic is scaled to fit when pasted into a rectangular selection area.

Note: If there is a rectangular selection area in the Paint layer when you choose **Paste**, the contents of the Clipboard are pasted into that area and scaled to fit.

Pasting into the Draw Layer

In the Draw layer, when you chose **Paste** from the Edit menu, or use the Command-P shortcut, a copy of the contents of the Clipboard is pasted into the center of the document window. Any currently active objects are deselected, and the pasted object(s) is active.

If the graphics on the Clipboard are bitmapped, they are pasted into the Draw layer as a single SuperBits object. (SuperBits objects are described in Part 4, Chapter 9.) If the Clipboard contains vector or Draw-type objects, they are pasted as individual objects and maintain their precision.

Undo

The standard Macintosh **Undo** command is available in the Edit menu. You can undo a transformation, a brush stroke, movement of a selection area, or virtually any action. You can even undo the last undo action (this is sometimes called "redo").

Choose **Undo** to reverse the action last performed, or use the Command-Z shortcut.

Transformations

The Transform commands let you alter the size, shape, and orientation of selections in the Paint and Draw layers. (The commands are available only when a selection is active.) You can scale, flip, rotate, slant, and stretch selections, and in the Paint layer you can also distort and apply a perspective effect. In the Draw layer, all transformations except **Scale Selection** can be removed using the **Remove Transformations** command.

Note: You can use the **Remove Transformations** command to remove **Rotate Right** and **Rotate Left** transformations for all objects in the Draw layer, except those drawn with the Perpendicular line, Horizontal line, Rounded Rectangle, Rectangle, Oval, Arc, and Bubbles tools.

The dimensions and rotation of a selection are displayed on the Coordinates palette, and updated when the selection is transformed. To open the Coordinates palette, choose **Show Coordinates** from the **Floating Palettes** submenu of the View menu. (In the Draw layer, this information is also available for a selected object in the Object Info dialog box.)

Original image.

Free-rotated selection.

Selection free rotated after a copy was created.

When a selection in the Paint layer is transformed, the selection is "cut" from the image and part of the "hole" may be visible, depending on the transformation. To transform a copy of the selection, press the Option key and click inside the selection area before choosing the Transform command.

In the Paint layer, fills and shapes are distorted by transformations. However, in color documents, transformed bitmapped graphics are automatically "anti-aliased" to reduce this distortion (i.e., pixels at jagged edges are blended, softening the transition between two colors).

Original graphic in the Paint layer.   Graphic stretched in the Paint layer.

In the Draw layer, fills are independent of objects and thus are not distorted by transformation. Also, transformed Draw-layer objects, including text, may appear distorted on the screen, but they still print smoothly at the highest resolution possible.

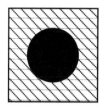 

Original graphic in the Draw layer.   Graphic stretched in the Draw layer.

Scale Selection

The **Scale Selection** command lets you change the size of the selection by specifying horizontal and vertical scaling factors.

To scale a selected area or object:

1. Choose **Scale Selection** from the Transform menu.

    The Scale Selection dialog box appears.

Scale Selection	
Horizontal	**Vertical**
○ 25% ○ 200%	○ 25% ○ 200%
○ 50% ○ 300%	○ 50% ○ 300%
◉ 100% ○ 400%	◉ 100% ○ 400%
○ Other: [100] %	○ Other: [100] %
	[Cancel] [OK]

2. Click one of the preset *Horizontal* scaling factor buttons, or type a factor in the *Other* text box.

    Scaling factors can range from 10 to 1000.

3. Click one of the preset *Vertical* scaling factor buttons, or press Tab to highlight the *Other* text box, and type a factor between 10 and 1000.

    To scale an object and maintain its proportions, be sure to use the same settings for both the *Horizontal* and *Vertical* factors.

4. Click *OK*, or press Return or Enter, to close the dialog box.

    The selected area or object(s) is reduced or enlarged by the specified factors. To bypass the dialog box and use the existing scaling factors, press the Option key while opening the Transform menu to choose **Scale Selection**.

Note: You can increase the resolution of a bitmapped graphic or a SuperBits object by scaling it down.

Rotate Selection

Available only in the Draw layer, the **Rotate Selection** command lets you rotate objects with precise control over the degree, direction, and point of rotation.

To rotate a selected object:

1. Choose **Rotate Selection** from the Transform menu.

    The Rotate Selection dialog box appears.

Original graphic.

After rotating 25 degrees clockwise around the center of the object.

2. Enter the number of *degrees* you want the object rotated.

    If you wish, change the direction of rotation by clicking the *Clockwise* or the *Counterclockwise* button.

    You can also change the point around which the object is rotated: the center, or one of the four corners of the object's bounding box.

3. Click *OK*, or press Return or Enter, to close the dialog box.

    The selected object(s) is rotated as specified. To bypass the dialog box and use the existing settings, press the Option key while opening the Transform menu to choose **Rotate Selection**.

Fixed Transformations

Original graphic.

Flip Horizontal.   Flip Vertical.

Rotate Left.   Rotate Right.

Four commands in the Transform menu have a fixed effect on the selection. Simply select an area or an object and choose one of these commands:

- **Flip Horizontal** produces a mirror image of the selection; the selection is flipped horizontally around its vertical axis (what was the left side of the selection is now the right and vice versa).

- **Flip Vertical** flips the selection vertically around its horizontal axis (what was the top of the selection is now the bottom and vice versa).

- **Rotate Left** rotates the selection counterclockwise 90 degrees around its center.

- **Rotate Right** rotates the selection clockwise 90 degrees around its center.

Interactive Transformations

Transform
Scale Selection...
Rotate Selection...
Flip Horizontal
Flip Vertical
Rotate Left
Rotate Right
✓Free Rotate
Slant
Stretch
Distort
Perspective
Remove Transformations

A check appears in front of the transformation mode that is "on."

Interactive transformations are those controlled by dragging a selection handle. You can perform the transformation repetitively, stopping and starting until you are satisfied. In other words, that transformation mode remains "on" until you turn it "off." (In the Draw layer, you can even select another object and perform the same transformation.)

When you choose one of the interactive commands, a check appears in front of the command in the Transform menu. The check remains until you select that command again, until you select another of the interactive transformations, or until you deselect the selection (by clicking outside it, or by selecting another tool).

Free Rotate, **Slant**, and **Stretch** work in both the Paint and Draw layers; **Distort** and **Perspective** are available only in the Paint layer. The commands are dimmed unless a selection is active.

In the Paint layer, when you choose one of the interactive commands from the Transform menu, the selection is surrounded by a dotted frame with handles at its corners.

In the Draw layer, when you choose an interactive transformation command, the pointer changes to a "starburst." If *Outlines* mode is in effect, only the object's outline is transformed until you release the mouse button (see "Moving Selected Objects" earlier in this chapter).

In both layers, the pointer becomes an arrow when positioned over a handle; transform the selection by dragging any handle.

A selection in the Paint layer after one of the Transform commands is chosen.

In the Draw layer, the transformation pointer is a "starburst."

In both layers, the pointer is an arrow when positioned over a handle.

Free Rotate

Selected graphic.

The **Free Rotate** command lets you drag a corner of the bounding box to rotate the selection clockwise or counterclockwise.

To free rotate a selected area or object:

1. Choose **Free Rotate** from the Transform menu.

   In the Paint layer, a transformation frame with handles at the corners appears. In the Draw layer, the pointer switches to the transformation starburst.

2. Drag one of the handles to rotate the selection.

   Rotation occurs around the center of the selection. In the Draw layer, you can press the Option key before beginning to cause the object to rotate around the corner opposite the handle being dragged.

   If you press the Shift key and drag a handle, rotation is constrained to fifteen-degree increments. If you press the Shift and Command keys and drag a handle, rotation is constrained to five-degree increments.

Free Rotate.

Slant

Slant.

The **Slant** command slants the selection as a parallelogram. When you use **Slant**, two adjacent handles are anchored and the other two slide parallel to them. The opposing sides of the selection remain parallel.

To slant a selected area or object:

1. Choose **Slant** from the Transform menu.

    In the Paint layer, a transformation frame with handles at the corners appears. In the Draw layer, the pointer switches to the transformation starburst.

2. Drag one of the handles horizontally or vertically to slant the selection.

Stretch

The **Stretch** command stretches (or shrinks) a selection vertically, horizontally, or in both directions.

Stretch.

To stretch a selected area or object:

1. Choose **Stretch** from the Transform menu.

    In the Paint layer, a transformation frame with handles at the corners appears. In the Draw layer, the pointer switches to the transformation starburst.

2. Drag one of the handles to stretch the selection.

    The handle diagonally opposite the one you are dragging is anchored.

Press the Shift key while transforming to restrict the selection to stretching only vertically or horizontally.

Distort

Distort.

Available only in the Paint layer, the **Distort** command lets you stretch a selection unevenly. The selection's fills are also distorted.

To distort a selected area:

1. Choose **Distort** from the Transform menu.

    A transformation frame with handles at the corners appears.

2. Drag one of the handles to change the frame's shape.

   The other three handles are anchored.

Press the Shift key while transforming to restrict the dragged handle to either vertical or horizontal movement.

Perspective

Perspective.

Available only in the Paint layer, the **Perspective** command can be used to create a two-dimensional perspective effect. When you drag one of the handles, two sides of the selection frame move toward or away from each other, creating a trapezoid (a four-sided figure in which only two sides are parallel).

To change the perspective of a selected area:

1. Choose **Perspective** from the Transform menu.

   A transformation frame with handles at the corners appears.

2. Drag one of the handles horizontally or vertically to change the frame's shape.

   The dragged handle and one of its adjacent handles slide toward or away from each other along the side connecting them. The other two handles are anchored. Which adjacent handle moves depends on the direction in which you are dragging.

Press the Shift key while transforming to restrict movement to only the handle being dragged.

Remove Transformations

The **Remove Transformations** command is available only in the Draw Layer. You can choose this command to remove all transformations made to the selected object with Transform menu commands. This can be more than simply undoing the last transformation: the object reverts to its *original* shape and size; that is, the effects of multiple transformations are removed.

Note: Remove Transformations also removes scaling and rotation applied with the **Replicate** command.

Chapter 8: Paint and Draw Commands

This chapter describes most of the commands found in the Paint and Draw menus, as well as those in the Reshape menu. At different times, the three menus occupy the same position in the menu bar.

The **Replicate** and **Duplicate** commands in the Edit menu are also discussed in this chapter.

Paint Commands

Paint
⬆Masking ▶
Fill Modes ▶
Paint Multiple
Brush Symmetry...
Airbrush Settings...
AutoTrace
AutoTrace Settings...
Create SuperBits...
Repeat Effect ⌘\
Invert
Fill
Spatter
Trace Edges
Brightness & Contrast...
Color Balance...
Darken
Diffuse
Lighten
Pickup

The Paint menu is available only when you are working in the Paint layer. The menu is divided into three sections. The top section includes commands that affect selection areas and the paint (brush) tools. All of these commands (except **Airbrush Settings**, which is described in Part 4, Chapter 6) are discussed in this chapter. The second section contains three commands that relate to transferring Paint-layer selections to the Draw layer; they are described in Part 4, Chapter 9. The third section of the Paint menu includes paint and image-processing commands, as well as any commands appended to the menu by Paint plug-in modules in the SP Pouch. These commands are also discussed in this chapter.

Masking

The commands in the **Masking** submenu of the Paint menu let you mask parts of your image to protect them from all image operations. For example, you could mask a shape and use the Airbrush to create a background effect without painting on the shape.

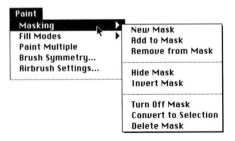

The first step in creating a mask is to define a selection area. The commands in the **Masking** submenu then let you make the selection into a mask, and turn it on and off, show or hide it, edit it by removing from or adding to it, invert it so the area behaves as a stencil, and finally convert the mask back into a selection or delete it. Only one mask can exist at a time.

Note: The **Undo** command has no effect on any of the **Masking** commands.

To create a new mask:

1. Select the area to be masked using any of the Paint-layer Selection Tools.

2. Choose **New Mask** from the **Masking** submenu of the Paint menu.

Original graphic.   Selecting part of graphic with Lasso.   Mask is indicated by diagonal lines.

The selection is converted to a mask, indicated by diagonal lines moving across the masked area. You can perform any image operations — use all of the line, shape, selection, and painting tools, and choose all of the Paint and Transform commands — and the masked area will not be affected.

Painting on original graphic.   Masked area cannot be painted.

Adding to the Mask

You can add to the area that is masked by selecting an additional area and choosing **Add to Mask**. The additional selection area need not intersect the existing mask.

1. Use any of the Paint-layer Selection Tools to define an area of the document to be added to the mask.

2. Choose **Add to Mask** from the **Masking** submenu.

   Repeat Steps 1 and 2 as necessary to reshape the masked area of the document.

The dolphin is masked.   The circle is selected with the Lasso.   Additional area added to original mask.

Subtracting from the Mask

You can subtract from the area that is masked by selecting an area to be removed and choosing **Remove from Mask**. The additional selection area should intersect the existing mask.

1. Use any of the Paint-layer Selection Tools to define an area of the mask to be deleted.

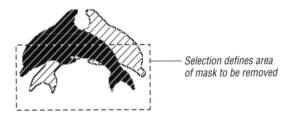

Selection defines area of mask to be removed

2. Choose **Remove from Mask** from the **Masking** submenu.

   Repeat Steps 1 and 2 as necessary to reshape the masked area of the document.

After choosing **Remove from Mask**.

Painting on previously masked area.

Hiding and Showing the Mask

To hide the moving diagonal lines while you work, choose **Hide Mask** from the **Masking** submenu. Although hidden, the mask remains active. The **Hide Mask** command becomes **Show Mask**, which causes the moving diagonal lines to re-appear.

 ———— Masked area

The mask can be hidden and still active.

Inverting the Mask

Inverting a mask protects the area previously unprotected and leaves unprotected the area previously masked. The effect is very much like using a stencil. To invert the mask, choose **Invert Mask** from the **Masking** submenu.

Original mask.

After choosing **Invert Mask**, the previously masked area is the only area that is not protected.

Turning the Mask Off and On

Turn Off Mask switches the mask off but does not delete it — the mask is retained in memory. When the mask is off, you can paint over the masked area. The command switches between **Turn Off Mask** and **Turn On Mask** according to the current state of the mask; the command is dimmed if no mask has been defined.

Converting the Mask to a Selection

Choose **Convert to Selection** to remove the protective masking, restoring the original selection area.

Note: This command, combined with the mask editing commands **Add to Mask** and **Remove from Mask**, provide the means by which you can reshape a selection area.

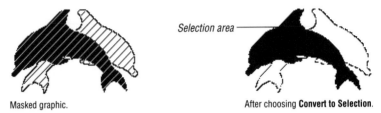

Masked graphic.

Selection area ——

After choosing **Convert to Selection**.

Deleting the Mask

To delete a mask completely, erasing it from memory, choose **Delete Mask** from the Masking submenu.

Fill Modes & the Fill Command

Original graphic.

The **Fill** command fills a selected area or the entire document with the current Area Fill; the fill has the property of the current Fill Mode (indicated by a check before the appropriate command in the **Fill Modes** submenu).

Fill Modes

Graphic selected with Lasso.

The current Fill Mode defines how the fill applied with the **Fill** and **Spatter** commands (and possibly other commands appended to the Paint menu by plug-ins) interact with the contents of the filled area. Choose a mode from the **Fill Modes** submenu before choosing **Fill** or **Spatter**.

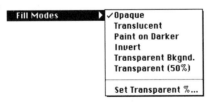

Selection filled with Opaque gray.

Note: The Fill Modes are similar to the Transfer Modes (found on the Line & Fill palette) described in Part 4, Chapter 4. The utility of two sets of modes is apparent within a selection area. If you create a floating selection area, you can select a Transfer Mode to specify how it interacts with the underlying image. You can also choose a Fill Mode and then fill the selection; the Fill Mode specifies how the fill interacts with the contents of the selection, effectively combining two modes.

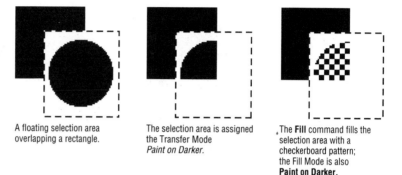

A floating selection area overlapping a rectangle.

The selection area is assigned the Transfer Mode *Paint on Darker.*

The **Fill** command fills the selection area with a checkerboard pattern; the Fill Mode is also **Paint on Darker.**

Original graphic.

There are four Fill Modes available in black-and-white documents (the commands **Opaque**, **Translucent**, **Paint on Darker**, and **Invert** in the **Fill Modes** submenu). In color documents three additional commands are available: **Transparent** and **Transparent Bkgnd.**, and the **Set Transparent %** command.

- **Opaque** – the applied fill completely replaces the contents of the selection or the document; this is the default Fill Mode.

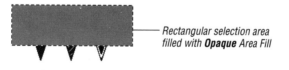

*Rectangular selection area filled with **Opaque** Area Fill*

- **Translucent** – the contents of the selection or the document are visible through the fill. The effect is similar to placing a film of the current Area Fill over the screen. Patterns and colors interact with existing patterns and colors to create new patterns and colors. The fill is opaque on areas of white.

*Rectangular selection area filled with **Translucent** Area Fill*

- **Paint on Darker** – the fill is visible only on areas that are darker than itself. If there is nothing darker in the selection or document, you will see no change.

Rectangular selection area filled with current Area Fill; *Paint on Darker* is the Fill Mode

- **Invert** – the fill reverses the black and white portions of the selection or document; colors produce complementary colors. (In an 8-bit document, the color's *index* is reversed and the result may not be strictly complementary. Refer to Part 4, Chapter 5 for more information.)

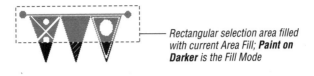
Rectangular selection area filled with current Area Fill; *Invert* is the Fill Mode

- **Transparent Bkgnd.** – the background of the Area Fill (white areas of the pattern) is transparent, allowing the contents of the selection or the document to show through. The foreground is opaque.

Rectangular selection area filled with a pattern of vertical black and white bars; Fill Mode is *Transparent Bkgnd.*

- **Transparent** – the contents of the selection or document are more or less visible through the fill; the percentage indicates the fill opacity — the lower the percentage the more transparent the fill.

Rectangular selection area filled with *Transparent (50%)* Area Fill

- **Set Transparent %** – displays the Set Transparent % dialog box in which you can change the **Transparent** percentage. Select one of the preset percentages, or enter a value from one to 99. (Transparency processing is faster when you use the preset values.)

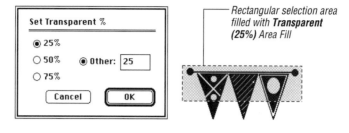

Rectangular selection area filled with **Transparent (25%)** Area Fill

Note: The **Transparent Bkgnd.**, **Transparent** and **Set Transparent** % commands are available only in color documents.

Paint Multiple

This logo was created with the Rectangle tool; Paint Multiple was chosen and grid snap was on.

The **Paint Multiple** option leaves intermediate lines and shapes on the screen as you drag a line or shape to the size you want. The effect is comparable to a rapid freeze-frame action that is controlled by the speed of the mouse. The command is checked when the option is on, and it works with all the Paint-layer line and shape tools except the Polygon and the Freehand tool.

You can achieve interesting effects by varying the Line Width, Area Fill, Line Fill, Transfer Modes, and by using the line tools with arrows and dashes.

The effect is quite different when **Paint Multiple** and **Paint from Center** are both chosen. (Double-clicking the Rectangle or the Oval icons on the Tools palette is a shortcut to and from Paint-from-Center mode.)

These stylized flowers were created with the Multigon tool after choosing both **Paint Multiple** and **Paint from Center**.

Brush Symmetry

The **Brush Symmetry** command lets you produce mirror effects, or up to nine radially related strokes simultaneously, with the brush-type tools (the Paint Brush, Airbrush, Spray Can, Sprinkler, and most of the Paint-only plug-in tools).

To turn on Brush Symmetry:

1.   Choose **Brush Symmetry** from the Paint menu to display the Brush Symmetry dialog box.

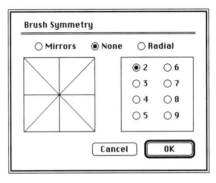

2.   Click *Mirrors* or *Radial* to specify the type of symmetry.

You can skip this step: if you define an option as described in Step 3, the appropriate type of symmetry is selected automatically.

3.   For the *Mirrors* option, turn on one or more of the mirror angles by clicking the lines in the box beneath the *Mirrors* button.

When you select an angle by clicking a line, the line becomes a bar, indicating it is selected; click the bar to deselect that angle.

Each line represents a "mirror" across the area displayed in the document window; any paint stroke on one side of the mirror is duplicated on the other side.

or

For the *Radial* option, click one of the numbered buttons to specify a number of arms for the radial pattern.

Each paint stroke produces a total of the specified number of identical strokes, evenly spaced about the center of the document window.

4. Click *OK*, or press Return or Enter, to close the dialog box.

A check appears before the command in the Paint menu when Brush Symmetry is on. To turn off the option, choose **Brush Symmetry** to re-open the Brush Symmetry dialog box, click the *None* button, and close the dialog box.

The flowers and leaves in this graphic using created with the Paint Brush with Brush Symmetry on. The black areas were filled with the Paint Bucket.

Paint-Effect Commands

The third section of the Paint menu includes paint, image-processing, and plug-in commands. (Any commands required by the Paint plug-in modules in the SP Pouch folder are appended to the Paint menu.)

Repeat Effect

Repeat Effect repeats the command last chosen from the commands that follow it in the Paint menu (**Invert, Fill, Spatter, Trace Edges, Brightness & Contrast, Color Balance, Darken, Diffuse, Lighten,** and **Pickup**). The result is the same as choosing the effect command again. To use **Repeat Effect**, choose it from the Paint menu or use the Command-\ shortcut.

As with the commands it repeats, **Repeat Effect** can be used on a selected area or the entire document. For example, to lighten your image, choose **Lighten** from the Paint menu. If the image was not lightened sufficiently, choose **Repeat Effect** (or use Command-\) to lighten it further.

Invert

Original graphic.

The **Invert** command in the Paint menu reverses the color of the pixels in the document or selection area. Black pixels become white, and white pixels become black. Colored pixels are converted to their complementary colors. (In 8-bit documents, the color's *index* is reversed, and depending on the color table in use, the resulting color may not be strictly complementary. Refer to Part 4, Chapter 5 for more information on color tables in 8-bit documents.)

Graphic enclosed by a rectangular selection area and **Invert** chosen.

Note: This command is similar to both the Transfer Mode *Invert* and **Invert** in the **Fill Modes** submenu of the Paint menu. The Transfer Mode controls the interaction of a selection area, or a fill applied with any of the tools, with the underlying image. The Fill Mode affects the interaction of a fill applied to the image, or a selected area, using Paint commands (especially **Fill**). This **Invert** command simply inverts the image or the contents of the selected area.

Spatter

Spatter randomly fills the document or selected area with pixels of the current Area Fill. The spattered fill has the property of the current Fill Mode.

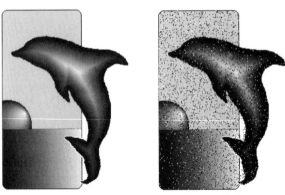

The original image was selected with the Lasso and "spattered" with an opaque Area Fill of solid black.

Trace Edges

The **Trace Edges** command outlines pixels or groups of pixels that contrast with their surroundings. The outline is a single pixel wide and its color is taken from the surrounded area (in some cases the color is inverted for contrast); the surrounded pixels are lightened or whitened.

Using **Trace Edges** with complex gray-scale or color images produces interesting results. The tracing can be repeated several times for maximum effect.

Original image.

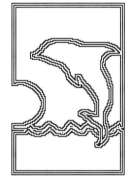

Trace Edges chosen three times.

Modifiers

If you are using **Trace Edges** repeatedly in a selection area, the boundary of the selection is expanded as necessary to accommodate repeated tracings. Anything under the expanded selection area is unaffected until you paste it down.

If you press the Option key and choose the **Trace Edges** command, the selection does not expand to accommodate the repeated tracings, although tracing within the selection does occur.

If you press the Shift key and choose **Trace Edges**, a shadowed tracing is produced. The tracing is two pixels thick to the right and below the surrounded pixels and one pixel thick to the left and above.

Image-Processing Commands

Image processing can be performed on a selection area or the entire document. The image processing commands are **Brightness & Contrast**, **Color Balance**, **Darken**, **Diffuse**, and **Lighten**.

These commands represent Paint plug-in modules. If any of these commands do not appear in the Paint menu, the corresponding plug-in module was not found in the SP Pouch folder.

For the information about plug-ins provided by their developers, choose **About SuperPaint** from the Apple menu. In the About SuperPaint dialog box, click the *Plug-ins* button. A scrolling list of the plug-ins in the Pouch is displayed; select a plug-in from the list and click *About*.

Brightness & Contrast

The **Brightness & Contrast** command displays a control window that lets you adjust the brightness and contrast for a selection or the entire document. The effect is similar to using the brightness and contrast controls on your monitor screen. Increasing the brightness makes the image lighter, while decreasing it makes the image darker. Increasing the contrast makes the dark colors darker and the light colors lighter, making the difference between them more apparent. (The Brightness & Contrast controls are not available in black-and-white documents.)

Before Brightness & Contrast adjustment.

After Brightness & Contrast adjustment.

To adjust the brightness and contrast of the document or a selected area:

1. Choose the **Brightness & Contrast** command from the Paint menu to display the Brightness & Contrast control window.

    Drag the control-window title bar to reposition it on the screen.

Brightness & Contrast
control window.

2. Drag the sliders to change the brightness and contrast of the image.

   As you move a slider, its effect is visible immediately, *over your entire monitor screen*. However, the effect is actually applied to only the document, or only the active selection if there is one, when you close the Brightness & Contrast control window.

3. Click *OK*, or press Return or Enter, to apply the changes and close the control window.

   Click *Cancel* to close the control window without applying changes. Click *Revert* to return the sliders to their original settings (the control window remains open).

Color Balance

The **Color Balance** command displays a control window that lets you adjust the color components of your image. You can change the color balance of the highlights, shadows, and midtones in your document by changing the red, green, and blue components of each. (Highlights are the lightest portions of the image. Midtones are the hues between highlights and shadows. Shadows are the darkest portions of an image.) The Color Balance controls are not available in black-and-white documents.

To adjust the color values for the highlights, shadows, and midtones of the document or a selected area:

1. Choose the **Color Balance** command from the Paint menu to display the Color Balance control window.

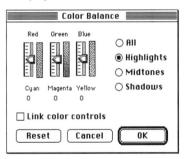

Drag the control-window title bar to reposition it on the screen.

2. Select *All*, *Highlights*, *Midtones*, or *Shadows* to specify the image elements to be adjusted.

    If you select the *Link color controls* option, the three sliders are linked to maximize each effect; that is, as you move one slider, the other two move in the opposite direction.

3. Drag the sliders to change the red/cyan, green/magenta, and blue/yellow components of the image element selected in Step 2.

    As you move a slider, its effect is visible immediately, *over your entire monitor screen*. However, the effect is actually applied to only the document, or only the active selection if there is one, when you close the Color Balance control window.

4. Click *OK*, or press Return or Enter, to apply the changes and close the control window.

    Click *Cancel* to close the control window without applying changes. Click *Reset* to return the sliders to their original settings (the control window remains open).

When you move a slider up, more of that color is added to the image. When you move the slider down, more of that color is subtracted (more of its subtractive counterpart is added). The numbers below the sliders indicate the relative intensity of each color. (Color and color models are discussed in Part 4, Chapter 5.)

Darken

In a black-and-white document, **Darken** adds a random spray of black pixels to the image or selected area. In a color document, it overlays the image or selected area with a translucent gray wash.

Press the Option key before choosing **Darken** to increase the darkening.

Original image.   **Darken** chosen once (1-bit document).   **Darken** chosen once (8-bit document).

Diffuse

Diffuse softens or defocuses the image, or selected area, by randomly scattering a small percentage of the pixels; the effect is apparent only at edges and other areas of contrast. The Twister tool produces a similar effect in a much smaller area.

Press the Option key before choosing **Diffuse** to increase the number of pixels scattered.

After **Diffuse**.

Lighten

In a black-and-white document, **Lighten** adds a random spray of white pixels to the image or selected area. In a color document, it overlays the image or selected area with a translucent white wash.

Press the Option key before choosing **Lighten** to increase the lightening.

Original image.

Lighten chosen once (1-bit document).

Lighten chosen once (8-bit document).

Pickup

The **Pickup** command replaces the contents of the selection area with a copy of whatever is under it in the Paint layer. You can use this command in conjunction with the Transfer Modes to produce some interesting effects.

To pick up the image area underlying the selection:

1. Define a selection area with any of the area Selection Tools (except the Two-Layer Selection tool).

2. Drag or Option-drag the selection area into position over the area of the image to be picked up.

3. Choose **Pickup** from the Paint menu.

   The selection is filled with a copy of the underlying image.

Original graphic.

Background texture.

Selected graphic is placed on background texture.

Graphic after picking up underlying texture.

Draw Commands

Draw

Bring to Front	⌘=
Send to Back	⌘-
Group	⌘G
Ungroup	⌘U
Lock	
✓**Unlock**	
Align Objects...	⌘M
Object Info...	⌘I
Reshape	⌘R
Convert to Bezier	▶
Bezier to Polygon	▶
Join Beziers	
Bezier Settings...	

The Draw menu replaces the Paint menu on the menu bar when you switch to the Draw layer. The Draw commands let you change basic object qualities, like size and shape, object relationships, such as position relative to each other, and the method used to define an object's shape.

Object Stacking Order

Within the Draw layer, each new object is created in its own plane "on top of" existing objects. Two commands in the Draw menu let you change the order of objects in this stack: **Bring to Front** and **Send to Back.** To move an object to the front or back of the stack, select the object and choose the appropriate command from the Draw menu. These commands move the selected object in the front of or in back of all other objects in the Draw layer.

Selected object is in front.

If more than one object is selected when you use the **Bring to Front** or **Send to Back** commands, the selected objects are sent behind or brought in front of all other objects as a group.

Note: You can also use Command-- (minus) to send the selected object to the back. Use Command-= (equals) to bring the selected object to the front.

The selected object after **Send to Back** is chosen.

Grouping Objects

The **Group** command combines a set of selected objects. The group behaves as a single object: it has a single set of handles, moves as a unit, and when you edit a grouped object, the editing is applied to all members. Transform commands, resizing, and changes to Line Fill, Area Fill, and line thickness affect the entire group.

To group multiple objects:

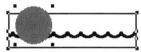

Three individual objects are selected. Note the three sets of handles.

1. Select the objects to be grouped.

    Either Shift-click each object, or use the Selection Arrow to drag a rectangular frame that completely encloses the objects to be selected.

The three objects are grouped. Note the single set of handles.

2. Choose **Group** from the Draw menu, or press Command-G.

To separate a group into its member objects, select the group and choose **Ungroup** from the Draw menu (or use the Command-U shortcut).

Note: The **Group** command is available only if two or more objects are selected. The **Ungroup** command is available only if a group is selected.

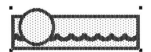

Changes to the Line Fill, Area Fill, and Line Widths are applied to the group.

Nested Groups

You can use the **Group** command to add objects, and even other groups, to an existing group to produce a "nested group."

When you ungroup an object that has been grouped in stages, the first **Ungroup** command separates only the most-recent grouping. The next **Ungroup** command separates the next-most-recent grouping, and so on.

Locked Objects

The **Lock** command locks an object so that it can't be moved or altered inadvertently. This lets you protect elements of your drawing while you work with other items.

Select the object or objects to be locked, and choose **Lock** from the Draw menu. Locked objects have gray handles when selected, and a check appears before the **Lock** command in the Draw menu.

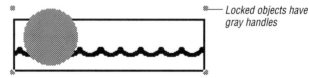

— Locked objects have gray handles

To unlock a locked object, select it and choose **Unlock** from the Draw menu. The object's handles become black and a check appears before the **Unlock** command in the Draw menu.

Aligning Objects

The **Align Objects** command displays a dialog box that you can use to align two or more objects in the Draw layer. (The command is dimmed if only one object is selected.) The objects are moved horizontally, vertically, or both to achieve the specified alignment. The command can be used, for example, to align text blocks to create rows and columns of text.

To align two or more selected objects:

1. Choose **Align Objects** from the Draw menu to display the Align Objects dialog box.

```
┌─────────────────────────────────────────────────┐
│ Align Objects                                    │
│ ┌─Horizontal alignment─┐ ┌─Vertical alignment──┐ │
│ │ ● No change          │ │ ● No change         │ │
│ │ ○ Left sides         │ │ ○ Tops              │ │
│ │ ○ Centers            │ │ ○ Centers           │ │
│ │ ○ Right sides        │ │ ○ Bottoms           │ │
│ └──────────────────────┘ └─────────────────────┘ │
│                            ┌─────────┐ ┌───────┐  │
│                            │ Cancel  │ │  OK   │  │
│                            └─────────┘ └───────┘  │
└─────────────────────────────────────────────────┘
```

2. Select a *Horizontal alignment* and a *Vertical alignment* option.

   The left sides, right sides, or centers of the objects' bounding boxes can be selected for horizontal alignment (one or more of the objects are moved horizontally). Vertical alignment can be along the objects' tops or bottoms, or through their centers.

3. Click *OK*, or press Return or Enter, to close the dialog box and align the selected objects.

   The axis of alignment for the objects is determined as follows: when you select one of the four sides options, one or more of the objects is moved to align with the specified side of the object furthest in the selected direction (i.e., one of the objects doesn't move). For example, with three objects active, *No change* selected for *Horizontal alignment*, and *Tops* selected for *Vertical alignment*, two of the objects would be moved upward until the tops of their bounding boxes align with the top of the highest object, which is not moved.

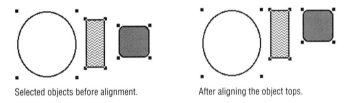

Selected objects before alignment.   After aligning the object tops.

Note: In the Align Objects dialog box, "horizontal" and "vertical" are the directions objects are moved to achieve the specified alignment, rather than the orientation of the axis of alignment.

When you select either of the *Centers* options, the axis of alignment is equidistant from the two object sides that are furthest apart (left and right, or top and bottom).

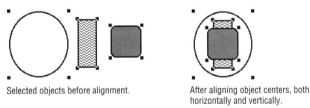

Selected objects before alignment.   After aligning object centers, both
                                                  horizontally and vertically.

If you select both a horizontal and a vertical alignment option, the objects will be placed on top of one another according to their stacking order.

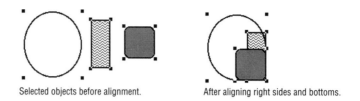

Selected objects before alignment.   After aligning right sides and bottoms.

Press the Option key before choosing **Align Objects** to suppress the dialog box and align the selected objects using the existing settings.

Note: You can also use the **Align to Grid** command to align objects. **Align to Grid** is described in Part 4, Chapter 2.

Object Info

You can determine and change the location, size, and rotation of the selected object in the Object Info dialog box. If the selected object is a SuperBits object, you can also change its resolution. To open the dialog box, choose **Object Info** from the Draw menu, or use the Command-I shortcut. To change an object's size, location, or rotation, enter the desired values in the dialog box.

```
┌─────────────────────────────────────────────────┐
│ Object Info                                      │
│ ─────────────────────────────────────────────   │
│  ┌─Location ──────┐   ┌─Size ──────┐             │
│  │ [2]     right  │   │ [2.25]  wide │ ┌──────────┐│
│  │                │   │            │ │ SuperBits...││
│  │ [4]     down   │   │ [1.75]  high │ └──────────┘│
│  └────────────────┘   └────────────┘             │
│  ┌─Rotation ──────┐                              │
│  │ [0]   degrees  │   Measure in: [ Inches ]     │
│  └────────────────┘                              │
│                        ┌────────┐ ┌──────────┐   │
│                        │ Cancel │ │    OK    │   │
│                        └────────┘ └──────────┘   │
└─────────────────────────────────────────────────┘
```

Note: If more than one object is selected, the **Object Info** command is dimmed.

The *Location* values are the horizontal and vertical distances, in current units of measurement, from the upper left corner of the document to the upper left corner of the object's bounding box. To move the object, enter new horizontal and vertical distances (you cannot enter values that would place the object entirely off the document).

The *Size* values are the width and height, in current units of measurement, of the object's bounding box. To change its size, enter a new width and height.

The *Rotation* value is the number of degrees the upper left corner of the bounding box is rotated relative to the upper right corner. A positive value indicates clockwise rotation; a negative value indicates counterclockwise rotation. To rotate the object to a new orientation, enter a positive or negative value.

Use the *Measure in* pop-up menu to change the units of measurement for the document.

Note: You can use the Object Info dialog box to makes changes to a locked object. Locking an object prevents *inadvertent* changes.

If the selected object is a SuperBits object, the *SuperBits* button is available. Click the button to open the SuperBits Info dialog box in which you can change the horizontal and vertical resolution of the SuperBits object. This is particularly useful with bitmapped graphics that have been cut or copied from the Paint layer or the Clipboard.

You can also cause the SuperBits object to be resized to match its resolution, and you can specify whether it is a black-and-white or a color object. (Refer to Part 4, Chapter 9 for a detailed explanation of SuperBits, resolution, and the two options.)

```
┌─────────────────────────────────────────────────────────┐
│  SuperBits Info                                           │
│ ═══════════════════════════════════════════════════════  │
│  ┌─Horizontal ─────────    ┌─Vertical ─────────           │
│   ○ 72 (Screen)              ○ 72 (Screen)                 │
│   ○ 144 (ImageWriter)        ○ 144 (ImageWriter)          │
│   ○ 216 (ImageWriter LQ)     ○ 216 (ImageWriter LQ)       │
│   ◉ 300 (LaserWriter)        ◉ 300 (LaserWriter)          │
│   ○ 360 (StyleWriter)        ○ 360 (StyleWriter)          │
│                                                           │
│   ○ Other: │ 300 │ dpi       ○ Other: │ 300 │ dpi         │
│                                                           │
│  ☒ Resize to match resolution                             │
│                                                           │
│                             ┌────────┐  ┌──────────┐      │
│  ○ Black & white  ◉ Color   │ Cancel │  │    OK    │      │
│                             └────────┘  └──────────┘      │
└─────────────────────────────────────────────────────────┘
```

Reshaping Objects

There are three types of objects in the Draw layer that can be reshaped: polygons, Bezier objects, and arcs. A polygon is composed of points joined by straight lines. A Bezier path is a series of straight- and curved-line segments, joined at anchor points. Both polygons and Bezier objects can be totally reshaped, and you can convert one type to the other. Arcs are a special case in that the range of reshaping is limited, and you cannot convert other objects to arcs (however, arcs can be converted to Bezier objects).

Polygon in Reshape mode.   Bezier path in Reshape mode.   Arc in Reshape mode.

The shapes produced by the Multigon, Arc, Polygon, Freehand tool, and the AutoTrace process (described in Part 4, Chapter 9) can be reshaped immediately. The Rectangle, Rounded Rectangle, and Oval produce specific shapes that cannot be reshaped (other than resizing) until they are converted to polygons or Bezier objects.

The commands in the last section of the Draw menu relate to reshaping and converting objects.

Reshaping Objects

To reshape the selected object, choose the **Reshape** command from the Draw menu to put the object into Reshape mode. Depending on the type of object selected, the command is **Reshape Polygon**, **Reshape Arc**, or **Reshape Bezier**. If a SuperBits object is selected, the command becomes **Edit SuperBits** (editing SuperBits objects is described in Part 4, Chapter 9). When **Reshape Bezier** is chosen, the Draw menu is replaced by the Reshape menu, described in detail later in this chapter.

To reshape an arc or a polygon:

1. Use the Selection Arrow to select the object.

2. Choose **Reshape Arc** or **Reshape Polygon** from the Draw menu (or use the Command-R shortcut).

   The handles at the corners of the bounding box disappear and reshaping handles appear on the outline of the object.

3. Drag one or more of the handles to reshape the object.

   Arcs have two reshaping handles, and their movement is limited to the outline of the oval of which the arc represents one quarter.

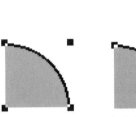 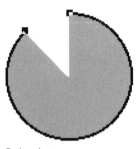

Selected arc.   Arc in Reshape mode.   Reshaped arc.

Polygons have multiple reshaping handles, each of which has an unlimited range of motion.

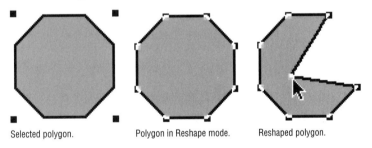

Selected polygon.   Polygon in Reshape mode.   Reshaped polygon.

4. To exit Reshape mode, click outside of the object, or select another tool.

Note: When reshaping a polygon, you cannot convert the straight lines to curves. To do so, the polygon would first have to be converted to a Bezier object.

Reshaping Bezier Objects

The outline of a Bezier object is called a path. A Bezier path is made up of *segments*. The point at which a segment joins another segment, or where a segment ends, is called an *anchor point*. The segments and the anchor points can be altered to reshape the path.

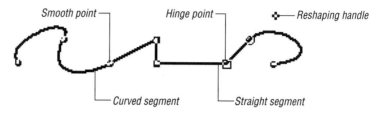

Note: To draw Bezier objects that are not closed, filled shapes, use the Freehand tool with the Area Fill set to *None*. Refer to Part 4, Chapter 6 for a complete description of the Freehand tool.

There are two types of anchor points and two types of segments. An anchor point is either a *smooth* or a *hinge* point, and they can be converted from one to the other. Segments are either *curved* or *straight*, and they also can be converted from one to the other. You can add or delete points, you can break the path at any anchor point, or you can close a path by joining its two endpoints. You also can join two Bezier paths into a single path.

To reshape a Bezier path:

Reshape
Bring to Front ⌘=
Send to Back ⌘-
✓Straight Segment
Curve Segment
Hinge Point
Smooth Point
Close Curve
Break Curve
Delete Point
Add Point

The Reshape menu.

1. Use the Selection Arrow to select a Bezier object.

2. Choose **Reshape Bezier** from the Draw menu (or use the Command-R shortcut).

    The handles at the corners of the bounding box disappear and filled anchor points appear on the outline of the object.

    The Reshape menu replaces the Draw menu.

3. Work with the segments, anchor points, and reshaping handles, as described in the following sections, to reshape the path.

4. To exit Reshape mode, click outside of the object, or select another tool.

Note: If the *Go into Reshape mode after drawing a Bezier* option is selected on the Draw Layer Settings page of the Preferences dialog box, the Bezier curves you draw with the Freehand tool in the Draw layer are automatically put into Reshape mode when you finish the curve. Refer to Part 4, Chapter 2 for more information.

In Reshape mode, filled circles and squares mark the Bezier path's anchor points: smooth points are indicated by circles, and hinge points are indicated by squares. A Bezier path is reshaped by moving its segments, moving its anchor points, and by altering the path of the curved segments.

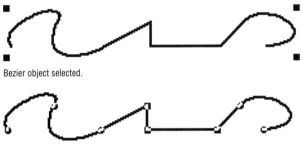

Bezier object selected.

Bezier object in Reshape mode.

Note: The **Bring to Front** and **Send to Back** commands in the Reshape menu are the same commands found in the Draw menu, and described earlier in this chapter.

Segments

To move a whole segment, position the tip of the Selection Arrow on the segment and drag it. The segment is selected and moved intact — the adjacent segment or segments stretch and swing (rather like elastic bands) to maintain contact with it. The anchor points on the path and the object's Area Fill disappear while you drag the segment.

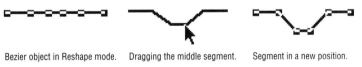

Bezier object in Reshape mode.   Dragging the middle segment.   Segment in a new position.

When a segment is selected, the anchor points at each end are also selected, and reshaping handles may be available to reshape the segment (as described in a subsequent section). To deselect any selected anchor points, simply select another segment or a single point on the curve. (To select a segment, click it anywhere between the two anchor points; to select multiple segments, Command-click the segments.)

To convert a selected segment from straight to curved, choose **Curve Segment** from the Reshape menu; to convert from curved to straight, choose **Straight Segment**. (You can also double-click a segment to convert it from one type to the other.) A check before the appropriate command indicates the type of the selected segment.

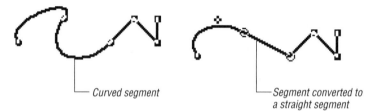

Curved segment   Segment converted to a straight segment

Note: If multiple segments are selected when you choose **Straight Segment** or **Curve Segment,** they are all affected by the command.

Anchor Points and Reshaping Handles

You can drag an anchor point to reposition it; the point is selected and the attached segments stretch and swing to maintain contact. (The anchor points and the object's Area Fill disappear while you drag the point.)

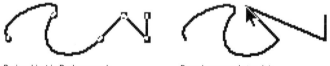

Bezier object in Reshape mode.   Dragging an anchor point.

To select anchor points: click a point; click a segment to select the points on its ends; Shift-click additional points to select multiple points; Command-click an unselected point to add it to those already selected (the same as Shift-clicking), or Command-click a selected point to deselect it.

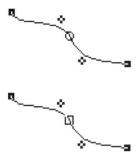

Top: A selected smooth point.
Bottom: A selected hinge point.

When an anchor point is selected, the circle or square becomes hollow, and one or two special reshaping handles may appear in the vicinity of the point. The handles look like a cross with a hollow center.

Reshaping handles are associated with curved segments and are used to alter the curves. Thus, an anchor point that connects two straight segments has no handles. An anchor point connecting two curve segments has two handles, and an anchor point connecting a curve segment and a straight segment has one handle on the side of the curve segment.

Drag a handle to reshape its curve segment; anchor points, handles and the object's Area Fill disappear, and the curve of the segment changes.

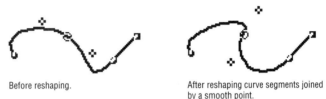

Before reshaping.

After reshaping curve segments joined by a smooth point.

The reshaping handle affects only the curve segment that is on the same side of the anchor point as the handle, except where two curved segments are joined by a smooth point. In that situation, the handles are related, and the curves on both sides of the anchor point are altered. Visualize a line that starts at one handle, goes through the anchor point, and ends at the other handle. As you drag one of the handles, the other one swings around too, with the invisible line anchored on the curve at the selected anchor point.

Converting Anchor Points

To convert the selected smooth point to a hinge point, choose **Hinge Point** from the Reshape menu; to convert the selected hinge point to a smooth point, choose **Smooth Point**. (You can also double-click an anchor point to convert it from one type to the other.) A check before the appropriate command indicates the type of the selected anchor point.

Before converting an anchor point.

After converting a hinge point to a smooth point.

Note: Changing an anchor point from smooth to hinge, or vice versa, may change the shape of attached curve segments.

Adding and Deleting Anchor Points

You can add anchor points to a Bezier path to provide more control over its shape. Points can also be deleted, should they prove unnecessary, or to change the shape of the object.

Original Bezier path.

To add an anchor point anywhere on a Bezier path, select a segment and choose **Add Point** from the Reshape menu. The anchor point is added to the middle of the segment; it is the same type as the next clockwise point. (An alternate method is to Option-click the spot at which you want the anchor point to appear.) The addition may slightly alter the shape of the Bezier path.

After adding a point.

If you choose **Add Point** when multiple segments are selected, a new point is added at each segment midpoint.

After deleting a point.

To delete a point, select it and choose **Delete Point** from the Reshape menu (or press the Delete key). If multiple anchor points are selected, all are deleted. Deleting anchor points may change the shape of the Bezier object.

Breaking and Closing a Path

You can break a Bezier path at any of its points, and you can close an open path by joining its two endpoints.

To break a Bezier path, select a point and choose **Break Curve** from the Reshape menu (or simply Option-click an anchor point). The path is broken at the selected point. If breaking the path produces two or more separate paths, Reshape mode is exited and each of the Bezier objects are selected. This occurs if the path is not closed (i.e., the object was created with an Area Fill of *None*), or when multiple points are selected.

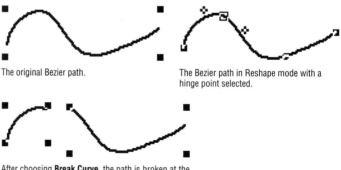

The original Bezier path.

The Bezier path in Reshape mode with a hinge point selected.

After choosing **Break Curve**, the path is broken at the selected point.

To close an open Bezier path, choose **Close Curve** from the Reshape menu. The two endpoints are joined with a straight segment.

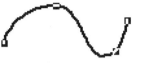

The original Bezier path in Reshape mode.

After choosing **Close Curve**, the endpoints are joined with a straight segment.

Exiting Reshape Mode

When you are finished reshaping the Bezier path, Reshape mode can be exited by selecting a tool from the Tools palette (the object is deselected), by clicking outside the object (the object is deselected), or by switching to the Paint layer. Reshape mode is also exited when you break a Bezier path into two or more separate paths (all objects are selected).

Converting Objects

You can convert any object produced in the Draw layer to a Bezier object, including objects produced with the Rectangle, Rounded Rectangle, and Oval tools. You also can convert any Bezier object to a polygonal object. Thus, complex shapes can be produced by converting and reshaping simpler objects, reducing the amount of drawing required. (SuperBits objects are not produced in the Draw layer and cannot be converted to any other type of object.)

Convert to Bezier

To convert the selected object or objects to Bezier objects, choose **Point-to-Point** or **Curve Fit** from the **Convert to Bezier** submenu of the Draw menu.

Draw	
Bring to Front	⌘=
Send to Back	⌘-
Group	⌘G
Ungroup	⌘U
Lock	
✓**Unlock**	
Align Objects...	⌘M
Object Info...	⌘I
Reshape Bezier	⌘R
Convert to Bezier ▶	Point-to-Point
Bezier to Polygon ↖▶	Curve Fit
Join Beziers	
Bezier Settings...	

Choosing **Point-to-Point** converts every point in the polygon to a hinge point in the Bezier object, and the lines joining the polygon points become straight segments; the appearance of the object doesn't change.

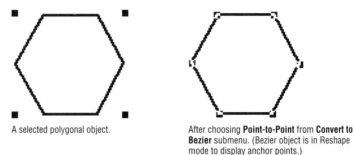

A selected polygonal object.

After choosing **Point-to-Point** from **Convert to Bezier** submenu. (Bezier object is in Reshape mode to display anchor points.)

When you choose **Curve Fit**, the current settings in the Bezier Settings dialog box are applied during the conversion, so the object outline may change slightly. Straight and curved segments, and smooth and hinge points are produced.

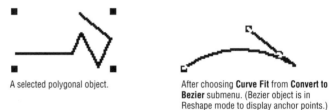

A selected polygonal object.

After choosing **Curve Fit** from **Convert to Bezier** submenu. (Bezier object is in Reshape mode to display anchor points.)

Bezier to Polygon

To convert the selected Bezier object or objects to a polygon or polygons, choose **Point-to-Point** or **Polygon Fit** from the **Bezier to Polygon** submenu of the Draw menu.

When you choose **Point-to-Point**, the Bezier anchor points are converted to polygon points and the segments joining them become straight lines. The appearance of the object most likely will change.

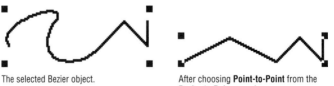

The selected Bezier object.

After choosing **Point-to-Point** from the **Bezier to Polygon** submenu.

When you choose **Polygon Fit**, points are added to the curved segments to maintain the object's shape (its appearance doesn't change).

The Bezier object in Reshape mode.

After choosing **Polygon Fit** from the **Bezier to Polygon** submenu. (The polygon is in Reshape mode to display its definition points.)

Joining Bezier Objects

The **Join Beziers** command links two open Bezier paths to produce a single path. The command is dimmed if more than two objects are selected.

To join two Bezier curves:

1. Select two Bezier objects.

    The two Bezier objects selected must be open paths.

2. Choose **Join Beziers** from the Draw menu.

    The two closest endpoints (one on each path) are joined with a straight segment.

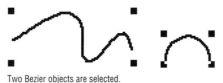

Two Bezier objects are selected.

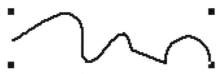

After choosing **Join Beziers**, the closest endpoints are joined with a straight segment.

Bezier Settings

The sliders in the Bezier Settings dialog box control the smoothing of Bezier outlines drawn with the Freehand tool and produced by conversion from polygons (i.e., existing Bezier objects are not affected). The settings control whether many or few points are used to define the path (thus influencing segment length), the possible mix of straight and curved segments, and the possible mix of hinge and smooth points.

Choose **Bezier Settings** from the Draw menu to display the Bezier Settings dialog box. Drag the slider bars to change the settings.

```
┌──────────────────────────────────────────────┐
│  Bezier Settings                               │
│  ───────────────────────────────────────       │
│       More              Less                   │
│       Points   [▦▮]      Points                │
│       per Line           per Line              │
│                                                │
│   All Straight [▮▦]      All                   │
│       Lines              Curves                │
│                                                │
│        Sharp   [▦▮]      No                    │
│      Corners             Corners               │
│                                                │
│     ( Revert )  ( Cancel )  (( OK ))           │
└──────────────────────────────────────────────┘
```

More points per line mean the segments can be shorter and follow the original outline more accurately. Fewer points mandate longer segments which follow the original outline more approximately.

All straight segments produce a polygonal path, anchored by all hinge points; more points are required to closely approximate curves on the original path. All curved segments will produce the most smoothing of the outline.

Sharp corners requires the anchor points to be all hinge points, while smooth corners makes them all smooth points. Smooth points produce rounding of sharp corners.

The three settings are related; that is, the combination of the settings defines their influence. Generally, however, positioning the sliders toward the left side of their ranges produces paths that are more faithful to the original outlines, but when output, the paths tend to be jagged and the larger numbers of points require longer to process. Moving the sliders to the right increases smoothing, producing outlines that are easier to process and more visually pleasing.

Note: A similar set of sliders is found in the AutoTrace dialog box; the two sets are not linked. See Part 4, Chapter 9 for a description of the AutoTrace feature.

Duplicating Objects

The duplicate is on top of and offset from the original.

The **Duplicate** command in the Edit menu creates a copy of the selected object or objects; the duplicate is selected and the original object is deselected. (**Duplicate** is available only in the Draw layer.)

To duplicate the selected object(s), choose **Duplicate** from the Edit menu, or use the Command-D shortcut. The duplicate appears on top of and offset slightly lower and to the right of the original.

Note: If grid snap is on, the upper left corner of the duplicate's bounding box is aligned to the next grid point down and to the right.

If you drag the copy to a new location and then duplicate the copy (without doing anything else in between), the second copy is offset from the first copy the same distance and direction that the first copy was moved from the original.

Replicating Objects

The **Replicate** command in the Edit menu provides a step-and-repeat function that is a shortcut to producing multiple, regularly spaced copies of objects. (**Replicate** is available only in the Draw layer.)

The original object.

After replication and rotation.

To use the **Replicate** command:

1. Use the Selection Arrow to select an object or objects.

2. Choose **Replicate** from the Edit menu to display the Replicate dialog box.

```
┌─────────────────────────────────────────────────────────┐
│  Replicate                                              │
│  ═══════════════════════════════════════════════════    │
│                                                         │
│   No. of copies: [█]      Measure in: [ Inches ]        │
│  ┌─Scale each copy:──────┐ ┌─Rotate each copy:──────┐  │
│  │                       │ │ ⦿ Clockwise            │  │
│  │  Vertical  Horizontal │ │   Counter-   [0]       │  │
│  │  [100] %   [100] %    │ │ ○ clockwise     degrees│  │
│  └───────────────────────┘ └────────────────────────┘  │
│  ┌─Move each copy:───────┐ ┌─Scale and rotate around:─┐ │
│  │            ○ Left     │ │ ○ Upper left ○ Upper right│ │
│  │ [0.00] inches         │ │      ⦿ Center            │ │
│  │            ⦿ Right    │ │ ○ Lower left ○ Lower right│ │
│  │ ·············         │ └──────────────────────────┘ │
│  │ [0.00] inches ○ Up    │   ┌──────────┐ ┌──────────┐  │
│  │            ⦿ Down     │   │  Cancel  │ │    OK    │  │
│  └───────────────────────┘   └──────────┘ └──────────┘  │
└─────────────────────────────────────────────────────────┘
```

3. Enter the number of copies, and press the Tab key to enter vertical and then horizontal scaling percentages, number of degrees each copy is to be rotated, and horizontal and vertical movement factors.

   Rather than using the Tab key to move from text box to text box, you can double-click or drag across the text box you wish to highlight. To maintain the original proportions of the object, enter the same values for the horizontal and vertical scaling factors.

   You can also use the *Measure in* pop-up menu to change the units of measurement for the document.

4. Click the appropriate buttons to change the direction of rotation, the direction of horizontal and vertical movement, and the point on the object's bounding box around which the copies are scaled and rotated.

5. Click *OK*, or press Return or Enter, to close the dialog box and replicate the selected object or objects.

The selected object or objects are replicated, with each successive copy offset, scaled and rotated by the amounts specified in the dialog box. The last copy of each original object is selected.

Chapter 9: AutoTrace and SuperBits

This chapter describes two features that integrate the capabilities of the Paint layer and the Draw layer.

The AutoTrace command quickly traces bitmapped graphics in the Paint layer, producing polygons or Bezier objects in the Draw layer.

The SuperBits feature lets you create and edit *bitmapped objects*, combining the creativity and pixel-by-pixel control of the Paint layer with the smooth precision and shapes orientation of the Draw layer. In addition, clip art and scanned images can be edited as SuperBits objects.

Bitmapped Graphics and Objects

Paint-layer graphics consist of many dots, which are displayed on your monitor by its picture elements or pixels. Each dot of a graphic is represented in memory as a string of bits, and is said to be mapped to the display — hence the terms "bitmapped image" and "bitmapped graphic."

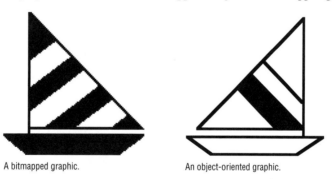

A bitmapped graphic.   An object-oriented graphic.

Draw-layer graphics are collections of mathematical shape descriptions. These graphics are referred to as "draw-type," "vector," "object-oriented" graphics, or simply as "objects." Since they are mathematically defined as outlines with fills, you can't edit objects one dot at a time, but you can easily resize or reshape them (while maintaining their resolution), make lines thicker or thinner, change fill patterns, and group them together to form larger objects.

There are advantages and disadvantages to both types of graphic:

- The Paint layer provides considerable control over details: the color of every single dot in the bitmapped image can be changed independently.

  However, bitmapped graphics don't include information that says "these dots are related." You may see a shape, but it is your eyes and brain doing the work. Thus, it can be difficult to select a "shape" in the Paint layer. And after the shape is deselected, you have to start all over to select it again.

  The dot-by-dot nature of the Paint layer also means you cannot print bitmapped graphics at a resolution higher than the resolution of the screen — 72 dots per inch — as the program has no means of knowing how you would want the additional dots placed or colored in each separate situation. In addition, enlarging bit-mapped graphics increases the saw-tooth effect (the "jaggies") found at their edges.

- Draw-layer graphics are individual entities: to select an object, you simply click it.

  Since the object shape is mathematically defined, it prints at the maximum resolution of any output device (meaning the "jaggies" are minimized, no matter how the object is scaled).

  The major disadvantage of object-oriented graphics is that they do not allow pixel-by-pixel editing. To change a portion of an object, you virtually have to recreate the whole object.

However, with the AutoTrace and SuperBits features, you can work with each pixel of your image in the Paint layer, and then, when it is exactly the way you want it, you can convert the image into object form to gain the advantages of the Draw layer. Or you can convert a Draw object into a bitmapped graphic and edit it dot by dot.

Note: Except in 1-bit documents, the Draw layer is always 32 bit. Therefore, in the Draw layer of 8-bit, 16-bit and 32-bit documents, you have access to nearly 16.8 million "true" colors. The discussions of bit depth and dithered colors pertain only to the Paint layer.

AutoTrace

The **AutoTrace** command traces each group of contiguous pixels of the same color within a selected area of the Paint layer, producing a separate, editable object for each in the Draw layer. The objects are outlined in black with an Area Fill of None; you can change the fills, the line thickness, and so on. The original image is not affected in any way.

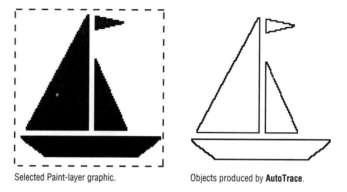

Selected Paint-layer graphic.   Objects produced by **AutoTrace**.

The groups of pixels traced and the type of objects produced by the **AutoTrace** command are affected by the settings in the AutoTrace Settings dialog box. Since **AutoTrace** can trace every distinct group of two or more pixels, complex images can require a great deal of time and produce a large number of small objects. You should give some thought to how much detail you want traced, use the AutoTrace Settings to optimize the tracing process, and perhaps pre-process the image (guidelines are provided later in the chapter).

Paint
Masking ▶
Fill Modes ▶
Paint Multiple
Brush Symmetry...
Airbrush Settings...

AutoTrace
AutoTrace Settings...
Create SuperBits...

Repeat Effect
Invert
Fill
Spatter
Trace Edges
Brightness & Contrast...
Color Balance...
Darken
Diffuse
Lighten
Pickup

To use **AutoTrace**:

1. Define a selection area in the Paint layer.

   Use any of the area Selection Tools (except the Two-Layer Selection tool). If an area has not been selected, the **AutoTrace** command is dimmed.

2. Choose **AutoTrace** from the Paint menu.

   Each group of pixels that meets the thresholds specified in the AutoTrace Settings dialog box is traced, producing an object in the Draw layer. Each object has an Area Fill of *None* and Line Widths of one pixel; all traced objects are selected when you switch to the Draw layer.

The Paint-layer selection can be deleted, dragged aside, or the Paint layer hidden so the original graphic doesn't interfere visually with the traced objects when you switch to the Draw layer, or print the image.

Note: Scanned images brought into SuperPaint are placed into the Draw layer. To AutoTrace them, you must first move them to the Paint layer. (Remember that when images are moved to the Paint layer, their resolution is 72 dpi.)

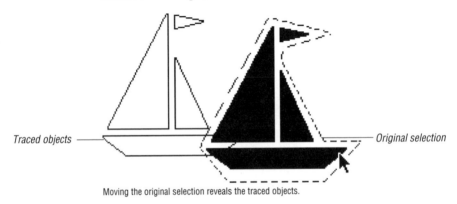

Traced objects ——————————— ————— Original selection

Moving the original selection reveals the traced objects.

AutoTrace Settings

Parameters for tracing the selected graphics are defined in the Auto-Trace Settings dialog box. If you simply select **AutoTrace** from the Paint menu, the existing settings are used.

To change the AutoTrace Settings:

1. Choose **AutoTrace Settings** from the Paint menu to display the AutoTrace Settings dialog box.

2. In the *Find objects at least* section, define a minimum height and width for groups of pixels.

Groups that do not meet these criteria will not be traced; larger values reduce the detail produced. Use the *and* and *or* buttons to further control the size of objects found. A group of pixels must be either the minimum height *and* width to be traced, or it must simply meet one *or* the other of the criteria.

3. Specify whether the traced objects are to be defined as polygons or by Bezier paths.

If you select *Polygons*, the tracing follows the edges of the pixel groups and results in objects defined by of straight lines. (The sliders in the *Beziers* section of the dialog box cannot be adjusted.)

Original Paint-layer graphic.

Traced to *Polygons*, with default *Find objects* settings of 5 pixels high or 5 pixels wide.

Traced to *Polygons*, with *Find objects* settings of 50 pixels high or 50 pixels wide.

Note that when tracing to *Polygons*, the jagged outline of each group of pixels is followed faithfully; use the **Reshape Polygon** or **Convert to Bezier** commands to smooth the objects.

Traced to *Beziers*, with the bottom slider set to *No Corners*.

Selecting *Beziers* activates the sliders in the *Beziers* section of the dialog box. Use the sliders to control how much smoothing is applied to the Bezier paths, and how closely the paths follow the outlines of the pixel groups. (Refer to Part 4, Chapter 8 for more information on Bezier curves.)

More Points per Line/Less Points per Line influences how many anchor points are used.

All Straight Lines/All Curves influences the mix of straight and curved segments in the traces.

Sharp Corners/No Corners determines the mix of smooth and hinge points. Selecting *No Corners* results in all smooth points; selecting *Sharp Corners* results in all hinge points.

4. Check *Outline only* if you wish to trace only the outlines of the selected graphic; groups of pixels completely enclosed are not traced.

   Outline only is available only in black-and-white (1-bit) documents.

5. Click *OK*, or press Return or Enter, to close the dialog box with the current settings.

   Click *Revert* to restore the original settings without closing the dialog box. Click *Cancel* to close the dialog box without changing the settings.

As with any polygonal or Bezier objects, the traced objects can be resized, the fills and the Line Widths changed, and they can be reshaped. Polygons can be converted to Bezier curves, and vice versa, with the **Convert to Bezier** and **Bezier to Polygon** commands in the Draw menu. Refer to Part 4, Chapter 8 for additional information.

Optimizing AutoTrace

AutoTrace is capable of very detailed tracing, which you will rarely need. For the best results, you should optimize the tracing process to achieve the detail you require, without producing an overwhelming number of objects and consuming more time than necessary. In addition to the control provided by the AutoTrace Settings, the following tips may help:

- Before tracing, you might "clean up" the image, deleting areas too detailed to trace, simplifying fills, and so on to reduce the number of small objects produced.

- Be sure to select only that portion of the document you want traced.

- You can trace individual sections of a complex image separately, optimizing the trace settings for each area. To rejoin the sections later, trace them as Bezier paths, or convert the polygons to Bezier paths, and then use the **Join Beziers** command from the Draw menu.

- AutoTrace produces a separate object for each color. In color documents, you can use the **Brightness & Contrast** and **Color Balance** commands before tracing to bring out certain image features, or posterize the image slightly to reduce subtle shadings.

- Tracing as polygons produces outlines that closely follow the shape of each group of pixels. A great many points are required to define the outlines, these objects can be difficult to reshape, and you may not require such detail. Bezier curves can be edited more extensively than polygons, but the tracing does not follow the shape of each group of pixels as closely. Thus, if you plan to edit the outlines extensively, tracing as Bezier curves may be more suitable. However, the straight-line composition of polygons may be preferable if you are using a non-PostScript printer.

SuperBits Objects

The SuperBits feature provides another means of producing a Draw graphic from a Paint graphic, increasing its resolution to match your output device, while retaining the ability to edit it pixel by pixel. In other words, the SuperBits feature allows you to combine the advantages of both layers.

In addition, the SuperBits feature is the basis of SuperPaint's image-processing and photomontage capabilities. Scanned photographs, sketches, and other images can be placed into the Draw layer as SuperBits objects and enhanced using all of SuperPaint's tools and commands.

Further, a SuperBits graphic can be exported as a TIFF or an EPS document to maintain the special effects of the graphic and the high resolution of the Draw layer in a format usable by other applications. Refer to Part 4, Chapter 3 for more information.

About Resolution

Computer images, whether on your monitor screen or the pages from your printer, are displayed as tiny dots. Different devices have dots that are different sizes. The term *resolution* refers to the number of dots a particular output device can fit into one inch.

For example, the Macintosh monitor resolution is 72 dots per inch (dpi), meaning that a single screen dot, or pixel, is $1/72$ inch in diameter. A single LaserWriter dot measures $1/300$ inch, since that printer's resolution is 300 dpi. (In these two instances, the horizontal and vertical resolution is the same, so only one figure is necessary.)

In the Paint layer, graphics are always 72 dpi because that is the resolution of the screen — you cannot "paint between the dots." At normal magnification, one pixel on the screen represents one dot in the image. (In magnified views, single dots are represented by blocks of pixels to allow easier viewing and manipulation.)

If the Paint-layer image is displayed on another, higher-resolution device, each dot is simply transferred or mapped to it, and $^1/72$ of an inch is occupied, regardless of the resolution of the device (the program has no way to determine how to "fill in" gaps).

Objects created in the Draw layer, however, are mathematical descriptions of shapes. As such, they can be displayed at the resolution of the device — on the monitor, represented by screen pixels, they are 72 dpi; on a LaserWriter they are printed at 300 dpi.

If a bitmapped image is moved into the Draw layer, it is converted into an object whose outline maintains the appearance of 72-dpi resolution, although potentially it can be output at any resolution. Since all bitmapped images are moved into the Draw layer as SuperBits objects, you can specify their resolution and edit them to take full advantage of higher resolution devices. (You can also increase the resolution of SuperBits objects by making them smaller.)

Bitmapped graphic, 72 dpi.

Edited 300-dpi SuperBits object.

Edited 1270-dpi SuperBits object.

Creating SuperBits Objects

All bitmapped images in the Draw layer are SuperBits objects. There are several ways to create a SuperBits object:

- Use the **Cut to Drawing** or **Copy to Drawing** commands in the Edit menu to move or copy the selected area from the Paint layer to the Draw layer as a SuperBits object.

- Paste a bitmapped image from the Clipboard into the Draw layer.

- Use the **Place** command in the Edit menu to place a bitmapped image produced by a scanner or another paint program into the Draw layer. Images can be scanned directly into SuperPaint (depending on the scanner plug-in module), or TIFF documents can be placed as SuperBits objects at the resolution at which they were scanned.

- Use the **Create SuperBits** command in the Paint menu to specify a resolution and copy the selected area in the Paint layer to the Draw layer as a SuperBits object.

- Duplicate an existing SuperBits object with the **Duplicate** or **Replicate** commands in the Edit menu.

You can set the resolution for a SuperBits object in the Create SuperBits dialog box, or by clicking the *SuperBits* button in the Object Info dialog box to display the SuperBits Info dialog box (both are described later).

You can edit a selected SuperBits object by choosing the **Edit SuperBits** command from the Draw menu. A SuperBits editing window opens on top of the active document window, and the SuperBits object is scaled so one screen pixel displays one dot from the object, regardless of the resolution of the object; this allows you to edit each dot individually. (Editing SuperBits objects is also described later in this chapter.)

Cut, Copy or Paste into the Draw Layer

When you move a bitmapped graphic from the Clipboard or directly from the Paint layer into the Draw layer, it becomes a SuperBits object:

- When there is a bitmapped image on the Clipboard and the Draw layer is active, choose the **Paste** command from the Edit menu. The image is pasted into the Draw layer as a 72-dpi SuperBits object.

- Select an area in the Paint layer and choose **Cut to Drawing** from the Edit menu. The selection is transferred to the Draw layer as a 72-dpi SuperBits object.

- Select an area in the Paint layer and choose **Copy to Drawing** from the Edit menu. The selection is copied to the Draw layer as a 72-dpi SuperBits object; the original selection remains in the Paint layer.

The resolution of these SuperBits objects can be changed by resizing or scaling them, or with the **Object Info** command, as described later in this chapter.

Placing an Image into the Draw Layer

Choose the **Place** command from the File menu to import an image into SuperPaint as a SuperBits object. The **Place** submenu includes options that allow you to import TIFF, EPS, StartupScreen and Mac-Paint documents. Other options depend on the image-acquisition plug-in modules in the SP Pouch folder. (If the plug-in provides the appropriate control, you can scan an image directly into SuperPaint as a SuperBits object. These plug-ins are usually provided by scanner manufacturers or third-party developers; refer to their documentation for more information.)

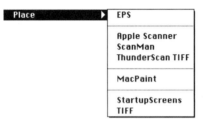

Choose **TIFF** from the **Place** submenu to import a 1-bit, 8-bit, or 24-bit TIFF document; the image can be at any resolution. Choose **Mac-Paint** to import a document in one of those formats; the image is placed into the Draw layer as a 72-dpi SuperBits object. (EPS images are placed as object-oriented graphics, not SuperBits objects.)

Note: The **Place** command is discussed in detail in Part 4, Chapter 3.

For example, to place a TIFF image as a SuperBits object:

1. Choose **TIFF** from the **Place** submenu of the File menu to display the Place TIFF dialog box.

```
┌─────────────────────────────────────────────────────────────┐
│  Place TIFF                                                   │
│  ─────────────────────────────────────────────────────────   │
│                      ┌─ My SuperPaint Graphics ─┐             │
│   ┌──────────────┐   │ ▯ dolphin. TIFF      ⇧ │   ▭ HD 100    │
│   │              │   │ ▯ map. TIFF            │               │
│   │              │   │                        │   ┌─────────┐ │
│   │              │   │                        │   │ Eject   │ │
│   │              │   │                        │   └─────────┘ │
│   │              │   │                        │   ┌─────────┐ │
│   │              │   │                        │   │ Drive   │ │
│   └──────────────┘   │                        │   └─────────┘ │
│  □ Image Preview     │                      ⇩ │   ┌─────────┐ │
│  ┌ Size in. ──────┐                              │ Cancel  │  │
│  │  Width:        │   ⊠ TIFF                     └─────────┘  │
│  │  Height:       │   ⊠ ThunderScan              ┌─────────┐  │
│  │     DPI:[    ] │   □ Digital Darkroom Archive │ Place   │  │
│  └────────────────┘                              └─────────┘  │
└─────────────────────────────────────────────────────────────┘
```

2. Use the *Drive* button, the pop-up menu, and the scroll bars to find and highlight the TIFF file you want to place.

    Click *Image Preview* to see a "thumbnail" preview of the image.

3. Click *OK*, or press Return or Enter, to close the dialog box.

The TIFF image is centered in the Draw layer of the active document window as a single SuperBits object. Its resolution matches the resolution of the document from which it was imported. If it is a color image, its bit depth changes to match the document into which is placed. For example, if you place a 24-bit image into an 8-bit document, the image is converted to an 8-bit image; that is, the image is dithered. Conversely, if you place an 8-bit image into a 24-bit document, the image is converted to 24 bits. The appearance of the image does not change; however, you will be able to use more colors when editing. (One-bit images remain black and white.)

The Create SuperBits Command

The **Create SuperBits** command in the Paint menu lets you copy a Paint-layer selection into the Draw layer, creating a SuperBits object at the resolution you specify.

To use the **Create SuperBits** command:

1. Use any of the area Selection Tools (except the Two-Layer Selection tool) to define a selection in the Paint layer.

    Any blank space included in the selection area becomes part of the SuperBits object. Minimize processing time and memory requirements for the SuperBits object by excluding as much "white space" as possible (the Lasso is often the best selection tool to use).

2. Choose **Create SuperBits** from the Paint menu to display the Create SuperBits dialog box.

```
┌──────────────────────────────────────────────────────────────┐
│  Create SuperBits                                              │
│  ══════════════════════════════════════════════════════════   │
│  ┌─Horizontal ──────────────┐  ┌─Vertical ──────────────┐     │
│  │  ○ 72 (Screen)           │  │  ○ 72 (Screen)         │     │
│  │  ○ 144 (ImageWriter)     │  │  ○ 144 (ImageWriter)   │     │
│  │  ○ 216 (ImageWriter LQ)  │  │  ○ 216 (ImageWriter LQ)│     │
│  │  ● 300 (LaserWriter)     │  │  ● 300 (LaserWriter)   │     │
│  │  ○ 360 (StyleWriter)     │  │  ○ 360 (StyleWriter)   │     │
│  │                          │  │                        │     │
│  │  ○ Other: │ 300 │  dpi   │  │  ○ Other: │ 300 │  dpi │     │
│  └──────────────────────────┘  └────────────────────────┘     │
│  ☐ Resize to match resolution                                 │
│  ☐ Smooth (300 dpi, B & W only)    ┌────────┐ ┌──────────┐    │
│  ○ Black & White  ● Color          │ Cancel │ │    OK    │    │
│                                     └────────┘ └──────────┘    │
└──────────────────────────────────────────────────────────────┘
```

3. Specify a horizontal and a vertical resolution for the SuperBits object.

    Click the appropriate resolution buttons, or type a horizontal value in the highlighted *Other* text box, press Tab, and type a vertical value.

    You can specify any resolution up to 3000 by 3000 dpi. However, setting the resolution above that of the intended output device will not change the appearance of the image, while its memory requirements and processing time will increase.

Note: Horizontal and vertical resolution are set separately. Specifying two different values may cause distortion of the image.

4. Select from the options available in the lower left portion of the dialog box.

    Select *Resize to match resolution* if you want the graphic resized according to its new resolution (refer to "Size and Resolution" later in this chapter for a discussion of this process). The SuperBits object will be smaller or larger than the original; if smaller, its edges will be smoother, requiring less editing, than if the object was not resized (although this may not be apparent on your screen).

If you have specified a black-and-white SuperBits object, and 300 by 300 dpi, you can also select the *Smooth* option. SuperPaint will then automatically add pixels to smooth the jagged edges of the SuperBits object, saving you some editing.

Select *Black & White* instead of *Color* to save memory and processing time if you are creating a black-and-white SuperBits object in a color document. This option is unavailable in black-and-white documents.

5.   Click *OK*, or press Return or Enter, to close the dialog box.

The SuperBits object is created in the Draw layer, with the upper left corner of its bounding box in the same location as the upper left corner of the bounding box of the selection area in the Paint layer. If *Resize to match resolution* was not selected, or if you specified 72 dpi for the horizontal and vertical resolution, the SuperBits object will be exactly beneath the Paint-layer selection area. Resized objects may be wholly or partially visible.

Unless you will need the Paint-layer selection again, delete it before switching to the Draw layer so it doesn't interfere visually with the SuperBits object.

Paint-layer graphic (72 dpi).

SuperBits object created at 300 dpi and smoothed; *Resize to match resolution* was not selected.

Paint-layer graphic (72 dpi).

SuperBits object created at 150 dpi, and resized to match resolution.

Changing SuperBits Resolution

You can change the resolution of the selected SuperBits object at any time by:

- Resizing the object by dragging its handles.

- Resizing the object by choosing the **Scale Selection** or **Stretch** commands from the Transform menu (described in Part 4, Chapter 7).

- Choosing the **Object Info** command from the Draw menu to display the Object Info dialog box, and then clicking the *Super-Bits* button to display the SuperBits Info dialog box. (You can open the SuperBits Info dialog box at any time to check the resolution of the selected SuperBits object.)

The Object Info Dialog Box

The Object Info dialog box lets you change the selected object's location, rotation, size, and the units of measurement for the active document. The Object Info dialog box also provides access to the SuperBits Info dialog box, in which you can check and change the resolution of the selected SuperBits object.

To change the resolution of the selected SuperBits object:

1. Choose **Object Info** from the Draw menu to display the Object Info dialog box.

2. Click the *SuperBits* button to display the SuperBits Info dialog box.

   The button is dimmed if the selected object is not a SuperBits object.

```
┌─────────────────────────────────────────────────┐
│ SuperBits Info                                  │
│ ┌─Horizontal ────────┐  ┌─Vertical ───────────┐ │
│ │ ◉ 72 (Screen)       │  │ ◉ 72 (Screen)        │ │
│ │ ○ 144 (ImageWriter) │  │ ○ 144 (ImageWriter)  │ │
│ │ ○ 216 (ImageWriter LQ)│ ○ 216 (ImageWriter LQ)│ │
│ │ ○ 300 (LaserWriter) │  │ ○ 300 (LaserWriter)  │ │
│ │ ○ 360 (StyleWriter) │  │ ○ 360 (StyleWriter)  │ │
│ │ ○ Other: [ 72 ] dpi │  │ ○ Other: [ 72 ] dpi  │ │
│ └────────────────────┘  └─────────────────────┘ │
│ ☐ Resize to match resolution                    │
│                          ┌────────┐ ┌────────┐  │
│ ○ Black & white ◉ Color  │ Cancel │ │   OK   │  │
│                          └────────┘ └────────┘  │
└─────────────────────────────────────────────────┘
```

3. Specify a new horizontal and vertical resolution for the SuperBits object.

   Click the appropriate resolution buttons, or type a horizontal value in the highlighted *Other* text box, press Tab, and type a vertical value.

   You can specify any resolution up to 3000 by 3000 dpi. However, setting the resolution above that of the intended output device will not change the appearance of the image, while its memory requirements and processing time will increase.

Note: Horizontal and vertical resolution are set separately. Specifying two different values may cause distortion of the image.

4. Select from the options available in the lower left portion of the dialog box.

   Select *Resize to match resolution* if you want the graphic resized according to its new resolution (refer to "Size and Resolution" later in this chapter for a discussion of this process). The Super-Bits object will be smaller or larger than the original; if smaller, its edges will be smoother, requiring less editing, than if the object was not resized (although this may not be apparent on your screen).

   Select *Black & White* instead of *Color* to save memory and processing time if this is a black-and-white SuperBits object in a color document. This option is unavailable in black-and-white documents.

5. Click *OK*, or press Return or Enter, to close the SuperBits Info dialog box.

6. Click *OK*, or press Return or Enter, to close the Object Info dialog box.

The resolution of the selected SuperBits object is changed as specified. If the *Resize to match resolution* option is selected, the size of the object is reduced or increased to reflect the increase or decrease in resolution. (The upper left corner of the bounding box does not move when the size of an object is changed.)

Original SuperBits object at 72 dpi.

The resolution of the SuperBits object was changed to 144 dpi, and the object resized.

Size and Resolution

Generally, when a SuperBits object is resized to match its resolution, the object is made smaller or larger by moving its dots closer together or further apart. For example, changing the resolution of an object from 72 dpi to 300 dpi means squeezing the dots closer together so 300 fit into one inch. Thus, one pixel on the screen may represent many dots in the object. Conversely, changing the resolution from 300 dpi to 72 dpi means moving the dots further apart so only 72 occur each inch. In both cases, the number of dots used to represent the object does not change.

SuperBits object at 72 dpi, (displayed in the Draw layer at normal magnification).

Object displayed in the SuperBits editing window (described in a subsequent section) at normal magnification — one pixel displays one object dot.

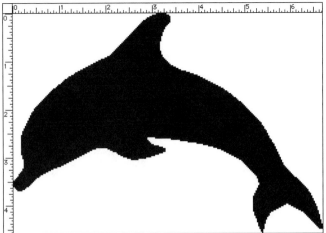

Resolution increased to 144 dpi, but the object was not resized (displayed in the Draw layer at normal magnification).

Object (144 dpi) displayed in the SuperBits editing window at normal magnification — one pixel displays one object dot. Notice the difference in size compared to the illustration on the previous page.

Similarly, when you change the size of a SuperBits object, either with the **Scale Selection** or **Stretch** commands, or by dragging its handles, its resolution is changed in the same manner.

However, when you create a new SuperBits object with the **Create SuperBits** command, or when you open the SuperBits Info dialog box from the Object Info dialog box, you can elect to maintain the original size of the object while changing its resolution. Changing the resolution of a SuperBits object this way does change the number of dots used to represent the object: when increasing the resolution, dots are added between existing dots; when decreasing resolution, dots are removed.

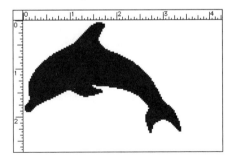

Resolution increased to 144 dpi, and the object was resized (displayed in the Draw layer at normal resolution).

Object (144 dpi, resized) displayed in the SuperBits editing window at normal magnification — one pixel displays one object dot. Compare to the previous illustrations.

Note: When increasing resolution, outlines and other border areas do not look dramatically different until the SuperBits object is edited and the borders smoothed.

Editing a SuperBits Object

When a SuperBits object is selected, the Reshape command in the Draw menu becomes the **Edit SuperBits** command.

Draw

Bring to Front	⌘=
Send to Back	⌘-
Group	⌘G
Ungroup	⌘U
Lock	
✓Unlock	
Align Objects...	⌘M
Object Info...	⌘I
Edit SuperBits	⌘R
Convert to Bezier ▶	
Bezier to Polygon ▶	
Join Beziers	
Bezier Settings...	

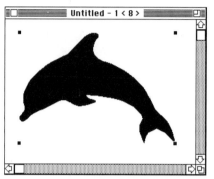

SuperBits object selected in the Draw layer.

To edit the selected SuperBits object:

1. Choose **Edit SuperBits** from the Draw menu (or use the Command-R shortcut).

    The SuperBits editing window appears on top of the active document window; only the SuperBits object is displayed. The object is expanded (or contracted if its resolution is less than 72 dpi) so one pixel displays one dot at normal magnification.

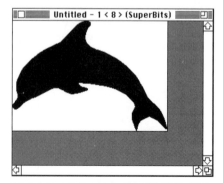

Selected object displayed in the SuperBits editing window.

Note: If the monitor bit depth does not match the document bit depth, or the document is not 1 bit, the program will not display white lines between pixels in magnified view.

2. Alter the SuperBits object — smooth outlines, change fills, and so on.

Most of the commands and all of the tools in both layers are available for use when editing the object. However, anything in the Draw layer of the SuperBits editing window is stamped to the Paint layer when the window is closed.

You can easily edit the SuperBits object pixel by pixel, as with normal Paint-layer graphics, at increased levels of magnification. (Editing a SuperBits object most commonly involves filling in the saw-tooth "jaggies" to smooth the outline of the object.)

SuperBits object as created.

SuperBits object after editing.

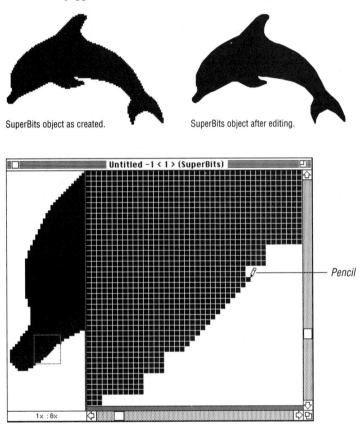

Pencil

Smoothing an edge with the Pencil in a magnified view of the SuperBits editing window.

3. To close the SuperBits editing window, choose **Close SuperBits** from the File menu, use the Command-W shortcut, or click the close box in the title bar of the editing window.

If you altered the SuperBits object, a dialog box appears asking if you want to save the changes.

```
Save changes to the SuperBits
object?

    Yes

    No              Cancel
```

4. Click *Yes*, or press Return or Enter, to close the SuperBits editing window and update the SuperBits object.

You are returned to the Draw layer of the active document.

Click *No* to close the window with no change to the SuperBits object; click *Cancel* to return to the SuperBits editing window.

SuperBits Editing with Limited Memory

SuperBits editing takes place in system memory (RAM), and depending on the object's size, resolution, and the amount of memory available in your system, it may not be possible to display the entire object in the SuperBits editing window. When this is the case, you can edit the object section by section.

When you choose **Edit SuperBits** and there is not enough memory available, the SuperBits Editing Area dialog box appears. A reduced view of the document and the SuperBits object is displayed in the dialog box. A selection frame of moving-dash lines, with handles at the corners, is displayed in the upper left corner of the reduced view.

The frame indicates how much of the object can be edited, based on available memory. Drag anywhere within the frame to position it over the portion of the object you want to edit.

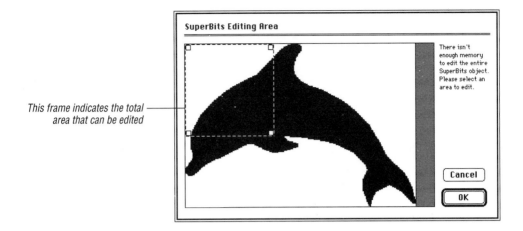

This frame indicates the total area that can be edited —

SuperBits Editing Area

There isn't enough memory to edit the entire SuperBits object. Please select an area to edit.

Cancel

OK

In addition, the handles at the corners of the frame can be dragged to reshape the frame; however, the total area enclosed cannot be increased. As you drag a handle in one direction, the frame automatically changes size in the other direction to enclose the largest possible editing area.

When you've framed the area you want to edit first, click *OK,* or press Return or Enter. The dialog box closes and the SuperBits editing window opens, with the selected area of the object displayed.

When you have completed editing the first portion of the object, close the SuperBits editing window and repeat the process, beginning with choosing **Edit SuperBits** from the Draw menu.

Chapter 10: SuperPaint Text

Using the Text tool to add text to a SuperPaint document was discussed in Part 4, Chapter 6. This chapter describes formatting the text.

Text and Fonts

In most respects, text is just like the other graphics in SuperPaint: Paint-layer text consists of bitmapped shapes, and a block of text in the Draw layer is an editable object. Text is filled with the current Area Fill, and selected and manipulated like any other graphic resident in either layer.

Natura   Natura

Paint-layer text.   Draw-layer text.

Yet text is also unique in that it is composed of shapes or characters taken from a predefined set or *font*. Further, this set of characters must be installed in your System for SuperPaint to access.

About Fonts

A bitmapped character.

A font is a set of characters of a specific typeface, such as Helvetica™ or Times,™ in a specific style, such as bold or italic, and of a specific size (10-point Times Italic is one font). This definition includes the collection of shape descriptions used by a machine to render a particular set of characters.

The category of Macintosh fonts can be separated into two types: bitmapped fonts and outline fonts. Each bitmapped font is a set of characters described in terms of blocks of dots. These fonts are used to display text on your monitor, and on pages printed by dot-matrix printers such as the ImageWriter. (Thus, the fonts are also called "screen" and sometimes "ImageWriter" fonts.)

An outline character is described by a Bezier path.

Outline fonts describe characters mathematically as scalable outlines that are independent of device resolution. These fonts are used by laser printers and imagesetters to print text. (In fact, any device that can interpret the outline descriptions can use the fonts.) Outline fonts are also referred to as "printer" fonts, and sometimes as "PostScript" fonts, because PostScript is commonly used to describe the outlines.

Thus, within SuperPaint, you could consider screen fonts to be Paint-layer fonts, and outline fonts to be Draw-layer fonts.

Using Available Fonts

Generally, character descriptions are transmitted from your Macintosh to your monitor or printer, as needed. This means that specific fonts must be installed in your System to be used. (Certain printers, such as the LaserWriter, have a small number of outline fonts resident in their memory. However, for fonts that are not resident and for devices that have no memory, the descriptions must be transmitted from the Macintosh.)

In the case of screen fonts, each specific typeface at each specific size must be installed in your System for the text on your screen to look good. Installed screen fonts can be enlarged or reduced to accommodate requests for a specific typeface in a size that is not installed; however, the appearance of enlarged characters will be poor. This is especially important in the Paint layer, since "what you see is what you get."

Left: Character displayed using an installed screen font (18 points).
Right: The same character enlarged to 54 points, which is not an installed size.

The list of typefaces displayed in SuperPaint's Font menu represents the screen fonts installed in your System. The corresponding outline fonts may or may not be available. If you are printing Draw-layer text to a laser printer or imagesetter, and a particular outline font is not present in the printer or in your System, another outline font is substituted, or the bitmapped approximation on the screen is used (producing characters with 72-dpi resolution).

Note: Apple's System 7.0 and TrueType™ are changing the way the Macintosh uses fonts. TrueType uses the same scalable outlines to produce both the characters on your screen and on the printed page, eliminating the need for two sets of the same font.

Formatting Text

The term *format* refers to the visual characteristics of a body of text, and includes collectively the settings or attributes of: typeface, type size, type style, text justification, and line spacing. There are two menus in SuperPaint that let you define these attributes. The Font menu displays a list of the typefaces installed in your system. The Text menu presents commands for specifying size, style, justification, and line spacing. (Justification refers to the horizontal alignment of rows of text, relative to some point in the document. Line spacing refers to the vertical distance between lines of text.)

You can choose format options from these menus before you start typing, and the subsequent text is formatted accordingly. You can also change the attributes of existing "active" text in the Paint layer, and existing "selected" text in the Draw layer. "Active" text is that which you are in the process of typing into the Paint layer. "Selected" text refers to: text in the Draw layer that you are in the process of entering, an existing text object that you clicked with the Selection Arrow, or text within an existing text object that you highlighted with the Text tool.

Formatting in the Paint Layer

The I-beam.

To enter text in the Paint Layer, select the Text tool from the Tools palette. When you move the pointer into the document window, it is represented by the I-beam (or text) cursor. Click to specify where you want to begin typing — a blinking vertical line known as the insertion point appears. Enter your text; press Return to begin a new line, and use the Delete or Backspace key as necessary to correct mistakes.

The insertion point ⌐

Magna est veritas|

Paint-layer text.

Note: You can use the Return and Backspace or Delete keys when entering text in the Paint layer; the arrow keys and the Tab key have no effect.

Formatting options chosen from the Font or Text menus affect the entire block of active text in the Paint layer unless you press Enter to "freeze" the text you've already typed. (Do not confuse the Return key with the Enter key; Return begins a new line.) Changes to text settings, Area Fill and Transfer Mode then affect only subsequent text. For example, you can change the type style in the middle of a phrase like this:

this is **bold** text

by typing:

this is [press Enter, choose **Bold** from the **Style** submenu of the Text menu] bold [press Enter, choose **Plain** from the **Style** submenu of the Text menu] text.

Keep in mind that you cannot edit the "frozen" text; pressing Delete or Backspace will not move the insertion point back past the point at which you pressed Enter.

As long as the insertion point is blinking, the current text is *active,* and you can edit the text and change its attributes. As soon as you select another tool from the Tools palette, or click the Text tool anywhere else in the document window, the text is deactivated and you can no longer edit it as text. It is "stamped" into the Paint layer, becoming bitmapped shapes.

Once deactivated, text in the Paint layer can be selected, moved, scaled, transformed, and otherwise manipulated like any other bitmapped graphics. If the Area Fill includes a gradient, the "elastic band" appears when the text is frozen or deactivated.

Note: When bitmapped graphics are transformed in color documents, they are automatically "anti-aliased" (pixels at the jagged edges are blended, producing a smoother appearance). This is particularly helpful when you use SuperPaint to give on-screen presentations or create slides with a film recorder.

Formatting in the Draw Layer

A text frame with insertion point.

To enter text in the Draw Layer, select the Text tool from the Tools palette. When you move the pointer into the document window, it is represented by the I-beam (or text) cursor. Click or drag to define a text frame. (Clicking produces a text frame one line tall that extends from the insertion point to a point one-half inch from the right edge of the document window. Dragging lets you create a frame of any height and width.) The insertion point appears within the text frame. Type your text; press Return to begin a new line, and use the Delete or Backspace key as necessary to correct mistakes.

Note: You can use Return, the arrow keys, and the Backspace or Delete key when entering text in the Draw layer. The keys Enter and Tab have no effect.

The height of the text frame
increases to accommodate
more lines.

As you type, the width of the frame remains constant, but its height increases to accommodate new lines of text. Text wraps to the next line automatically in the frame, or you can press Return to begin a new line.

When you're finished entering text, deselect the text frame by clicking another location in the document to create another text frame, or by selecting another tool from the Tools palette.

Filling Draw-Layer Text

Text in the Draw layer of a color document can be filled with a solid color, a solid texture, or a solid gradient; patterns cannot be used. In the Draw layer of a black-and-white (1-bit) document, text can be filled with a solid texture, a solid gradient, or a pattern (foreground and background color assignments can be made to the pattern). If the 1-bit document is converted to a color document, pattern fills are converted to solid grays. Transfer Modes cannot be assigned to Draw-layer text in any document.

Editing Draw-Layer Text

The changes you can make to Draw-layer text depend on how you select it. With the Text tool:

Verbum sat sapienti est.

Positioning the insertion point in
existing Draw-layer text.

- Click to position the insertion point anywhere in the existing text (the gray text frame reappears around the text block). Delete or add characters or words; the arrow keys can be used to move the insertion point.

Verbum sat sapienti est.

Individual words can be selected
for editing.

- Double-click a word to highlight it, or drag to highlight a phrase or block of text (the gray text frame reappears around the text block). You can change the style, size, and font, or you can cut, copy, and paste words or blocks of text.

Verbum sat sapienti est.

Text object selected with the
Selection Arrow.

Select text as an object by clicking it with the Selection Arrow to:

- Change the formatting of the entire block of text.

- Change the Area Fill.

- Move, group, copy, and transform the text object.

Draw-layer text can still be edited after being transformed. If an outline font was used, transformed text prints at high resolution on any PostScript printer.

Note: Changes to spacing and justification are applied to the entire text object, whether selected as text or as an object. Changes to the formatting of grouped text objects are applied to all the component text objects at once. But grouping does not create a single continuous text block: changing the line spacing for two grouped text objects may cause one to overlap the other.

Expanding and Fixed-Size Text Objects

A text object selected with the Selection Arrow has handles at the corners and a symbol centered on the top of its bounding box. The symbol (an arrow or a rectangle) indicates the type of text object: expanding or fixed. An expanding text object, indicated by the arrow, expands vertically as you add lines of text. A fixed-size text object, indicated by the rectangle, remains a constant size, and added lines will push text below the bottom edge of the bounding box. This hidden text is not lost and can be displayed by dragging a handle to enlarge the text object, or by converting the text object to the expanding type. To change a text object from one type to the other, click the symbol centered at the top of the object.

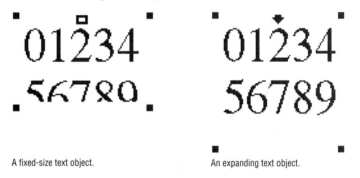

A fixed-size text object.   An expanding text object.

Superimposing a duplicate, fixed-size text object with a different Area Fill on the original text object.

Resizing Text Objects

You can resize either type of text object by dragging one of its handles with the Selection Arrow. Both the height and width of a fixed text object can be changed, while only the width of an expanding text object can be changed — its height is altered by "squeezing" the width. In both cases, the text re-wraps to accommodate the new line length. The size of the characters does not change when the object is resized with the Selection Arrow.

To resize a text object, select it and drag one of the handles.

The text reflows to fill the resized object.

Text objects also can be resized by means of the Object Info dialog box, the **Scale Selection** and **Stretch** commands in the Transform menu, and the **Replicate** command in the Edit menu. These methods change the size of the object as a graphic, so the size of the characters is changed also (with outline fonts, there is no loss of resolution when the characters are printed on a PostScript printer). This can be useful, for example, if you want to stretch a headline to fill a column without changing the font size.

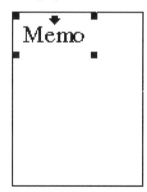

Text block in the Draw layer before stretching (on screen).

Text block after stretching (printed).

Copying and Pasting Draw-Layer Text

When you copy a selected text object to the Clipboard, it is copied as a text object. When you select text within a frame before copying, only the selected characters are copied to the Clipboard. Formatting and fill information is copied with the text.

If the Clipboard contains a text object, when you choose the **Paste** command, the text object is pasted into the Draw layer in the center of the document window (unless a text fame is active — a text object cannot be pasted into a text frame).

If the Clipboard contains selected text, you can paste it into the Draw layer into a new text object, or into an existing text frame. If a text frame is active when you choose **Paste**, the text is pasted into the text frame at the insertion point. The pasted text assumes the justification and line spacing of the text in the frame; it retains its own font, size and style. If no text frame is active when you choose **Paste**, a new text object is created in the center of the document window. If there is hidden text in the pasted selection, it becomes visible when pasted.

The Font Menu

Font
Chicago
Courier
✓Geneva
Helvetica
Monaco
Symbol
Times

The Font menu lists all the screen fonts (typefaces) installed in your system. To select a typeface for use in either layer, choose it from the Font menu. The currently selected typeface is checked in the menu.

The printer outline fonts that correspond to the screen fonts listed in this menu may or may not be installed. If you are printing to a Post-Script printer, and a font is used in the Draw layer for which there is no corresponding outline font, a similar outline font will be substituted if *Font Substitution* is selected in the LaserWriter Page Setup dialog box (refer to Part 4, Chapter 11 for more information). Otherwise, the bitmapped screen representation is used.

The appearance of text printed on an ImageWriter depends on a number of factors, including the print mode (*Faster* or *Best*) and the installed font sizes. ImageWriters reduce a large bitmapped font when printing to minimize distortion. For example, for best results when printing at *Best* quality to an ImageWriter, an installed screen font twice the size of the selected text should be available. When printing at *Best* quality to an ImageWriter LQ, an installed screen font size three times the size of the selected text should be available. Otherwise, another size will be scaled, with often noticeable character distortion. Refer to the ImageWriter user manual for more information.

Note: A multitude of fonts, as well as font management and font manipulation packages, are available from third-party sources. The appearance of your Font menu is undoubtedly different from the illustrations on these pages; this will not affect SuperPaint's text-handling capabilities.

The Text Menu

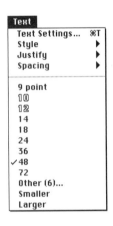

The Text menu lets you specify a type style and type size for the typeface chosen from the Font menu, as well as text-justification and line-spacing options.

Text Settings

The first command in the Text menu, **Text Settings**, displays a dialog box that lets you set all the text attributes at once: font, size, style, spacing, and justification. The dialog box also displays a text sample with the current settings.

To specify text attributes in the Text Settings dialog box:

1. Choose **Text Settings** from the Text menu (or press Command-T).

    The Text Settings dialog box appears.

```
Text Settings

Font:   [ Helvetica     ]   Spacing: [ Single   ]
Size:   [ 12 ] ▼ points     Justify: ◉ ▤  ○ ▤  ○ ▤
Type style:
⊠ Plain      ☐ Italic     ☐ Underline
☐ Bold       ☐ Outline    ☐ Shadow

[ The quick brown fox jumped over the lazy dog's back  ]
[ 1234567890 times.                                    ]
                                        [ Cancel ]
                                        [   OK   ]
```

2. Choose a typeface from the *Font* pop-up menu.

    The typefaces listed are the same as those displayed in the Font menu.

3. Select a line-spacing option from the *Spacing* pop-up menu.

The spacing options (*Single*, *1-1/2*, *Double*, and *Custom*) are the same as those found in the **Spacing** submenu of the Text menu, which is described in a subsequent section.

```
┌─────────────────────────────────────────────────────────┐
│  Text Settings                                           │
│  ─────────────────────────────────────────────────────   │
│                                    ┌─ ✓Single ──┐        │
│  Font:  [ Helvetica        ]  Spacing:│  1-1/2  ▲ │       │
│                                    │  Double    │  ○ ▤   │
│  Size:  [12  ] ▼ points    Justify:│  Custom (2 pt)│     │
│                                    ├────────────┤        │
│  Type style:                       │  Custom... │        │
│  ⊠ Plain    □ Italic    □ Underline└────────────┘        │
│  □ Bold     □ Outline   □ Shadow                         │
│  ┌─────────────────────────────────────────────┐        │
│  │ The quick brown fox jumped over the lazy dog's back   │
│  │ 1234567890 times.                             │        │
│  │                                               │        │
│  │                              ┌──────────┐     │        │
│  │                              │  Cancel  │     │        │
│  │                              └──────────┘     │        │
│  │                              ┌──────────┐     │        │
│  │                              │    OK    │     │        │
│  └──────────────────────────────└──────────┘────┘        │
└─────────────────────────────────────────────────────────┘
```

4. Choose a type size from the *Size* pop-up menu, or enter a size in the *Size* text box.

The pop-up menu contains the standard suite of sizes between 9 and 72 points; outlined numbers indicate screen fonts that are installed in your System. You can also type a number between one and 16,000 into the highlighted text box.

5. Select a justification option.

The justification options (*Left*, *Center*, and *Right*) are the same as those found in the **Justify** submenu of the Text menu, which is described in a subsequent section.

6. Select a type style.

Multiple styles can be selected; for example, *Bold*, *Italic*, and *Underline* can all be on at the same time. Selecting *Plain* turns off all other styles. The styles are described in more detail in the following section.

7. Click *OK*, or press Return or Enter, to close the dialog box and apply the current settings to active, or selected, and subsequently typed text.

Justification and spacing settings are applied to the entire block of text.

Style

You can select type styles in the Text Settings dialog box, or you can choose them from the **Style** submenu of the Text menu. There are six style commands in the submenu: **Plain, Bold, Italic, Underline, Outline,** and **Shadow.** These styles are independent of the font selection. This means, for example, that you can italicize an italic typeface.

```
Text
Text Settings...  ⌘T
Style            ▶   ✓Plain
Justify          ▶    Bold
Spacing          ▶    Italic
                      Underline
                      Outline
                      Shadow
```

You can apply more than one style to text at the same time:

Bold Italic   _Italic Outline_   _Italic Underline_

Styles that are "on" are checked in the menu. Choosing **Plain** turns off all other styles.

As an alternative to applying styles by choosing them from the **Style** submenu, you can use the following keyboard shortcuts:

Plain	Command-Shift-P
Bold	Command-Shift-B
Italic	Command-Shift-I
Underline	Command-Shift-U
Outline	Command-Shift-O
Shadow	Command-Shift-S

Like the submenu commands, the keyboard shortcuts switch styles on and off. For example, Command-Shift-B initiates text bolding. Pressing the key sequence again turns off the bolding. Style changes are applied to all "unfrozen" and subsequent text in the Paint layer. In the Draw layer, style changes are applied to all selected and subsequent text.

In the Paint layer, with the **Outline** and **Shadow** styles, the characters are filled with the current Area Fill, and the outlines and shadows are always black. In the Draw layer, if a color is selected as the Area Fill foreground, it is applied to the outlines and shadows, and the characters have no fill. If a texture or gradient is selected, the characters are filled, and the outlines and shadows are black. In both layers, the thickness of the outlines and shadows cannot be changed automatically.

Justify

There are three commands in the **Justify** submenu that let you define text alignment: **Left**, **Center**, and **Right**. In the Paint layer, text is aligned to the point first clicked with the Text tool. In the Draw layer, text justification occurs within the text frame.

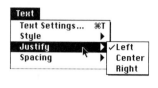

Entering right-justified text in the Draw layer (left), and the Paint layer (right). The insertion point represents the point first clicked in both cases.

You can use the following keyboard shortcuts to change text justification:

Left	Command-Shift-L
Center	Command-Shift-C
Right	Command-Shift-R

Spacing

Spacing is applied to the entire text block, rather than to selected lines or paragraphs only. Like font size, spacing is measured in points (one point equals $1/72$ of an inch). Normally, line spacing is 1 to 1.5 points larger than the current font size. Thus, the spacing that results from the commands in the **Spacing** submenu of the Text menu depends on the currently selected font size. For example, if you select a 10-point font and **Single** spacing, the distance between the bottom of the characters in two adjacent lines is approximately 11 points.

Single spacing.   One and one-half spacing.   Double spacing.

The **Custom** command displays the Custom Line Spacing dialog box, in which you specify a number of points (between one and 72) to be added to the single spacing for the current font size. (The current custom spacing is noted in parentheses after the **Custom** command.) For example, with the same 10-point font and a custom spacing of two points, the distance between the bottom of the characters in two adjacent lines is approximately 13 points.

Note: To apply the existing custom line spacing without opening the Custom Line Spacing dialog box, press Option while choosing **Custom** from the **Spacing** submenu.

Font Sizes

Text	
Text Settings...	⌘T
Style	▶
Justify	▶
Spacing	▶
9 point	
10	
12	
14	
18	
✓24	
36	
48	
72	
Other (6)...	
Smaller	
Larger	

You can define the point size of your text by choosing one of the standard sizes between 9 and 72 listed in the Text menu. You also can use the **Other**, **Smaller** and **Larger** commands to specify a custom font size. The currently selected size is checked in the menu.

The standard sizes listed as outline numbers are those screen fonts actually installed in your System. When you select another size, it is generated by the system from one of the installed fonts. The on-screen appearance of installed fonts is generally better than that of generated fonts. (There are applications available that let you enhance the appearance of generated screen fonts.)

Custom Font Sizes

The **Other** command displays the Other Font Size dialog box, in which you can specify a custom font size between one and 16,000 points. The current custom size is listed in parentheses next to the **Other** command.

Note: To select the current custom size without opening the Other Font Size dialog box, press Option while choosing **Other** from the Text menu.

The **Smaller** and **Larger** commands in the Text menu reduce or enlarge the currently selected font size by one point. Choose the commands from the Text menu, or use the keyboard shortcuts Command-Shift-> for **Larger** and Command-Shift-< for **Smaller**.

Chapter 11: Printing

This chapter describes printing SuperPaint images.

Note: The illustrations of the System-related dialog boxes in this chapter represent their appearance under System 6.0; their appearance under System 7.0 may be slightly different, but the options are the same and they work in the same manner.

Printing Guidelines

Printing your image is a simple operation, controlled by two commands: **Page Setup** and **Print**. With slight variations, these are the same commands and dialog boxes found in most Macintosh applications. Thus, printing from SuperPaint is similar to printing from other applications, especially if you follow these guidelines:

•   Be sure the correct printer is chosen.

    To select a printer, open the Chooser control window (choose **Chooser** from the Apple menu), click the icon for the appropriate type of printer, and select the name of the printer you want to use. Click the close box in the title bar to close the Chooser. Once a printer has been selected, it remains selected until you change it. (Refer to the Macintosh user manual for more information about the Chooser.)

Chooser control window.

Printing your images on an imagesetter, color printer, or slide maker is as simple as printing them on a LaserWriter. With the appropriate printer driver in your System folder, open the Chooser and select the device as you would any printer.

The type of printer currently chosen is displayed in the Document Info dialog box, as is the current paper size (choose **Document Info** from the File menu). If you print your image from another computer, make sure the correct printer is chosen.

• Be sure that the page orientation in the Page Setup dialog box is the same as the image orientation selected in the Document Info dialog box.

If you try to print a portrait image on a printer set up for landscape pages, a portion of your image will be printed on another page if the image is "taller" than the paper.

• If you're printing Draw-layer text to a PostScript® device such as a LaserWriter, be sure PostScript outline fonts ("printer" fonts) are available for printing. (Printing Draw-layer text on a laser printer with bitmapped fonts can result in loss of print quality.) If you're printing to an ImageWriter, use ImageWriter fonts or other bitmapped fonts that look good on the monitor screen. Refer to Part 4, Chapter 10 for additional information about fonts.

QuickDraw versus PostScript Printers

Most Macintosh output devices fall into two categories, according to the method of image rendering used: QuickDraw or PostScript. QuickDraw is screen based, and therefore QuickDraw printers are limited to bitmapped, 72-dpi output. As a result, for example, QuickDraw printers do not handle rotated text well. The ImageWriters are QuickDraw-based printers.

The PostScript language is a method of page description that is mathematically based, and independent of the resolution of the output device. Graphics and text are described by curves and straight lines, and can be transformed without loss of smoothness. LaserWriters and Linotronic™ imagesetters are examples of PostScript-based printers.

Note: Used in the Draw layer, the Transfer Modes display correctly on your monitor screen, and print correctly on QuickDraw printers, but do not print correctly on PostScript printers. This is a limitation of PostScript that may be remedied by a future version of the language. To work around this limitation, you can cut the appropriate objects to the Paint layer (with an attendant loss of resolution).

Note: When printing to PostScript printers, Draw-layer objects that have been assigned Transfer Modes other than Opaque will not print as they appear on your screen. To preview how such objects will look when printed, select all the objects, then choose Opaque from the Transfer Modes pop-up palette. If the effect you see is not satisfactory, cut all the selected objects to the Paint layer; they will then print with the assigned Transfer Mode(s) as they appear on your screen, but with a loss of resolution.

Setting Page Options

To change paper size, page orientation, and other specific printer options, choose **Page Setup** from the File menu. The contents of the Page Setup dialog box vary slightly, depending on the output device and printer driver you are using. (A printer driver is a file in the System folder that allows your Macintosh to work with a particular type of printer. The LaserWriter driver is used with many other laser printers and imagesetters.) The ImageWriter and LaserWriter Page Setup dialog boxes are described here.

Note: SuperPaint saves Page Setup settings with each document.

LaserWriter Page Setup dialog box.

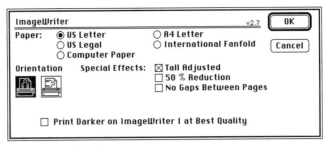

ImageWriter Page Setup dialog box.

Page Setup Options Common to ImageWriters and LaserWriters

A selection of paper sizes and a choice of orientations are found in both the ImageWriter and LaserWriter Page Setup dialog boxes.

Paper

The *Paper* option lets you choose from several paper sizes (according to the type of printer), including:

US Letter:	8.5 x 11 in.
US Legal:	8.5 x 14 in.
A4:	210 x 297 mm
Computer Paper:	11 x 14 in.
International Fanfold:	210 x 305 mm
B5:	176 x 250 mm
Tabloid	11 x 17 in.

Note: If you are using LaserWriter driver version 6.0, or later, with a printer that accommodates additional paper sizes, the *Tabloid* button is replaced by a pop-up menu that lists additional standard page sizes.

There is no relationship between page size and document size. The size of a SuperPaint document is the size of the area in which you can create and work on an image; document size is set in the Document Info dialog box (choose **Document Info** from the File menu). Paper size, or page size, is the size of the paper on which the document will be printed; paper size is specified in the Page Setup dialog box.

If your image is larger than the paper in the printer, SuperPaint automatically prints it on several pages in a process called "tiling." The pages can then be joined to form the complete image. The printing order for the pages is left to right, top to bottom.

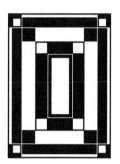

Oversize image.   Image printed on four pages.

The number of printer pages required by the current document is displayed in the Document Info dialog box.

Document Information

┌─ Document is... ─┐
- ⦿ **Black & White (1-bit)**   Measure in: [Inches]
- ○ Color: [8-bit]

┌─ Make the document... ─┐   Width: Height:
[Narrower] [Wider]   [16.00]   [21.50]   Pages: 4
[Shorter] [Taller]   Orientation: ⦿ Tall ○ Wide

Chosen printer: LaserWriter   [Cancel]   [OK]
Printer page: 8.00 x 10.78

Document Info dialog box.

Note: Most laser printers are physically incapable of printing on a strip approximately one-quarter of an inch around the edges of a page. Other printers may also have different print area restrictions; check your printer manual for more information.

Orientation

Portrait and landscape icons.

The *Orientation* option lets you specify whether the document is printed in portrait orientation, or in landscape. Tall (portrait) mode prints the image vertically on the paper; wide (landscape) mode prints the image horizontally on the paper. Click the appropriate icon.

Just as document size is independent of page size, print orientation is independent of the orientation of the document. If you print an 8 x 10 inch landscape document on a printer set up to print portrait pages on 8.5 x 11 inch paper, the document will be tiled, with the rightmost two inches of the image appearing on the second page. So, be sure the document orientation matches the printer page orientation.

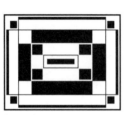

Original image.

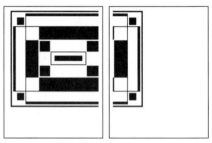

Pages printed with mismatched orientation.

ImageWriter-Only Page Setup Options

The options found only in the ImageWriter Page Setup dialog box are *Tall Adjusted*, *50% Reduction*, and *No Gaps Between Pages*. (The *Print Darker* option at the bottom of the dialog box is relevant only to early versions of the System software; selecting it has no effect.)

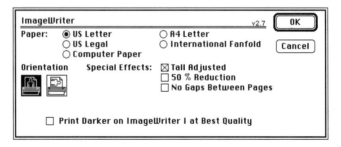

Tall Adjusted causes the printed image to be the same size as the screen image. Otherwise, when the option is off, the screen image is reduced 10% horizontally for printing. (ImageWriter resolution is 72 by 80 dpi; the reduction maintains image resolution.) The default setting is off.

The *50% Reduction* option scales your image to half size. The default setting is off.

No Gaps Between Pages begins printing at the top of the page, leaving no top margin. The default setting is off.

LaserWriter-Only Page Setup Options

The options found only in the LaserWriter Page Setup dialog box are *Reduce or Enlarge*, *Font Substitution*, *Text Smoothing*, *Graphics Smoothing*, and *Faster Bitmap Printing*.

```
┌─────────────────────────────────────────────────────────┐
│ LaserWriter Page Setup                    6.0    ┌──────┐ │
│ Paper: ⦿ US Letter  ○ A4 Letter                  │  OK  │ │
│        ○ US Legal   ○ B5 Letter  ○│ Tabloid │    └──────┘ │
│        Reduce or ┌───┐           Printer Effects: ┌────────┐│
│        Enlarge:  │100│%          ⊠ Font Substitution? │Cancel││
│                  └───┘           □ Text Smoothing?  └────────┘│
│        Orientation               □ Graphics Smoothing? ┌───────┐│
│        ┌──┐┌──┐                  ⊠ Faster Bitmap Printing? │Options││
│        └──┘└──┘                                      └───────┘│
│                                                      ┌──────┐│
│                                                      │ Help ││
│                                                      └──────┘│
└─────────────────────────────────────────────────────────┘
```

Reduce or Enlarge scales the image by the percentage entered (from 25% to 400%). For example, enter 50 to reduce the image to half its original size; enter 150 to enlarge the same image by half. If you enlarge the page so much that it will be tiled when it is printed, page breaks are shown on the screen. The default is 100% (normal size).

Font Substitution causes an outline (PostScript) font to be substituted for any screen font used in the Draw layer when the corresponding outline font is not installed. For example, Times replaces New York when a New York screen font was used in the document, but the New York outline font is not in the System. The default setting is on.

If *Font Substitution* is off, the text will be printed exactly as it appears on the screen (72 dpi), and the document will take longer to print. With *Font Substitution* on, outline fonts are always used to print Draw-layer text, the text will be 300 dpi, and the document will print more quickly. However, depending on the fonts, the text could take up more or less space on the page than on the screen.

Note: As a general rule, use only outline fonts when you intend to print Draw-layer text to PostScript devices such as the LaserWriter.

Text Smoothing causes smoothing of the edges of bitmapped characters to improve their appearance when printed on a LaserWriter. The default setting is off.

Without Text Smoothing.   With Text Smoothing.

Graphics Smoothing causes smoothing of the edges of all bitmapped graphics in your image. Generally this improves their appearance, but the graphics will not match exactly those on the screen, and they will take longer to print. Default is off.

Without Graphics Smoothing.   With Graphics Smoothing.

Faster Bitmap Printing speeds the printing of bitmapped images by increasing the data transmission rate; however, some documents may not print. Default is on.

Important Note: If you are having a problem printing a SuperPaint document, turn off *Faster Bitmap Printing,* turn your printer off and then back on, and try printing again.

Additional LaserWriter Options

The LaserWriter Page Setup dialog box also contains an *Options* button and a *Help* button. The *Help* button opens an information box that contains brief descriptions of the LaserWriter options (similar to those found here). The *Options* button opens the LaserWriter Options dialog box, containing six additional options.

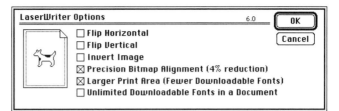

LaserWriter Options dialog box.

Original icon.   Flip Horizontal.

Flip Horizontal – when this option is selected, a mirror image of the document is printed (the image is flipped about its vertical axis: the left side becomes the right, and vice versa). The default setting is off.

Flip Vertical.

Flip Vertical – when this option is selected, an upside-down version of the image is printed (the document is flipped about its horizontal axis: the top becomes the bottom, and vice versa). The default setting is off.

Invert Image.

Invert Image – when this option is selected, a negative image is printed (i.e., blacks are printed as whites, and whites are printed as blacks). The default setting is off.

Precision Bitmap Alignment – when this option is selected, the image is shrunk four percent to prevent banding or a checkerboard pattern (known as a moiré pattern) in the printed image. This pattern is caused when the resolution of the image is not evenly divisible into the resolution of the output device (a 72-dpi image on a 300-dpi LaserWriter, for instance). Default is on.

The DogCow is slightly smaller

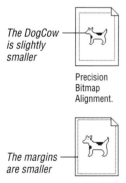

Precision Bitmap Alignment.

Note: To ensure that the measurements of the screen and printed images match, you should also select the *Measurements match Precision Bitmap Alignment* option on the Miscellaneous Settings page of the Preferences dialog box.

The margins are smaller

Larger Print Area.

Larger Print Area (Fewer Downloadable Fonts) – when this option is selected, some of the printer memory set aside for fonts is used for the image, allowing a larger image area on the page (within the physical limits of the printer). If a number of non-printer-resident fonts are used in the document, it will print more slowly if this setting is on. The default setting is on.

Unlimited Downloadable Fonts in a Document – if a number of non-printer-resident fonts are used in the document, turn on this option to set aside additional printer memory for the fonts. However, the document will take longer to print. The default setting is off.

Printing

To actually print an image on the currently chosen device, choose the **Print** command from the File menu to display the Print dialog box. The contents of the Print dialog box vary slightly, depending on the output device and the printer driver you are using. The ImageWriter and LaserWriter Print dialog boxes are described here. (The Laser-Writer driver is used with many other laser printers and imagesetters.)

To print the active document:

1. Choose **Print** from the File menu to display the Print dialog box.

   Be sure the correct printer is selected in the Chooser: the name of the current printer is shown at the top of the Print dialog box.

2. Select the options, described in the following sections, that you require.

3. Click *OK*, or press Return or Enter, to begin printing.

   To close the Print dialog box without printing, click *Cancel*.

   To abort printing in progress, press Command-period.

1	2	3
4	5	6
7	8	9

Tiling order.

The upper left corner of your document is positioned in the upper left corner of the page (i.e., the image is not centered on the page). If your document is too big to print on one page, it is tiled (printed over several pages) in the order shown at left.

Print Options Common to ImageWriters and LaserWriters

The following options are found in both the ImageWriter and the LaserWriter Print dialog boxes.

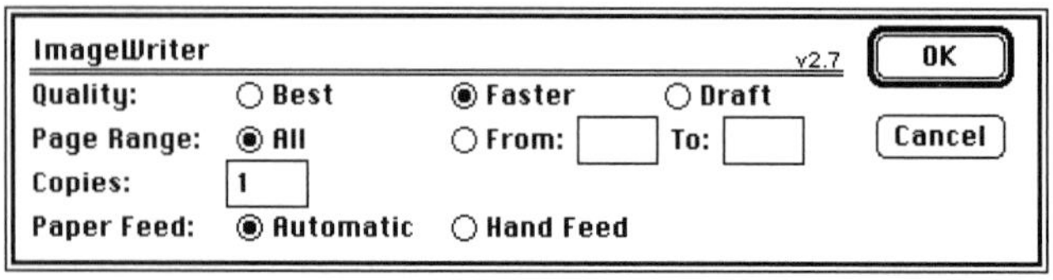

ImageWriter dialog box.

```
┌─────────────────────────────────────────────────────────────┐
│ LaserWriter "Marketing"                        6.0  ┌───────┐│
│                                                     │  OK   ││
│ Copies: 1        Pages: ◉ All  ○ From: [    ] To: [  ]└──────┘│
│                                                     ┌───────┐ │
│ Cover Page:  ◉ No ○ First Page  ○ Last Page        │Cancel │ │
│                                                     └───────┘ │
│ Paper Source: ◉ Paper Cassette  ○ Manual Feed      ┌───────┐ │
│                                                     │ Help  │ │
│ Print:       ◉ Color/Grayscale ○ Black & White     └───────┘ │
│                                                              │
│ Printer Type: ◉ Black & White    ○ Color                    │
└─────────────────────────────────────────────────────────────┘
```

LaserWriter dialog box.

Copies

The *Copies* option lets you specify the number of copies to be printed. Enter a number from one to 999; the default is one.

Pages

Labeled *Page Range* in the ImageWriter Print dialog box, this option lets you print all or part of an image that covers several pages.

If you enter a number in the *From* text box and leave the *To* text box blank, SuperPaint prints from the specified page to the end of your document. If you enter a number in the *To* text box and leave the *From* text box blank, SuperPaint prints from the first page through the specified page.

Paper Source

Labeled *Paper Feed* in the ImageWriter dialog box, this option lets you select how the paper will enter the printer: continuous or single-sheet feed. Select *Automatic* if you are using fanfold paper or an automatic cut-sheet feeder with an ImageWriter, or select *Paper Cassette* for automatic feed from the LaserWriter paper tray.

To feed paper by hand, one sheet at a time, select *Hand Feed* or *Manual Feed*; you will be prompted for each sheet. For paper such as letterhead and heavy stock, you may want to feed the pages singly.

ImageWriter-Only Print Options

The ImageWriter Print dialog box has only one exclusive option. The *Quality* option lets you select print quality from the *Best*, *Faster*, and *Draft* buttons.

```
┌────────────────────────────────────────────────────────┐
│ ImageWriter                            v2.7  ┌────────┐ │
│ Quality:      ○ Best      ◉ Faster   ○ Draft │   OK   │ │
│ Page Range:   ◉ All       ○ From: ▢   To: ▢  └────────┘ │
│ Copies:       ▢ 1                            ┌────────┐ │
│ Paper Feed:   ◉ Automatic ○ Hand Feed        │ Cancel │ │
│                                              └────────┘ │
└────────────────────────────────────────────────────────┘
```

Best quality provides the darkest output with the best detail possible, but prints slowly. *Faster* quality provides an acceptable image, and prints more quickly. *Draft* quality is for text only, and is not supported by SuperPaint.

Note: ImageWriters reduce large bitmapped fonts when printing text to minimize distortion of the characters. For example, at *Best* quality, the ImageWriter requires a bitmapped font twice the size of the selected text. Be sure the appropriate fonts are installed in your System.

LaserWriter-Only Print Options

There are four options exclusive to the LaserWriter Print dialog box: *Cover Page* options, *Print* image type, a *Printer Type* option, and a *Help* button.

```
┌────────────────────────────────────────────────────────┐
│ LaserWriter  "Marketing"                6.0  ┌────────┐ │
│ Copies: ▢1          Pages: ◉ All ○ From: ▢   │   OK   │ │
│                              To: ▢           └────────┘ │
│ Cover Page:   ◉ No ○ First Page ○ Last Page  ┌────────┐ │
│ Paper Source: ◉ Paper Cassette ○ Manual Feed │ Cancel │ │
│ Print:        ◉ Color/Grayscale ○ Black & White └─────┘ │
│ Printer Type: ◉ Black & White   ○ Color  ┌────────┐     │
│                                          │  Help  │     │
│                                          └────────┘     │
└────────────────────────────────────────────────────────┘
```

Cover Page

The three *Cover Page* buttons allow you to select *No* cover page, or an informative cover page can be printed as the *First Page* or the *Last Page*. The cover page contains the user name (from the Chooser), the document name, the date, and the time. The default setting is *No*.

The Print Option

This option causes PostScript printers to use a smooth range of half-tone grays to depict an image, rather than dithering black and white. The appearance of color and gray-scale images is improved, but printing takes longer.

Select *Color/Grayscale* when printing a color or gray-scale image on a PostScript printer.

Select *Black & White* when printing black-and-white documents. Printing a color or gray-scale document on a LaserWriter or an imagesetter with *Black & White* selected will cause posterization.

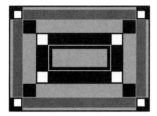

Gray-scale image printed with
Color/Grayscale selected.

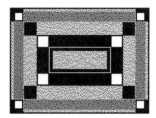

Same image printed with *Black & White* selected.

Printer Type

When printing a color document on a black-and-white PostScript device, such as a LaserWriter, the colors are converted to shades of gray. Normally, this task is performed by the printer; however, to speed printing, SuperPaint performs the conversion. When printing to a device that is capable of printing in color, select *Color* for this option to prevent the conversion.

The Help Button

Click the *Help* button to display an information box that briefly explains the LaserWriter Print options and manually feeding paper into the printer.

Destination

If you are operating under System 7.0, the dialog box includes a *Destination* option. Changing the *Destination* to *PostScript File* causes the PostScript commands necessary to print the active document to be saved, rather than being transmitted to the printer. A standard dialog box lets you name and specify a location for the file.

Note: You can use Command-period to stop printing at any time.

Part 5: Tips & Techniques

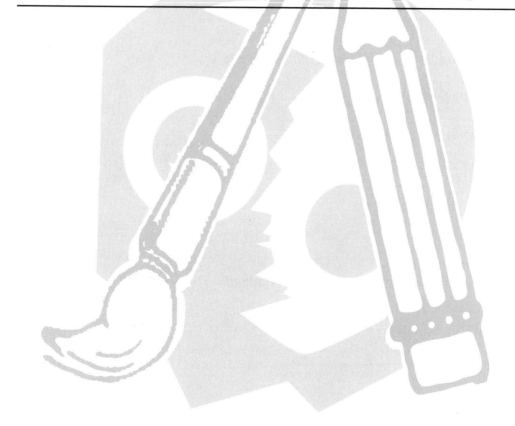

Tips & Techniques

This section contains simple techniques to help you achieve effects like drop shadows or broken shadows, as well as more sophisticated techniques for painting with custom textures. The descriptions assume you already have a degree of familiarity with the Macintosh and with SuperPaint 3.0.

Simple Drop Shadows

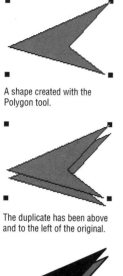

A shape created with the Polygon tool.

The duplicate has been above and to the left of the original.

The final drop shadow is complete.

There's a quick and easy way to create simple drop shadows in the Draw layer. You can also use this technique with shapes created in the Paint layer and cut to the Draw layer, or with images imported into SuperPaint with the **Place** command.

As an example, let's create a basic shape in the Draw layer, then add a drop shadow. From the Colors palette, select a medium gray as the current Area Fill (on black-and-white machines, select a medium gray pattern from the Patterns palette), and select 1 pt. for the Line Width. Make sure Opaque is selected as your current Transfer Mode.

1. Use the Polygon tool to create a simple shape.

   It's filled with the medium gray; this will be the "shadow."

2. Choose **Duplicate** from the Edit menu, or press Command-D.

   A duplicate of your shape is created, offset slightly lower and to the right of the original.

3. Use the Selection Arrow to move the duplicate so that it's offset slightly above and to the left of the original.

   All that's left is to fill the duplicate with another color, gradient, or texture.

4. Make sure the duplicate is still selected, then select as your current Area Fill the color, gradient, or texture you'd like to use as the fill for the object casting the shadow.

   The duplicate is filled with your new Area Fill and the drop shadow effect is complete.

Painting Gradients on Black-and-White Images

Using one of SuperPaint's gradient fills and the **Paint on Darker** command in the Paint menu, you can add some razzle-dazzle to black-and-white images — without masking, and without painstaking, time-consuming detail work. Once you've selected the appropriate settings, this effect can be applied in the time it takes to choose a menu command.

To try this technique, you need a black-and-white image to work on; any piece of clip art will do.

1. Open the image in the Paint layer and select it, using any of the Selection tools.

The original image.

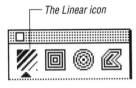

The Linear icon

2. Select a gradient from the Gradients palette on the Line & Fill palette.

    This example uses the "rainbow" gradient because the effect is quite striking, however a black-and-white gradient works equally well. Select the *Linear* icon from the top of the Gradients palette.

    Note: In color documents, SuperPaint's Custom Gradients dialog box allows you to create your own gradients, which you can store and use. For more information on custom gradients, see Part 4, Chapter 4.

3. Choose **Paint on Darker** from the Fill Modes submenu in the Paint menu.

    When you use **Paint on Darker**, the fill you apply is visible only on areas darker than itself. If there is nothing darker in the selection or document, you will see no change.

    Note: When using this technique with an object on a background, first select the object and mask it by choosing **New Mask** in the Masking submenu of the Paint menu. Then choose **Invert Mask**, and your background will not be affected. For more information on masking, see Part 4, Chapter 4.

    Now you're ready to apply the gradient to your image. The image should still be selected, since all graphics are selected when they are pasted down. If it's not, select it using any of the selection tools.

4. Choose **Fill** from the Paint menu. An elastic band stretches from the cursor to the image so you can choose the direction of your gradient fill. Position the cursor in the direction you want the gradient to go, and click.

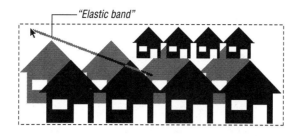

"Elastic band"

The black pixels in your image are now filled with a gradient.

Note: You can achieve detailed colorizing effects using the Paint on Darker Transfer Mode when applying paint with any of the brush tools. For example, use the Paint Brush to apply gradient enhancements only where you want them on your black-and-white image.

This technique makes it easy to create poster-type effects on any black-and-white image. When using one-color gradients, you can enhance the effect of any shadows that may appear on your image by directing the gradient ramp toward the supposed "light source."

For color machines

Creating a Glow Effect

Using one of SuperPaint's gradients and *Paint on Darker* from the Transfer Modes menu, you can create a "halo" around an object of almost any shape. The result is that your image seems to emit a "glow."

If you have access to some clip art, browse through it and locate a suitable picture. For this example, we're going to use an image of the planet Saturn.

1. Start with a bitmapped image in the Paint layer of a new document. Make sure it is deselected.

The original image.

The Circular icon —

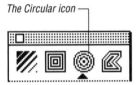

2. Select a gradient from the Gradients palette. This example uses a custom black-to-blue gradient because of the eerie "glow" it creates in an outer-space context. Select the Circular icon from the Gradients palette to specify gradient type.

    Note: In color documents, SuperPaint's Custom Gradients dialog box allows you to create your own gradients, which you can store and use. For more information on custom gradients, see Part 4, Chapter 4.

3. Choose *Paint on Darker* from the Transfer Modes palette and set the Line Fill to *None*.

    When you use **Paint on Darker**, the fill you apply is visible only on areas darker than itself. If there is nothing darker in the selection or document, you will see no change.

4. Double-click the Rectangle tool to activate its Draw-from-Center mode. Now, instead of starting to draw a rectangle from the corner, the rectangle you create will be drawn from its center outward.

    You're ready to apply the effect.

5. Place the pointer on the center of your image (in this case, the center of Saturn) and draw a rectangle to the edges of the document window (or as far as you want the halo effect to appear).

6. When you release the mouse button, the elastic band that stretches from the cursor to the image lets you choose the direction of your blue gradient fill. Position the pointer in the center of your image (Saturn), and click.

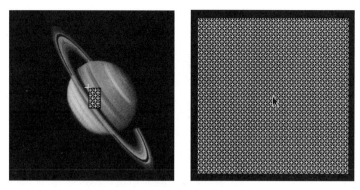

Left: the crosshair begins to drag the mesh-filled rectangle across the image from the center.
Right: the image is obscured by the mesh-filled rectangle, with pointer in the center.

The mesh disappears and a blue "halo" radiates from Saturn.

The glow effect you've produced seems to emanate from the center of your object. That's because you clicked the object's center when selecting the direction of the gradient fill. When you choose the Circular gradient type and click to select the gradient's direction, you're specifying the start of the color at the right end of your gradient; when the right-end color is the lightest color in your gradient, this appears to be the point where light hits your object and falls away.

Final image with gradient "halo."

For a variation on this effect, try masking your object before using the technique; the halo seems to radiate from behind the object. Or, try applying any of the plug-in filters supplied with SuperPaint to the image after you've created the halo and see what unique and surprising effects you can create.

For color and black-and-white machines

Creating Symmetrical Curved Objects

It can be difficult to create symmetrical curved objects such as a vase or a heart shape by simply drawing with the Freehand tool, since making both halves of the object identical is nearly impossible. Instead, you can create half of the object, duplicate it, then flip it to create the other half. As an example let's create a heart that we can use later in a logo.

1. In the Draw layer, use the Perpendicular Line tool to create a vertical line slightly longer than the height of your object. You don't need to be precise, because this line is just a reference mark to make sure that the beginning and end points of the object you create are on the same vertical axis. You'll delete the line later.

   If you want to be precise, you can press Command-Shift-M to display the rulers, or choose **Show Coordinates** from the **Floating Palettes** submenu in the View menu.

2. Select the Freehand tool from the Tools palette.

3. Since you're creating only one half of the object, you want the "inside" of the object to be open. Select *None* as your current Area Fill.

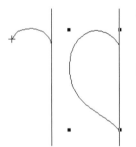

4. To create the left half of the object, position the Freehand cursor on the vertical reference line, and draw the curve you want, making sure the end point of your object is also on the reference line.

5. If you're not completely satisfied with the proportions of this half of the heart you can edit the Bezier curve you created; make sure the object is selected and choose **Reshape Bezier** from the Draw menu (or press Command-R).

Left: drawing the curve that begins on the reference line. Right: left side completed.

Note: You can double-click on the points to change them to smooth points, then drag the handles to smooth the curve further. For more information on reshaping Bezier curves, see Part 4, Chapter 8.

6. When you're satisfied with the shape, click anywhere outside the object to deselect it and take it out of reshape mode.

   Now you're ready to complete the shape.

7. Select the vertical reference line and delete it.

8. Select your Bezier curve and press Command-D to create a duplicate of it.

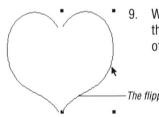

9. While this duplicate is still selected, choose **Flip Horizontal** from the Transform menu. This flips the duplicate so it is a mirror image of the original curve.

The flipped duplicate

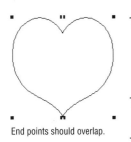

End points should overlap.

10. Now move this flipped duplicate so its end points overlap the end points of the original curve. For finer control, use the Arrow keys to move (nudge) the selected curve one pixel at a time.

    All that's left is join both halves of the heart to make one object.

11. While the flipped object is still selected, Shift-click the left side of the heart to select it too.

12. Choose **Join Beziers** from the Draw menu. The final, symmetrical object is now one Draw object and will be treated as such when you apply a fill or texture. Also, since it is a Draw object it prints at the resolution of the printer, and can be resized without losing resolution.

Note: You can use SuperPaint's gradient fills to create a three-dimensional effect like the one shown here. See Part 4, Chapter 4 for more information on creating and using gradients.

For color machines

Simulating Neon

Using custom gradients, grid snap, and the Paint Brush in the Paint layer, you can quickly and easily create a "neon" effect to enhance posters, letterheads, logos, even advertisements.

1. Select Gradients from the Options menu. The Gradients dialog box appears, with the currently selected gradient displayed in the Gradient bar.

    Click *New*. The Gradient bar and the Start Color and End Color boxes at either end are filled with white instead of the currently selected gradient.

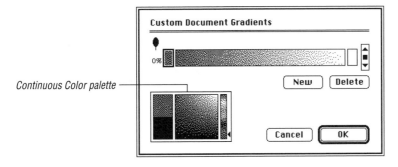

Continuous Color palette

2. Select the Start Color box by clicking it, then select a bright pink from the Continuous Color palette. The Gradient Bar is filled with a pink-to-white gradient. Click *OK*.

For more information on creating gradients, see Part 4, Chapter 4. For more information on using a Continuous Color palette, see Part 4, Chapter 5.

The pink-to-white custom gradient is now your current Area Fill.

The Peaked icon ⎯

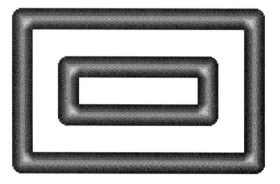

3. Open the Gradients palette and select the *Peaked* icon. Now your gradient will be applied from the area's outer boundaries toward the center.

4. Press Command-Shift-G to turn on the Grid snap. Anything you create in the document will be automatically aligned to the invisible grid points (if you want to see the grid, press Command-Shift-V; the grid will not print).

The final step before applying the neon effect is configuring the Paint Brush.

5. Double-click the Paint Brush icon in the Tools palette. In the resulting dialog box, click the largest round brush size, so that the image you create will be bold enough to show off the neon effect. Corners will be rounded to simulate the bending of neon-filled glass tubes. Click O*K*.

6. Paint any "neon" shapes you like in the document window. When you release the mouse button, the gradient effect is applied.

Grid snap enhances the neon simulation by restricting your painting to geometric patterns with straight, even edges. You can paint letters to spell out words, create pictures, or abstract designs.

Experiment with other custom-gradient ideas, as well as other brush sizes and shapes to vary the technique.

Creating Broken Shadows

When your illustration includes an object casting a shadow against a vertical surface, such as a wall, a broken shadow is required. To achieve this, you can make a two-piece shadow, each piece having a different orientation. A shadow against a background pattern should be translucent so the background can show through.

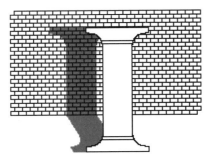

The column and brick wall used in this example are easy to create: set your text parameters to Times Outline, 126 pt., and type a capital "I" for the column; draw horizontal rules across it to complete the effect. Drag a rectangle (choose zero line width) of the "brick" pattern to make the background wall; edit the ends to match the illustration if desired.

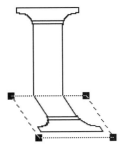

Slant the bottom half of the copy.

1. In the Paint layer, use the Lasso to select the object, then Option-drag a copy to one side.

2. Select the bottom half of the copy with the selection Rectangle, cutting the copy at the point where the shadow meets the background wall.

3. Choose the **Slant** command from the Transform menu. Drag one of the corner handles of the resulting bounding box to slant the bottom half of the shadow in the appropriate direction. If necessary, choose **Stretch** from the Transform menu to shorten it slightly.

4. Re-align the selected, slanted bottom half of the shadow with the top half. Use the Pencil in magnified mode to close any gaps in either half of the shadow; be sure to seal the edges where the shadow breaks.

5. Use the Lasso to select the entire shadow.

6. From the Colors palette, select a medium gray for the shadow (in black-and-white documents, select a medium gray pattern), make sure Opaque is selected as the current Fill Mode, then choose **Fill** from the Paint menu. While the shadow is still selected, choose **Translucent** from the Transfer Modes menu on the Line & Fill palette.

7. Drag the shadow into place against the vertical background surface.

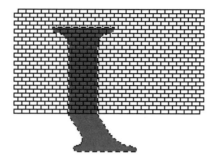

8. Lasso the original object, and drag it on top of the slanted shadow, aligning the points where they meet. It may be necessary to erase part of the shadow where it meets the original object.

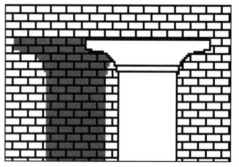

Close-up of background wall pattern showing through the shadow.

A Circle of Objects

A circle or ring of objects can lend a nice touch to a logo or business graphic. One way to create a circle of objects is by copying and then pasting and rotating each object separately as many times as needed to complete the circle. A shortcut and far easier method is to draw one object and use the **Replicate** command in the Edit menu to create the circle of objects.

You can use this technique for any Draw-layer object, or any Paint-layer graphic you select and then copy or cut to the Draw layer.

1. If you have a graphic you want to use as a sample, open that document, select and copy the graphic, then create a new SuperPaint document and paste the graphic into the Draw layer.

Star created with AllGon tool.

If you don't have a suitable graphic available, you can create a star using the Draw-layer AllGon tool. Open a new document, go to the Draw layer and double-click the AllGon tool to open the AllGon dialog box. Select *Pointz* as the style, type 5 for the number of points, and select Level 1. Click *OK* to close the dialog box. Select white as your current Area Fill and, while pressing the Shift key, draw a half-inch diameter star. (Pressing the Shift key constrains the AllGon tool so the bottom star points are horizontal. This isn't absolutely necessary, but it does produce a nice effect when the circle of stars is complete.)

Half-inch star with two-inch vertical line.

2. Use the Perpendicular Line tool to draw a vertical line from a point within the object (see the illustration) down. This line will be the diameter of the circle inside which the objects will be replicated and rotated. If you're using the star we created in Step 1, make the line two inches long.

Note: make sure the line is long enough to keep the bottoms of the stars from overlapping when they form a circle. A good rule is to make the line at least three times the height of the object. Use the Coordinates palette, the rulers, or the **Object Info** command in the Draw menu to determine the size of the object and the length of the line.

3. While the line is still selected, use the Selection Arrow to Shift-click the object to select it too.

4. Choose **Group** from the Draw menu to join the line and the object as one object.

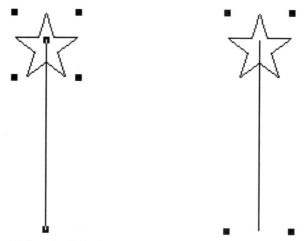

Left: line and star both selected as individual objects. Right: both objects grouped.

5. Choose **Replicate** from the Edit menu.

6. When the Replicate dialog box opens, select *Rotate Around Center* (rotating around the center of the object means that the length of your line determines the diameter of the circle) and *Clockwise*.

7. Determining the number of copies and the angle at which each copy will be made is more or less trial and error. You want to make sure that the stars don't overlap as they are copied around the circle. For your star and line, enter 11 as the number of copies and 30° for the degree of rotation of each copy.

    Since your object may have a different size, and the length of your line may be different than the star and line in this example, some additional trial and error may be necessary to achieve the same effect shown here. However, by trying different settings and experimenting with scaling and movement settings, you may discover other useful special effects.

8. When the settings are made, click *OK*. SuperPaint automatically replicates the object the specified number of times and rotates each one to keep it perpendicular to the circumference of the circle. If the results aren't what you expected, choose **Undo** from the Edit menu, then choose **Replicate** again, and change the settings.

Since the line and the star were treated as one object (you grouped them, remember), you now have a lot of lines you don't want. You can delete these lines, after first ungrouping the objects.

9. Use the selection Rectangle to select the entire circle of replicated stars and lines, then choose **Ungroup** from the Draw menu. Deselect the group by clicking anywhere outside the circle.

10. Select and delete all the lines one by one (or Shift-click several lines and then delete them all at once).

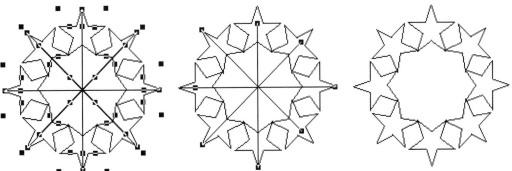

Ungrouped lines and stars, all selected.   Image with only lines selected.   Completed circle of stars with no lines.

When you've finished, your circle of stars is complete.

For color and black-and-white machines

"Pop" a Graphic Image Out of the Background

SuperPaint's masking functions can be used to "pop" a graphic image out of the rest of the image. This technique is useful when you're working with a scanned photograph, for example, and you want to emphasize something in the foreground by downplaying the picture's background. Masking the foreground area lets you apply one or more effects to the background of your photograph while leaving the foreground image sharp and clear.

The original image.

The selected image within photograph is outlined by "marching ants."

Assuming you've already scanned the photograph you want to use, you need to bring the scanned image into SuperPaint.

1. Choose **Place** from the File menu to place an existing TIFF, Mac-Paint, StartupScreen, ThunderScan TIFF, or EPS document (or choose the appropriate scan format [e.g., Apple Scanner, ScanMan] to import, if your scanner manufacturer provides a plug-in module for direct scanning into SuperPaint).

    Select the appropriate format from the **Place** submenu, then locate and place your scanned image into your SuperPaint document.

Note: The **Place** command automatically places an image in the Draw layer as a SuperBits object. The file's resolution is maintained, and you can see the actual size at which the image will print.

2. If your image's resolution is greater than 72 dpi, choose **Edit SuperBits** from the Draw menu (or press Command-R) to edit the image at the resolution of your scan. (If the image is 72 dpi or you don't need greater resolution, press Command-Y to cut the image to the Paint layer and continue with steps 3 through 10.)

    Your image appears magnified in the Edit SuperBits window — you can now edit it using any of the Paint tools, without losing resolution.

3. Select the area to be masked.

    You can use any of the Selection tools; which one depends on the shape of your foreground image, and how precise you want to be. The Freehand selection tool lets you trace every nuance of a shape. However, the Polygon selection tool lets you select freeform shapes with more control. Use the Polygon selection tool to trace the shape you want to mask. Since you're tracing the shape in straight-line segments, creating short lines may provide better accuracy.

4. Choose **New Mask** from the Masking submenu to cover the selection area with a mask. Your selected area is filled with animated diagonal lines, indicating that its mask is active.

    You can now apply any effects you like to the rest of your picture; the masked image will remain untouched. You can paint with sweeping strokes that pass right across your image, or apply fills to the entire document without affecting the masked area. You can also use any of the plug-in filters in the SuperPaint pouch to create a variety of effects in the background of your picture.

The Spatter effect is applied to the background; the foreground image is masked.

For this example, let's spatter the background with a magenta from the Colors palette (black-and-white users can select a gray pattern from the Patterns palette), then apply an even "wash" of color.

5. Select a magenta (or pattern) with which to spatter your background.

6. Choose **Spatter** from the Paint menu. Your entire picture, except the masked portion, is randomly filled with magenta (or patterned) pixels.

The remaining steps are for color users only.

7. From the Colors palette, select a light gray; it replaces the magenta in the Colors and current Area Fill displays; the magenta moves to the Frequent Fills palette.

8. Choose **Set Transparent %** from the Fill Modes submenu in the Paint menu, and select 25% in the Set Transparent % dialog box. In order to keep this effect very subtle, you're going to apply only a percentage of your light gray to the background.

Transparent gray has been added to the magenta spatter for a "muted" effect.

```
 Set Transparent %

 ● 25%
 ○ 50%     ○ Other: [ 25 ]
 ○ 75%

     [ Cancel ]    [  OK  ]
```

The Set Transparent % dialog box.

9. Choose **Fill** in the Paint menu, and watch how the magenta spatter on your background is "muted."

Note: You can first make a selection within the document and apply the effect only to that area, if you don't wish to spatter the entire document.

All that's left is to remove the mask from your foreground image.

Note: If you've been working in the Paint layer, you can either save the mask with your SuperPaint file, or you can delete it. But masks are not saved within SuperBits; as soon as you close the Edit SuperBits window, the mask is lost.

10. From the Masking submenu in the Paint menu, choose either: a) **Turn Off Mask** if you want to save the mask with your file, or b) **Delete Mask** if you don't think you'll need the mask again. Simply close the Edit SuperBits window without saving the mask if you are working with SuperBits.

The animated diagonal lines on your foreground image disappear.

The final altered photograph.

Notice how the graphic you've just unmasked "pops" from the muted background. With all of SuperPaint's available colors, textures, fill modes, filters, and gradients, your imagination is the only limit to what you can do to differentiate a foreground image from its background.

Experiment with the procedure suggested here to create your own masking effects. Try choosing **Invert Mask** from the Masking submenu once you've masked your foreground image, and apply effects only to the image while leaving your background untouched. You can hide masked areas when you want to concentrate on other parts of your image, and you can add to or remove parts of your mask. For more information on masking, see Part 4, Chapter 8.

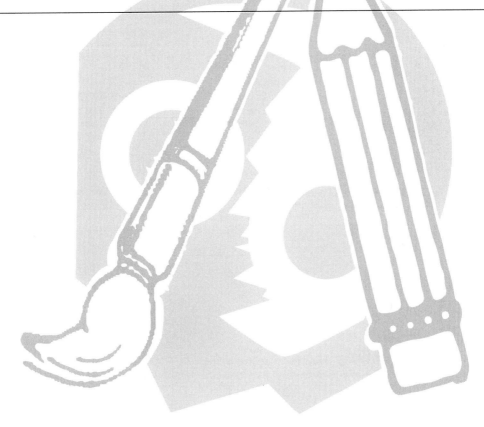

Part 6: Index

Index

Symbols

1-1/2 command 3-24
1-bit document 4-88, 4-91, 4-93
  color assigment 4-92
16-bit document 4-88, 4-91
16.8 million colors 4-89, 4-95,
  4-97, 4-109
24-bit color 4-88
256 colors 4-90
3-D Box 3-7, 4-123
32-bit
  document 4-88, 4-91
  QuickDraw 1- 8, 4-90, 4-91
32-bit document 4-109
8-bit
  document 4-88, 4-91, 4-101

A

About SuperPaint
  command 3-7, 3-13, 4-10,
    4-180
  dialog box 4-180
    Plug-ins button 4-10,
      4-123, 4-134, 4-180
active
  display 4-62
  document 4-48, 4-53
  layer 4-7
  text 4-226
active document
  document 4-211
Add Point command 3-23, 4-196
Add to Mask command 4-170
additive colors 4-107
Airbrush 3-9, 4-110, 4-111,
  4-168, 4-176
Airbrush Settings 4-129
  command 3-20, 4-129, 4-168
  dialog box 3-9, 3-20, 4-
    128, 4-130
  Dot Size 4-129, 4-130, 4-132
  Flow 4-129, 4-130, 4-131
  keyboard controls 4-130
    alphabet keys 4-131
    number keys 4-131
    symbol keys 4-132
  Nozzle Shape 4-129

Spray Area 4-129, 4-130,
  4-131
  Spray Pattern 4-129
Aldus FreeHand 4-69
Aldus Gallery Effects 4-9
Aldus PageMaker 4-59
Aldus Personal Press 4-59, 4-95
Aldus PrePrint 4-59
Aldus Preprint 4-109
Align Objects
  command 3-21, 4-186, 4-188
  dialog box 3-21, 4-186, 4-187
Align to Grid command 3-15,
  4-24, 4-188
AllGon 3-7, 4-123, 4-124
AllGon Settings dialog box 3-7,
  4-124
anchor points 2-26
  hinge 2-26, 4-195, 4-196
  smooth 2-26, 4-195, 4-196
anchor points (Bezier) 4-192
  hinge 4-192, 4-193, 4-194
  smooth 4-192, 4-193, 4-194
anti-aliasing 4-227
Apple
  Color Picker 4-74
  menu 3-7, 4-180
Apple Color Picker 4-93, 4-94,
  4-95, 4-97, 4-98, 4-105,
  4-107
Apple System colors 4-95
Arc 4-190
  angle 4-28, 4-29
  reshaping 4-29
  tool 3-10, 4-29, 4-115,
    4-117, 4-121
arcs 4-191
  reshaping 4-190
Area Fill 2-10, 3-8, 4-29,
  4-33, 4-61, 4-62, 4-63,
  4-64, 4-66, 4-67, 4-70,
  4-71, 4-75, 4-80, 4-111,
  4-148, 4-155
  as paint 2-13
  display 2-12, 3-11, 4-62
  text 4-234
arrow keys 2-35, 4-154
Arrows 3-17, 4-33
  Arrow on End 3-17
  Arrow on Start 3-17
  Arrows on Both 3-17
  command 4-81
  custom 4-82

Custom Arrows 3-17
  default 4-81
  No Arrows 3-17, 4-82
  submenu 4-81
autoscrolling 4-32, 4-44, 4-114
AutoTrace 4-190, 4-204
  command 2-33, 3-20,
    4-205, 4-206
  optimizing 4-208
AutoTrace Settings
  command 3-20, 4-205
  dialog box 3-20, 4-33,
    4-205, 4-206, 4-207, 4-208
    Beziers or Polygons 4-207
    Outline only 4-208

B

background 3-11
  color 2-13, 4-66, 4-92
Basic element(s). *See* Element(s)
Bezier objects 2-24, 3-10,
  3-23, 4-117, 4-122,
  4-192, 4-193, 4-208
  anchor points 2-26, 4-192
    hinge 4-192, 4-193,
      4-194, 4-195, 4-196
    smooth 4-192, 4-193,
      4-194, 4-195, 4-196
  converting 3-22, 4-197, 4-198
  joining 3-22, 4-199
  path 4-192
  reshaping 2-25, 3-22, 4-30,
    4-190, 4-195, 4-196
  segments 2-26, 4-192
    curved 4-192, 4-194,
      4-195
    straight 4-192, 4-194,
      4-195
Bezier Settings
  command 3-22, 4-122, 4-200
  dialog box 3-22, 4-33,
    4-122, 4-198, 4-200
Bezier to Polygon
  command 4-198, 4-208
  Point-to-Point 3-22
  Polygon Fit 3-22
  submenu 4-198
binary digit 4-87
bit depth 4-38, 4-39, 4-41,
  4-42, 4-47, 4-87, 4-90
  changing 4-89
  default 4-31, 4-38, 4-89

P

page
  breaks 4-33, 4-43, 4-46
  orientation 4-238, 4-240, 4-43
  size 4-38, 4-41, 4-43
Page Setup
  command 3-14, 4-237, 4-239
  dialog box 3-14, 4-231,
    4-238, 4-240, 4-33, 4-38,
    4-41, 4-42, 4-43
    ImageWriter 4-239,
      4-240, 4-242
    LaserWriter 4-239,
      4-240, 4-243, 4-244
Paint
  commands 4-168, 4-177
  fill 4-62
  graphics 1- 3, 4-210
  layer 2-3, 4-5, 4-204, 4-206
    selection area 4-147, 4-205
    selection arrow 4-148
  menu 4-9, 4-168, 4-172,
    4-177, 4-178, 4-179,
    4-184, 4-205, 4-206
  mirror effects 4-176
  plug-in modules 3-8, 3-20,
    4-134, 4-168, 4-172,
    4-176, 4-177, 4-179
    Calligraphy Brush 3-8,
      4-134, 4-138
    Charcoal 3-8, 4-134, 4-139
    Dry Brush 3-8, 4-134,
      4-139
    Smudge tool 3-8, 4-134,
      4-139
    Spin Tool 3-8
    Spin tool 4-140
    Sprinkler 3-8, 4-134,
      4-141
    Texture Brush 3-9,
      4-134, 4-143
    Twister 3-9, 4-134, 4-145
Paint Brush 3-8, 3-18, 4-112,
  4-134, 4-135, 4-138, 4-176
Paint Bucket 3-9, 4-23, 4-110,
  4-111, 4-133
Paint from Center
  command 3-18, 4-117, 4-175
  mode 4-119, 4-120
Paint from Corner
  command 3-18
  mode 4-119, 4-120

Paint Multiple command 3-20,
  4-23, 4-175
Paint on Darker
  Fill Mode 3-19, 4-173, 4-174
  Transfer Mode 3-11, 4-76
Paint/Draw Layer switch 2-5,
  2-8, 3-5, 4-6
palettes 3-3
  Brush Tools 3-8, 4-14,
    4-134, 4-157
  close box 4-14
  closing 2-17, 4-110
  Colors 3-11, 4-14, 4-32,
    4-62, 4-66, 4-91, 4-92,
    4-94, 4-95, 4-98, 4-103
  Continuous Color 4-93,
    4-94, 4-95, 4-96, 4-98
  Coordinates 2-31, 3-12,
    3-23, 4-13, 4-15, 4-20,
    4-22, 4-25, 4-26, 4-29,
    4-161
  Draw & Paint Plug-ins 3-7,
    4-14
  floating 3-3, 3-16, 4-14, 4-93
    captured defaults 4-14
  Frequent Fills 2-7, 2-17,
    3-3, 3-12, 4-13, 4-15, 4-80
  Gradients 3-11, 3-18, 4-14,
    4-62, 4-66, 4-70, 4-102
  hot keys 4-11, 4-14
  Line & Fill 2-3, 2-7, 2-10,
    3-3, 3-18, 4-13, 4-15,
    4-33, 4-62, 4-64, 4-66,
    4-71, 4-75, 4-78, 4-90,
    4-92, 4-147, 4-152
  Line Widths 3-12, 4-14,
    4-62, 4-78, 4-79
  moving 4-14, 4-110
  Patterns 2-10, 3-11, 3-17,
    4-14, 4-62, 4-64, 4-65, 4-66
  pop-up 2-3, 3-4, 4-14,
    4-15, 4-93
  primary 4-13, 4-15, 4-32
  selecting from 4-15
  Selection Tools 3-6, 4-14,
    4-147, 4-157
  showing and hiding 4-15
  Textures 3-11, 4-14, 4-62,
    4-66, 4-67, 4-68, 4-102
  title bar 4-14
  Tools 2-3, 2-7, 3-3, 3-4,
    4-6, 4-13, 4-14, 4-15, 4-33

Transfer Modes 4-14, 4-62,
  4-75, 4-147, 4-152
panes 2-22, 3-16
paper
  feed 4-247
  size 4-237, 4-240
Paste Color command 4-105
Paste command 3-14, 4-8,
  4-159, 4-210, 4-211
pasting
  Draw layer 4-160
  Paint layer 4-160
pasting selections 4-23
Path point handle(s). See Handle(s)
Patterns 3-11
  background component
    2-13, 4-61, 4-64, 4-66
  command 3-17, 4-65
  creating 4-65
  default 4-66
  editing 4-65, 4-66
  foreground component 2-13,
    4-61, 4-64, 4-66
  palette 2-10, 3-11, 3-17,
    4-14, 4-62, 4-64, 4-65, 4-66
  picking up 4-65
  selecting 4-64
  solid 2-15, 4-63
Patterns palette
  hot key 4-64
Peaked gradient 4-71
Pencil 3-9, 4-19, 4-110, 4-111,
  4-112, 4-132, 4-136, 4-143
  using to erase 2-22
Permanent Fills 2-15, 3-11, 4-63
Perpendicular Line tool 3-9,
  3-17, 4-81, 4-84, 4-115,
  4-116
Personalization dialog box 2-7
Perspective command 3-23,
  4-164, 4-167
picking up
  a pattern 4-65
  color 4-115
Pickup command 3-21, 4-177,
  4-183
PICT 4-40, 4-54, 4-55
PICT2
  see PICT 4-55
pixels 2-4, 4-5, 4-87, 4-203,
  4-207, 4-210
  editing 4-204